ROYAL AUSTRALIAN ARTIL

ACTION! ACTION! ACTION!

A SHORT HISTORY OF THE EMPLOYMENT OF AUSTRALIAN ARTILLERY

1871 – 2021

Nicholas Floyd and Paul Stevens

All inquiries should be made to the publishers.
Big Sky Publishing Pty Ltd
PO Box 303, Newport, NSW 2106, Australia
Phone: 1300 364 611
Email: info@bigskypublishing.com.au
Web: www.bigskypublishing.com.au

A catalogue record for this book is available from the National Library of Australia

Cover design and typesetting by Think Productions, Melbourne

Contents

Foreword

The senior serving Officers and Warrant Officers of the Royal Regiment of Australian Artillery's (RAA) Regimental Committee and the RAA's History Committee expressed a desire for a brief history of Australian Artillery. The premise was that serving Gunners deserve a broad understanding of their considerable history to complement their professional education. No single, up to date, succinct and accessible reference was available; a new approach to make available the broad sweep of 150 years of the history of Australian Artillery became the challenge that resulted in this book.

Regimental Master Gunner Warrant Officer Class One Anthony Hortle (left) uncases the Queen's Banner (1871-1971) during the presentation and consecration of the Queen's Banner (1871-2021) to the Royal Regiment of Australian Artillery at Victoria Barracks, Sydney (Courtesy Defence Image Gallery, 20221105adf8638673_1012)

Action! Action! Action! provides the essentials of a rich and substantial history, not only for all Gunners, but also the wider Army, the Services, and the Australian community.

It is not easy to decide the essentials to be distilled from the long history of artillery service to the nation to be included in a 200-page brief history. A full history includes thousands of missions, thousands of units raised and disbanded, involving hundreds of thousands of Gunners, across a hundred or so theatres of conflict. This book fulfils the Regiment's requirement through a select focus on what Australian artillery comprised and how it was employed against threats in differing era and theatres. It is a highly accessible overview of each major period in the 150-year history, with insights into tactics, people, organisations, tasks, and icons.

When British garrison forces were withdrawn in 1870 the Australian colonies were forced to consider their responsibility for their defences. The colony of Victoria was first to announce a permanent artillery force in 1870, however it was not sustained continuously. The colony of New South Wales proclaimed its first permanent battery of NSW artillery on 1 August 1871, and continuously sustained permanent force artillery capabilities through to Federation in 1901. The Royal Australian Artillery has thus adopted 1 August 1871 as its origin date.

Action! Action! Action! traces how Australian Artillery has operated in multiple theatres of war in different roles and adapted its operational employment and tactics. It is a journey of rises and declines in artillery capabilities. When major conflicts were imminent or erupted the growth in artillery capability was extraordinary. The more serious the fighting, the more the need for artillery. When real or perceived threats to Australian territory arose, coast defence and air defence artillery rapidly assumed priority for investment to deter and defeat raids. In benign periods, artillery capability was reduced to minimalist forms.

The book covers how artillery has employed anti-aircraft, anti-tank, anti-ship, counter battery, close and depth support field capabilities, while touching on specialist areas such as ammunition logistics, meteorology, radar, searchlights, survey and dedicated headquarters and liaison staffs. Artillery is a combat arm; the combined arms team has been at the heart of Australian Army tactics for a century. Planning for all phases of conflict has required highly trained artillery staff officers with specialist knowledge. The ability of artillery to operate across boundaries at long ranges in all weathers with highly adaptable and rapidly reconfigurable command and control arrangements provides commanders with options of where and when to mass effects. The long range of artillery and the size of areas of operations frequently resulted in artillery being at the joint interface with other Services and coalition forces.

Whether the reader 'dips in and out' of sections of interests, or skim reads the book, they will gain a clear understanding of how artillery has been employed in differing circumstances of national need. Break-out boxes and images provide context and enlighten readers about technical and tactical aspects of artillery, and of individual Gunners key to the story. Valuable snapshots of artillery organisations at select historical junctures are provided in a set of tables; in sum they tell a powerful story. A list of 'dates of significance' provides an insight into the changing nature or Australia's artillery through the historical evolution of organisational names across the Colonial to Federal transition, and before, during and after periods of conflict.

The power of artillery lies not only in its lethality but also in the extent to which its presence complicates an enemy's options. Artillery saves lives through its responsiveness and force protection missions. The nature of perceived threats, and national defence strategies such as local key port and settlement defence, forward defence and continental defence have each determined artillery capability needs. Over the 150 years the many changes in military technologies and capabilities had profound impacts. Branches of artillery have come and gone, and the return of anti-ship defence in a modern form is now imminent, as a new national defence strategy evolves.

Critical to the success of this ambitious book was close collaboration between the Royal Regiment of Australian Artillery, the RAA Regimental History Committee, the RAA Historical Company, and the Australian Army History Unit. No less so was the decision to establish a project team supporting two experienced authors with extensive knowledge of artillery. The joint authors, Major General Paul Stevens (Retd) and Lieutenant Colonel Nick Floyd have set a benchmark in a style of communication of history of a corps for serving members of the Army. The style entices readers to seek more knowledge across areas of their particular interest.

Action! Action! Action! satisfies a requirement by the Royal Regiment of Australian Artillery to understand the essentials of its past. It is intended to be a 'Gunner's friend', that provides a strong sense of the arc of their profession's history. It might assist leaders perceive possible futures. While primarily targeted at aspiring professional Gunners, this book will remain a close companion of all Gunners, whether serving or later in life as veterans. It will also provide family and friends of Gunners some understanding of service as a Gunner.

Brigadier John Cox AM (Retd)
Chair, RAA Regimental History Committee
History Director, RAA Historical Company

CHAPTER 1

An Introduction to Artillery

Action! Action! Action! The History of Employment of Australian Artillery 1871–2021 has been written to trace the evolution of Australia's artillery over the last 150 years. It is aimed at assisting readers to understand how and why this combat arm has been employed in the past. Equally, it provides a foundation for modern Gunners to build on in designing and planning the future employment of Australian artillery as part of a wider war fighting force.

Gunners have been part of Australia's armed forces since colonial self-government. For decades they formed the principal element of the permanent forces. Their universal presence in one form or another earned the battle honour *Ubique*, or 'everywhere'. Their devotion to duty and the profession of arms and their sense of pride and esprit de corps is reflected in their motto: *Quo Fas Et Gloria Ducunt* – 'Where Right and Glory Lead'.

The readiness and sustainability of Australian artillery, and the nation's resolve to deploy it, have depended on Australia's strategic and economic circumstances. The nature of the conflict to which Australian artillery has been deployed has determined its employment and command and control arrangements. Put another way, the value and priority afforded to the artillery has depended on the political context of the prevailing conflict.

This book covers the development, role and employment of the different forms of Australian artillery through the years, addressing the issues of national aspiration, technology and tactics, command and control, performance, and the role of individuals. Accompanying text boxes add further detail, and key data on organisations are contained in the appendices.

What is Artillery?

To many, the word artillery conjures an image of Napoleonic-era cannon, mounted on a carriage with spoked wheels and spouting flames and smoke, or its modern equivalent. The gun is indeed an iconic and sentimental image of artillery, but in the same way that a cricket bat is but an evocative symbol of a more complex game, so the gun does not tell the whole story.

At its simplest, artillery should be conceived as a system, aiming to apply a weakening or destructive power – often termed 'firepower' – in order to create a battle-winning advantage. The elements of this system include:

- A tactical **commander** who can visualise and pursue this battle-winning advantage;
- a means to **observe**, identify, acquire and select **target**s for the weapon system;
- a weapon to **deliver** the type of effect required;
- a means to **compute** the information needed to direct the delivery system onto the target;

- a tactical decision-maker to **control** when, where and how to apply the effect; and
- a logistics apparatus that **sustains** the availability of ammunition, stores, equipment and personnel essential to the task.

In the early days of direct-fire field and coast guns, the artillery system was relatively simple. As gun and ammunition design led to longer ranges and the potential for a variety of effects, it became more and more complex. Today the effects available range from the precise destruction of targets and personnel to the widespread suppression or neutralisation of an adversary, including the profound psychological effects of sustained bombardment. Artillery can also blind, obscure, illuminate, and mark targets. As the recent war in Ukraine has demonstrated, it is a potent weapon to be carefully and professionally wielded, and this requires extensive technical and tactical training.

In its operation, the artillery resembles the combat systems of a modern warship – the bridge, the fire control room, the magazines and the weapons launchers – but with its components dispersed across the battle space. This dispersion is both an advantage and disadvantage: it decreases the vulnerability of the whole to a single strike, and increases it in terms of its reliance on communications.

Each component of the artillery system has its own sub-systems involving humans and machines working in close concert, like the members of a rowing eight, or the crew of a racing yacht. Accordingly, teamwork is valued highly in the artillery, as is technical proficiency.

Proficiency in the use of artillery is a blend of the art of employing it tactically with the science of ensuring its effects are applied accurately and consistently. In land warfare, the relationship between the artillery and the 'manoeuvre' arms of infantry and mounted forces has traditionally been symbiotic, with one arm supporting the other in the pursuit of mutual objectives. This has led to the liaison arrangements through which artillery commanders provide advice to other arms.

Such advice covers not only the effects that can be achieved with artillery, but also its command and control. Because the longer ranges of artillery weapons allow them to support multiple manoeuvre units without having to move, unlike the direct fire or short-range capabilities of the supported arms, a distinction has to be drawn between the command of artillery resources and the control of their fire. The preferred practice, based on operational experience, is to group artillery units under a single command at the highest level while allotting control of their fire and effects to subordinate units. With communications assured, artillery command can remain centralised, while control is able to be decentralised to permit the maximum exploitation of the system: maximum flexibility of its application, and lethal concentration of its effects.

At the start of World War I, the 'underlying principle of all field artillery tactics' was:

> *To help the infantry to maintain its mobility and offensive power by all the means at its disposal. The primary objects of artillery fire should therefore be: to assist the movements of its own infantry; and to prevent the movements of the enemy's infantry.*[1]

Later, the role became expressed in broader terms, so that it could be applied equally to anti-tank artillery, to coast artillery guarding seaborne approaches, and to anti-aircraft artillery defending its allotted airspace. By 1969, the artillery's 'tactical function' was to 'support other arms and services by establishing such fire supremacy in the battle area that the enemy can neither interfere with our operations nor develop his own effectively.'[2]

Today, the 'the role of the Royal Regiment of Australian Artillery is to maximise the combat power of the Australian Defence Forces through the provision of offensive support coordination and indirect firepower, surveillance and target acquisition and ground-based air defence'.[3] This broader expression allows for the capability of artillery to be employed beyond close support.

Technical proficiency in the employment of artillery is bound up in what is known as 'solving the gunnery problem': being able, at a distance, to achieve the effect required with the opening rounds of an engagement. To be able to do so requires accurate location of both the weapon and its target, and a guidance system or, more commonly, precise computation of firing data including allowances for external factors influencing the projectile in flight. As technology and the character of warfare have evolved, improvements to fixation, targeting, and intelligence collection have helped transform artillery processes, but the gunnery problem itself, as a fundamental concept in the employment of artillery, remains.

Artillery firepower is about establishing a competitive advantage, or even an overmatch. It is a potent instrument to be used in preserving the lives of our own forces while shattering the morale, cohesion and will of an enemy. For its effective use four principles of employment of artillery have evolved over time:[4]

1. Cooperation. At the tactical level, artillery is a supporting arm, working to achieve the superior commander's intent, while freeing manoeuvre commanders of the need to know the detail of artillery processes – although they should understand artillery effects and how to apply them. Cooperation is equally relevant to the liaison required between air defence artillery and air force assets. Similarly, artillery surveillance and target acquisition elements provide combat information to manoeuvre units without direct command relationships.

2. Concentration. Artillery in all its forms is most effective when the weight of effort from multiple units is focussed on the area most in need. In the face of competing calls for support, commanders must make clinical, dispassionate decisions on prioritising where and when artillery is employed to maximise its effects.

3. Economy of effort. This principle asserts that, where practicable, artillery's fire and effects should be repositioned, rather than its units. Artillery's intrinsic range and flexibility allows its effects to be switched and reapplied far more rapidly than moving the unit itself. Additionally, each target should be engaged with sufficient resources to achieve the desired effect.

4. Sustainment. Sustainment is a self-evident requirement in providing necessary persistent and pervasive artillery support. The provision of responsive, reliable, all-weather, all-conditions fire support is central to artillery's commitment to the manoeuvre arms. Unbroken ammunition supply, logistics and maintenance chains are therefore fundamental.

In summary, the artillery is not just its more visible weaponry, but a multifaceted fire-support system that establishes advantage on the battlefield through fire supremacy. Today's system stretches across the land, maritime, air environments, and reaches in part into the cyber, space and electromagnetic realms. Even with advancements unimaginable to the early Gunner serving his old-fashioned cannon, the fundamentals of providing proficient support remain to be solved. How the Australian artillery has gone about that throughout its history is the basis of this book.

Artillery Technology: Evolution of the Gunnery Problem

Traditional form

In historical field artillery settings, 'delivery systems' (that is, the guns) would be deployed alongside infantry and cavalry on the battlefield. Observers were co-located with the guns.

Direct engagement would occur between the delivery system and target. This meant the guns were aimed directly at targets visible to them. Computation of firing data was minimal, consisting mainly of determining the distance (and potentially difference in elevation) from gun to target.

The Traditional Gunnery Problem

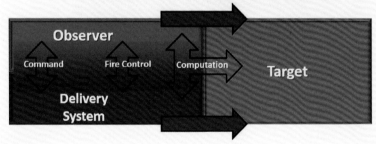

Modern form

The modern gunnery problem sees the observer, target and delivery system dislocated, with the latter two no longer intervisible.

The application of an *indirect* form of engagement between delivery system and target generates a competitive advantage in that artillery systems can engage targets at long range, and retaliation is complicated.

The ranges and displacements between the observer, delivery systems and the target are considerable. Complex computations are therefore required to account for all components of the artillery system. Accounting for factors such as geographic fixation of system components, orientation of delivery systems (when using unguided munitions), and trajectory variables is essential.

In the modern era, Observers may also be radars, uncrewed vehicles or similar automated sensors. These sensors transmit data collected from ships, aircraft or complex intelligence platforms.

Command and fire control functions are now also dispersed. This allows for rapid engagement, switching and massing of fires. Detailed processes for recording and sharing of targets are employed.

The Modern Gunnery Problem

Anti-tank application

Anti-tank artillery employed high-velocity, flat-trajectory delivery systems, against a new target genre of fast-moving, armoured vehicles a return to *direct* engagement between gun (and later, rocket and missile) delivery systems and targets. In modern times, the anti-tank role (gun, rocket and missile systems) has been transferred to other combat arms.

Anti-aircraft application

Anti-aircraft artillery also employed high-velocity, flat-trajectory delivery systems, against a new target genre of fast-moving airborne targets. The aircraft's appearance equally demanded a return to *direct* engagements between gun and short-range missile delivery systems and targets, and the application of additional computation to account for the target's three-dimensional motion. Later, the introduction of guided long-range missiles saw the reintroduction of *indirect* engagement between delivery system and target.

Deep battle application

The difficulty of locating targets deployed in depth led to the introduction of aerial observation, and novel target acquisition methods such as sound ranging, flash spotting, radar, acoustic, seismic, and laser sensors. The target locations so produced, and those predicted by analysis of available information, are engaged by what is termed *indirect* fire.

Targeting analysis techniques that can generate 'predicted' locations also augment immediate target computation methods. This allows more deliberate and more complex recording, sharing and engagement of deep targets. The extended ranges involved in the 'deep battle' have seen the proliferation of delivery systems such as rockets and missiles.

CHAPTER 2
Colonial Times: 1788–1901

From their establishment in the late 18th century until Federation in 1901, the Australian colonies relied on British imperial might, particularly that of the Royal Navy, for their ultimate defence. Coastal artillery forts were first erected to counter the threat of naval raids against the settlements, and, later, to secure the coaling stations and waterways that the Royal Navy might require. By the mid-19th century some local volunteer artillery units had been formed. Following the withdrawal of British garrisons in 1870, all the colonies raised artillery units to man their forts, in some cases also forming field batteries to assist in protecting the forts from the landward side.

The 19th century was marked by constant development of coast defences, and by technological advances in ship and gun design. Field artillery elements were twice deployed overseas. Even so, as Federation approached, the majority of permanent Gunners were those manning the coast artillery, and it was from their ranks that the first regiments of the Royal Australian Artillery were created.

The Birth of Australian Artillery: 1780s–1880

View from Fort Denison c. 1859–60, overlooking Farm Cove, 'Man o' War Roads' and Sydney Cove (Courtesy Dictionary of Sydney)

As the early colonial settlements came into being, the most likely external threat they faced was from isolated attacks by foreign warships. In response, British garrisons established batteries of smooth-bore muzzle-loading cannon, such as those at Dawes and Bennelong Points in Sydney and at Battery Point in Hobart.[1]

These defences were strengthened during Britain's wars with France (1793–1815) and America (1812) and at subsequent times of international tension or rumour of war. During the Crimean War in the 1850s, the colonies, enriched by the gold rushes and pastoralism and concerned about raids by the Russian Pacific Fleet, began to look to their own protection. The first local volunteer artillery units were raised to supplement the British troops on hand.

The Formation of a Permanent Artillery

When British land forces were withdrawn in 1870, Tasmania, South Australia (SA), Western Australia (WA) and Queensland, lacking the resources to create permanent forces, relied initially on volunteers to man their defences. Victoria, however, created alongside its volunteers a permanent 'Victorian Artillery Corps', which existed for a decade before being temporarily disbanded.[2]

New South Wales (NSW) also undertook the formation of a permanent artillery regiment, raising the first battery in 1871. This battery took over the forts from the Ordnance Department and manned field guns for cooperation with the volunteers. Regimental Headquarters and a second battery were raised in 1876, and a third battery was formed in 1877 in preparation for providing a detachment to the forts at Newcastle.[3]

Hobart Town Volunteer Artillery on a gun emplacement at Queen's Battery, August 1869 (Courtesy AWM AO4781)

That same year, amidst international tension and adverse commentary on the state of the local defences, Victoria, Queensland, SA and NSW engaged Colonel Sir William Jervois and Lieutenant Colonel Peter Scratchley, Royal Engineer officers with fortifications expertise, to advise on schemes of defence. Their report confirmed that raids by naval cruisers, perhaps accompanied by temporary lodgement of troops, were the principal threat. They recommended forts manned by permanent artillery at the principal ports along with the formation of small field forces of infantry, artillery, engineers and cavalry. The fixed defences should consist of minefields protected by guns and searchlights, with other guns and lights covering the approaches.

In response, fortifications in NSW were expanded at Middle and South Heads, Botany Bay, Newcastle and Wollongong. Victoria improved the works at the heads of Port Phillip Bay. SA built forts at Semaphore and Largs. Fort Lytton on the Brisbane River was completed in 1882, and in Tasmania the batteries around Hobart were consolidated into those at Queen's north of the city, Alexandra to its south, and Kangaroo Bluff at Bellerive.

The recommendations to establish permanent artillery forces also bore fruit. Alongside those already in existence in NSW, the permanent 'Victorian Artillery', numbering just over 100 personnel, was re-formed in 1882, and the volunteer system was replaced with a militia (paid part-time) force two years later. South Australia also formed a small permanent unit in 1882. A permanent battery was established in Queensland in 1885,[4] and a small permanent detachment in Tasmania in 1886.[5]

Twenty-five-ton gun at Middle Head, 1886 (Courtesy AWM ART94389)

New Weapons

These developments coincided with the emergence of armoured, steam-powered warships capable of bombarding shore targets at longer range, supplemented by auxiliary vessels and torpedo boats that might attempt to run past the forts. Such advances made smooth-bore cannon obsolete, and they were replaced or supplemented at Sydney, Port Phillip, Adelaide and Brisbane by rifled-muzzle-loading (RML) ordnance firing cylindrical anti-armour, common (explosive) or shrapnel (anti-personnel) projectiles.

Over time, breech-loading (BL) guns offering higher rates of fire superseded the RMLs. Breech loaders employed a system where the projectile and propellant cartridges were loaded separately, and the breech closed by a screw fitted with seals to prevent the rearward escape of gas on firing. Many colonies ordered 'disappearing' BL guns on hydro-pneumatic mountings that recoiled into the gun pit for re-loading and protection. For their inner defences, some colonies also procured some smaller-calibre quick firing (QF) weapons, so called because their projectiles were mated to a brass cartridge case containing the propellant, and loaded as one. The cartridge case constrained the propellant gases, allowing a simpler breech mechanism and a higher rate of fire. QF gun carriages also incorporated mechanical and hydro-pneumatic devices to absorb the force of recoil and return the barrel to the firing position without the carriage moving.

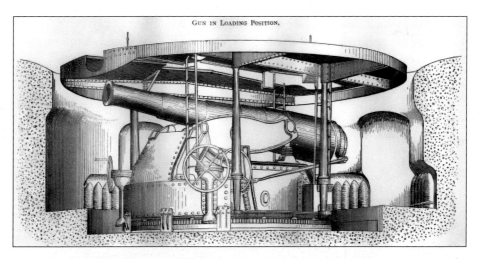

Pencil diagrams of disappearing BL 9.2-inch gun in firing and load positions, c. 1885 (Courtesy RAAHC)

The mounting, maintenance and service of these more complex weapons made training essential, a NSW Defence Enquiry Commission of 1881 noting that 'the fully instructed artilleryman is in reality an artisan of high order, and time, habit and systematic teaching are necessary to make him thoroughly competent'.[6] Most colonies engaged active or former Royal Artillery personnel to command, advise and conduct periodic 'schools'. NSW engaged the services of three British officers and a warrant officer master gunner, using them to establish the NSW School of Gunnery, the forerunner of the Commonwealth School of Artillery, in 1885.[7]

War in the Soudan: 1885

Portrait of the Australian Artillery Contingent, Handoub, the Soudan, 1885 (Courtesy AWM PO4535.003)

At this time, in north-east Africa, Britain was facing a rebellion in the Soudan. When Khartoum fell and General Sir Charles Gordon perished, four colonies offered contingents for the British campaign of 1885. The home government accepted a field battery, an infantry battalion and field ambulance from NSW, and within a fortnight, the battery of 190 men had been found from the permanent and volunteer artillery. Reaching the Soudan, it trained with the 9 pounder (pr) RML field gun, but saw no action before returning home, leaving behind Gunner Edward Lewis, the first Australian artilleryman to die on active service.[8] The campaign echoes to this day in that the 9-pounder is the gun on the artillery cap badge.

Artillery Leader: The 'Father of Australian Artillery': Hon. Second Lieutenant Henry Green, MSM

Henry Green has the distinction of being the first soldier enlisted in the NSW Permanent Artillery – Service Number '1'. During his 25 years of subsequent service during the earliest days of the permanent Australian Artillery, Green's profound knowledge of gunnery, operational experience and personal example was instrumental in forming the force's professional foundations. Consequently, many Gunners, especially in the regular RAA units, consider him the 'father of Australian Artillery'.

Green joined on 7 August 1871, after migrating from Britain, where he had spent 21 years in the Royal Artillery, reached the rank of sergeant, gained field and garrison artillery experience, and served in Crimea and India.

On enlistment in NSW, he was promoted to staff sergeant and appointed as the Battery Sergeant Major. The principal role of his battery was to establish and operate the fortifications of Port Jackson, with a secondary duty of turning out a field battery during volunteer camps. As the only senior member of the permanent NSW Artillery with previous Gunner experience – his enlistment papers recorded him as an artillery instructor – he was well suited to lead in these tasks.

When an artillery brigade was raised with the formation of a second battery of permanent artillery in 1876, Green became the Brigade Sergeant Major and was promoted warrant officer in 1884. The next year, he deployed supernumerary with the field battery of the NSW Artillery to the Soudan.

As the artillery Brigade Sergeant Major, Green was quartered with his family alongside the clock over the archway of Victoria Barracks, Sydney. He continued his duties until 1896 when, on retirement, he was awarded the Meritorious Service Medal, and promoted honorary second lieutenant. His service is commemorated by one of the two Norfolk Island pines planted on the high ground south of the Flag Station at the Barracks.

Henry Green following retirement from the New South Wales Artillery (Courtesy Victoria Barracks–Sydney Sergeants' Mess)

Towards Federation: 1890–1900

Between 1885 and the turn of the century, the colonies moved slowly towards federation and defence cooperation. In 1889, at the request of the colonial governments, Major-General J. Bevan Edwards, a former engineer and commander of British Forces in China, conducted a review of the organisation of the colonial forces. He recommended amalgamation of the permanent artilleries; that Tasmania and WA convert their unpaid volunteer forces to a militia (paid) basis; and that the four larger colonies organise their militia infantry, cavalry and field artillery into brigades able to serve in any of the other colonies.[9]

At subsequent inter-colonial military conferences, the colonial commandants urged the Premiers to adopt cooperative defensive arrangements. No action was taken because of the prevailing economic depression, and a view that civil federation should precede military federation. Nevertheless, in 1893, Britain and the colonies collectively contributed to coastal fortifications at the coaling station at Albany and on Thursday Island in the Torres Strait, to assist in maintaining naval freedom of action.[10]

Later in the decade, sparked by an initial request from NSW in 1897, a proposal was put to Queen Victoria for the permanent artilleries of that colony, Victoria and Queensland, to be designated as three regiments of Royal Australian Artillery (RAA). On 14 July 1899, the Secretary of State for the colonies conveyed royal consent, and the three separate regiments formally came into existence in August and September of that year.[11]

Coastal protection remained the principal task, and from 1892, as Britain regularised its garrison artillery procedures, Australian fortress Gunners were able to apply the resulting *Garrison Artillery Drill* manuals to local conditions. The doctrine covered the organisation of forts into sections, fire commands, batteries and groups, with batteries assigned to either counter-bombardment or close-defence tasks.[12]

While the fortresses grappled with engaging moving targets at increasing ranges, the field artillery continued to use direct fire controlled by the battery commander, even though, during the Franco-Prussian War of 1870–71, the range of Prussian BL field guns, modern rifles and nascent machine guns had made guns deployed in plain view vulnerable.

Following that war, increasing gun range, more powerful propellants and improved breech designs resulted the widespread adoption of BL field guns. Great Britain introduced 12- and then 15-pounder models, predominantly firing shrapnel, and 5-inch howitzers firing shrapnel and explosive. The guns, with their higher muzzle velocity and flatter trajectory provided the kinetic energy for shrapnel to attack opposing troops. The howitzers, with lower muzzle velocities, arcing trajectories and explosive shells allowed the attack of positions. The larger Australian colonies purchased some of these field guns, with NSW also acquiring a battery of 5-inch howitzers.[16]

Artillery Tactics: The Coast Defence Artillery System

In colonial times, fortified harbours around Australia included Army-operated forts with coast artillery batteries and minefields, in addition to Navy-operated floating defences and torpedoes. For Australian colonial governments, any foreign incursion into their littoral waters was cause for alarm, and particularly so after 1870, when colonial expansion into the Indo-Pacific accelerated. Foreign expansion drove local defence planning, acquisition and fortification of key harbours.

The colonies recruited the leading British advisor, military engineer Major-General Jervois, to plan their harbour defences. Jervois had a considerable international reputation, and was regarded by many as England's equivalent to the great French fortifications builder, Vauban. The 1875–6 Royal Commission into the Colony of Victoria's defences initiated a world-class system, based on modern technology and military engineering. Fixed defence planning across all Australasian colonies adhered to the prevailing British doctrine of harbour defence. Forts were supported by naval defences and underwater minefields.

The new Armstrong rifled guns were the prevailing ordnance of interest, and highly sought-after by the colonies, but initially unavailable. The first rifled guns used were muzzle-loading, but advancements soon introduced breech-loading versions, with higher rates of fire. Ammunition variations arose, including a quick-firing, mated shell. Nine-inch and 10-inch rifled muzzle-loading and 6-inch breech-loading guns were in operation by 1891. To assist with accurate counter-bombardment, the forts were equipped with range finders, and fire commanders applied estimated corrections to both bearing and range to account for propellant performance, the effect of wind, and the target's course and speed. Rapid, effective engagement called for well-drilled teams.[13]

The importance of naval support and the underwater minefields, alongside the heavier rifled guns, was a consequence of the ironclad warship developments. Harbour defence submarine mines (alongside fixed defences) were also the responsibility of the Army. The Military Torpedo Corps oversaw submarine mines, and included electricians, mechanics and boatmen. The Port Phillip Bay Heads fortification (completed early 1890s) was particularly progressive, and considered by some as the 'Gibraltar of the South' for its impressive construction.

These fortifications provided safe haven for the Royal Navy's maintenance, supply, communication, and training across the Australia Station. The Royal Navy continued to remain the centre of local defence efforts for the self-governing colonies, as it had been since their individual settlements.[14]

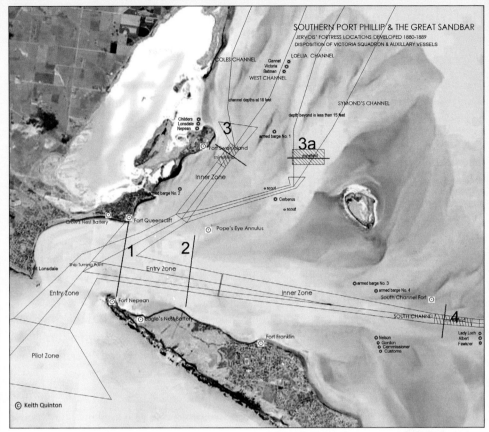

Port Phillip Heads Defence Zones – circa 1885-1887. Zone 1: Lonsdale/Queenscliff/Nepean experimental line of submarine mines (1887). Zone 2: Proposed Queenscliff-Observatory Point Line of submarine mines (1887). Zone 3: Swan Island (1885). Zone 4: South Channel (1885). Courtesy Keith Quinton, Military History & Heritage Victoria)[15]

Artillery Technology: Conventional Ammunition and Fuses

The smooth-bore cannon of Australia's early colonial defences predominately fired solid, round shot. Spherical shrapnel shells packed with a small charge of gunpowder and a number of musket balls were also available.

Cylindrical projectiles entered service with the introduction of rifled-muzzle-loading and breech-loading weapons. Because of their more streamlined forms and greater weight, these projectiles ranged further. Generally, they were shells with a hollow interior. Muzzle-loaded shells had protruding lugs to engage the rifling, whereas those loaded at the breech had soft metal 'driving bands' fitted near the base.

Shrapnel shells carried a (gun) powder burning fuse allowing variable time settings to burst the projectile in the air. The fuse also functioned on impact. Exploding shells, first filled with gunpowder, and then from the late 1890s with high explosive (HE), were fitted with nose impact fuses, or base impact fuses if of armour-piercing design.

Early in World War I, impact fuses functioned too slowly to prevent HE rounds burying before exploding, lessening their anti-personnel effect, and making them unsuitable for cutting barbed wire. The latter could only be achieved by mortar or very deliberate shrapnel fire, leading by 1917 to the development of the instantaneous fuse.

The war saw TNT (trinitrotoluene) or TNT compounds replace picric acid as the HE shell filling. It also witnessed the introduction of specialised projectiles such as white phosphorous smoke shells, illuminating shells containing magnesium flares, gas shells and incendiary shells.

These shell types, supplemented by base-ejection carrier and armour-piercing projectiles, and with improved streamlining to enhance range, persisted through World War II and beyond.

Clockwork time fuses replaced powder-burning fuses before that war, and towards its end the first proximity fuses were introduced. They transmitted a continuous radio signal, and functioned when a reflection from an object was detected, improving the chances of anti-aircraft fire inflicting damage, and allowing the field artillery to burst shells above targets without having to establish the exact range for the fuse setting.[17]

Ammunition factory turning fuse caps for artillery shells (Courtesy AWM 000007/08)

Breech-loading 5-inch howitzer (Courtesy Artillery in Canada (9) Nova Scotia: Halifax, Royal Artillery Park

A Foundation Force

In their service from the mid-1800s, the colonial artilleries laid the foundations on which the national artillery would be built. From among them arose the first regiments of the RAA, and a permanent school of gunnery. Each of the artilleries comprised a small permanent force to man the higher-readiness fixed defences, and a citizen force to assist with garrison work and provide a field element. Victoria had the largest field component, but only NSW initially maintained a permanent field battery, designated A Battery in 1893.[18] Although organisations and equipment varied between the colonies, service in their artilleries provided valuable experience to many, including some who would soon rise to prominence, such as William Throsby Bridges in NSW, John Monash and Charles Rosenthal from Victoria, J.J. Talbot Hobbs and Alfred Bessell-Browne in Western Australia, and Cyril Brudenell-White and Walter Alfred Coxen from Queensland.

As the century drew to a close, while the garrison service led the way in the search for accuracy at longer ranges, it would be Australian field Gunners in the South African War who first saw action.

The South African War: 1899–1902

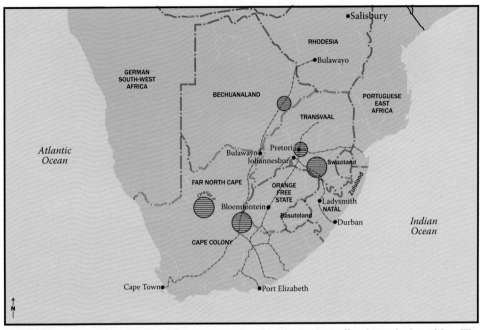

Map 2.01: Southern Africa, 1902. Australian Artillery support to the Imperial war effort during the Second Boer War was primarily in the Cape Colony and the Transvaal, as indicated by the hatched areas.

In September 1899, simmering tension between Britain and the two Boer republics in southern Africa, the Orange Free State and Transvaal, erupted into war. The Australian colonies, and after federation the Commonwealth Government, joined other members of the British Empire in sending contingents to support the British forces. Two units drawn from Regiments of the RAA served, as did over 200 Gunners who volunteered as Special Service Officers or as individuals in other colonial or national contingents.[19]

The first of the RAA units was a machine gun section of the Queensland Regiment RAA, armed with .303-inch maxim guns on travelling carriages, which deployed with the 1st Queensland Contingent. The guns proved insufficiently mobile, and the Gunners served as mounted infantry.

The second was A Battery, NSW Regiment RAA, which sailed for South Africa in December 1899 under Colonel Sydenham Smith, RA, with Warrant Officer William Coleman as Battery Sergeant-Major. The battery was armed with six 15-pounder field guns firing case shot for close protection and shrapnel shells with a range of 3750 metres.

Five Australian Gunners with a 15-pounder field gun in South Africa, 1901 (Courtesy AWM P02307.003)

Throughout 1900, commonly split into sections, A Battery supported columns skirmishing against a Boer diversionary force in the North West of Britain's Cape Colony. In January 1901, one section joined an attack on a Boer commando column attempting to enter the Cape Colony, and in subsequent action silenced the Boer guns on one occasion, and caused them to be abandoned on another. In its final months of service, the majority of the battery formed part of a column under Lieutenant Colonel MF Rimmington in the Transvaal. Rimmington praised the battery for its 'excellent horse management and accurate shooting', and his artillery commander remarked 'Australia might well be proud of such a battery'.[20]

The South African War provided valuable experience to the Gunners who participated, and in recognition of their services the RAA was presented with a King's Banner, an 'honorary distinction', in 1904.[21] While there had been little opportunity for the Australians to learn about higher command of artillery, wider lessons were evident. On occasion, in the larger battles, Boer guns and riflemen in protected positions were able to pick off exposed attackers, making direct artillery fire unsustainable, and leading some British batteries to turn to indirect fire with the guns under cover and their fire directed by an observer linked to the gun position by telephone cable. The need for a heavier component of field artillery was also identified, and for this purpose the Royal Artillery deployed 4.7-inch naval guns on land carriages.

The King's Banner of the Royal Australian Artillery held at the Australian War Memorial. The Royal Australian Artillery was represented in South Africa by A Battery from NSW. This banner was one of 20 presented to regiments and corps at a royal review in Melbourne in Melbourne 1904 on behalf of the King for recognition of their service in the war (Courtesy AWM RELAWM17231.001)

CHAPTER 3
Creating a National Artillery: 1901–1914

After Federation in 1901, Australian continued to rely on British imperial power to deter major aggression, and local coastal fortifications and field forces to deter threats posed by naval raids. Accordingly, garrison Gunners provided the first line of military defence, and formed the bulk of the permanent forces.

The period saw the creation of a national army, the rationalisation of the multiplicity of colonial equipment, the adoption of modern weapons, and the creation of new organisations. Unit structure, training and equipment reflected imperial defence ties, and the overall size of the army reflected the national reaction to changing strategic circumstances. When war broke out in 1914, Australia, long concerned by the rise of Japan and European rivalry in the Pacific, was in the process of creating a citizen-army field force of six divisions with attendant artillery components, manned through compulsory service.

Towards a National Army: 1902–1904

At the formation of the Commonwealth of Australia on 1 January 1901, there were just over 29,000 members of the previous colonial forces. Among them, the permanent artillery comprised 50 officers and 1170 other ranks, the part-time garrison artillery 1878 all ranks, and the part-time field artillery 1030 all ranks.[1]

Major-General Sir Edward Hutton took command of the Commonwealth Military Forces in January 1902 and began the organisation of a national army within an imperial security relationship with Great Britain that guided structure, equipment, training and techniques. In the July of that year, Hutton formed the three state regiments of the Royal Australian Artillery and the permanent artilleries of the other states into the Royal Australian Artillery Regiment (RAAR), the first unified Australian artillery regiment. Initially comprising 11 garrison companies, two field batteries, and the Commonwealth School of Gunnery, the RAAR persisted until 1911, at which point it was divided into the Royal Australian Field Artillery (RAFA) and the Royal Australian Garrison Artillery (RAGA).[2]

The *Defence Act 1903* authorised volunteer naval and military forces with permanent and citizen force components, the latter comprising militia (paid), volunteer (unpaid) and reserve elements. Section 31(2) of the Act limited the permanent military forces to administrative and instructional staffs, garrison artillery, fortress engineers and submarine mining engineers. While the permanent forces were liable for active service, the citizen forces were exempt, unless 'called out' by the Governor-General in time of war. Section 49 precluded members of the military forces, unless as volunteers, serving beyond the limits of Australia and its territories.[3]

Raids by foreign ships accompanied by small lodgements of troops remained the most plausible threat. Against this background Hutton established Military District staffs in each State, garrison forces for the defence of strategic centres, and a field force for the defence of the Commonwealth as a whole. The artillery composition is at Appendix 1, Table 1.[4] When Hutton's tenure expired in 1904, a Military Board assumed command of the Army, with artillery matters under the Chief of Ordnance. A Director of Artillery provided advice to the staff from 1907 onwards.[5]

The Garrison Forces

The Garrison Forces contained RAAR companies, citizen force Australian Garrison Artillery (AGA) companies, and 'District Reserves', essentially a small field element, for local protection of the forts. In the RAAR component, company officers could be designated 'sub-district officers', with responsibility, along with qualified master gunners and gunners on a separate District Establishment, for the mounting of the guns in designated forts, their care and maintenance, and the care of ammunition. Army Ordnance Department Inspection Services, the forerunner of Proof and Experimental Establishments, were also established.[6]

Forts of the time are shown at Map 3.01. Those at Townsville, Thursday Island and Albany were equipped with 6-inch breech-loading (BL) guns along with quick-firing (QF) guns of lesser calibre, as were elements of the Sydney and Port Phillip defences. However, in total there were 162 guns of 20 different types and models, many of them obsolete. Hutton produced a table to guide the rationalisation process, and by 1909 only 65 guns of nine different types remained in service.[7]

The Field Force

Colonial field batteries had been equipped with a mixture of 15-pounder, 12-pounder, and 9-pounder BL guns, with NSW also possessing four 5-inch BL howitzers, Victoria 40-pounder RBL guns, and Tasmania two mountain and two siege guns.[8]

Hutton's Field Force comprised six light horse and three infantry brigades supported by 12 four-gun field batteries, one mountain battery, and two 'position' batteries, one of 5-inch howitzers, the other of 4.7-inch guns. Two of the field batteries were permanent sub-units, designated as 'Instructional Cadre RAAR' to meet the strictures of the Defence Act, and the others were citizen force Australian Field Artillery (AFA) batteries. Artillery Brigade staffs were established in NSW, Victoria and Queensland for administration rather than operations.[9]

RAAR and AFA batteries standardised on the 15-pounder BL gun, the most modern in the existing arsenal. Internationally, however, the pre-eminent field gun was the French *Canon*

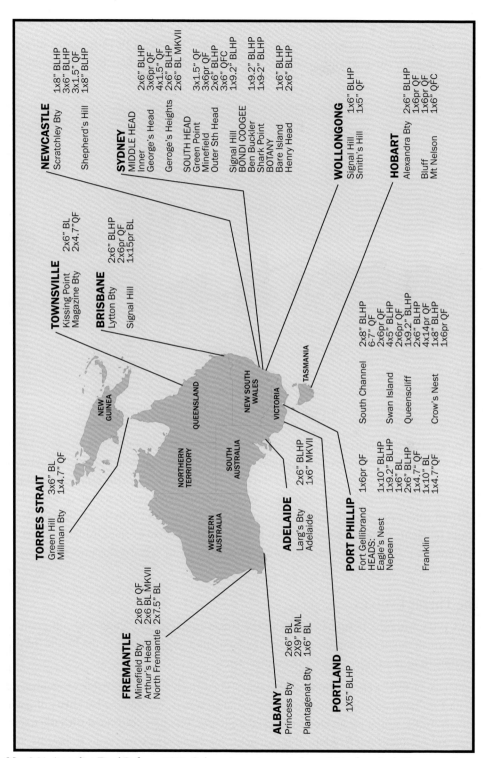

Map 3.01: Australian Fixed Defences 1903. Only service equipment is shown. Many forts also held reserve and obsolete equipment.

NEWCASTLE
Scratchley Bty	1x8" BLHP
	3x6" BLHP
	3x1.5" QF
Shepherd's Hill	1x8" BLHP

SYDNEY
MIDDLE HEAD	
Inner	2x6" BLHP
Geroge's Head	3x6pr QF
	4x1.5" QF
Geroge's Heights	2x6" BLHP
	2x6" BL MKVII
SOUTH HEAD	
Green Point	3x1.5" QF
Minefield	3x6pr QF
Outer Sth Head	2x6" BLHP
	3x6" QFC
Signal Hill	1x9.2" BLHP
BONDI COOGEE	
Ben Buckler	1x9.2" BLHP
Shark Point	1x9.2" BLHP
BOTANY	
Bare Island	1x6" BLHP
Henry Head	2x6" BLHP

WOLLONGONG
Signal Hill	1x6" BLHP
Smith's Hill	1x5" QF

HOBART
Alexandra Bty	2x6" BLHP
	1x6pr QF
Bluff	1x6pr QF
Mt Nelson	1x6" QFC

TOWNSVILLE
Kissing Point	2x6" BL
Magazine Bty	2x4.7"QF

BRISBANE
Lytton Bty	2x6" BLHP
	2x6pr QF
Signal Hill	1x15pr BL

PORT PHILLIP
Fort Gellibrand	1x6pr QF
HEADS:	
Eagle's Nest	1x10" BLHP
Nepean	1x9.2" BLHP
	1x6" BL
	2x6" BLHP
Franklin	1x10" BL
	1x4.7" QF
South Channel	2x8" BLHP
	6-7" QF
Swan Island	2x6pr QF
	4x5" BLHP
Queenscliff	2x6pr QF
	1x9.2" BLHP
	2x6" BLHP
Crow's Nest	4x14pr QF
	1x8" BLHP
	1x6pr QF

TORRES STRAIT
Green Hill	3x6" BL
Millman Bty	1x4.7" QF

ADELAIDE
Larg's Bty	2x6" BLHP
Adelaide	1x6" MKVII

FREMANTLE
Minefield Bty	2x6 pr QF
Arthur's Head	2x6 BL MKVII
North Fremantle	2x7.5" BL

ALBANY
Princess Bty	2x6" BL
Plantagenat Bty	2x9" RML
	1x6" BL

PORTLAND
1X5" BLHP

de 75 Modèle 1897, a QF weapon with on-carriage recoil and recuperation that gave it a high rate of fire. Britain's response was to introduce the Ordnance QF 18-pounder, initially armed only with shrapnel shell. Australia began to order 18-pounders in 1904, acquiring 36 by 1909.[10]

Military exercises during the visit of Lord Kitchener. Gunners with QF 18-pounder in action near Harris Creek, NSW, 1910 (Courtesy AWM P00595.023)

Training, guided by British manuals, was conducted against a debate as to whether direct fire remained practical given the experiences of recent wars, and whether the deployment of field guns alone, as practised by the French, was sufficient. British gunners generally favoured indirect fire, but, envisaging a war of manoeuvre, many senior commanders preferred direct fire. As the debate continued, the question of whether field howitzers should be retained was resolved in 1910 with the introduction of the Ordnance QF 4.5-inch howitzer, firing both shrapnel and high explosive, to replace the now-obsolescent 5-inchers.[11]

The Threat Evolves

From 1905 onwards, Japanese success in the Russo-Japanese War along with uncertainty over German intentions and the presence of a German naval squadron in the Pacific led the government to reconsider its defence arrangements.

Many coastal forts were re-armed at this time. The 6-inch BL gun, capable of combating the heaviest naval guns likely to appear in Australian waters, became the backbone of coast gunnery. In the search for greater accuracy, the garrison Gunners continued with the use of range and position finders; adopted instruments for calculating corrections to bearing and range to account for target travel, meteorological effects and propellant temperature; and began incorporating allowances for the actual muzzle velocity of each gun.[12]

Members of the Short Course at the South Head Commonwealth School of Gunnery moving a 6-inch Elswick Ordnance Company Pattern K gun barrel towards its mounting position, 24 April 1910. A 9-inch, 12-ton rifled muzzle loading (RML) gun is in the background (Courtesy AWM P00991.108)

Compulsory Military Training: 1911–1929

In the uncertain strategic circumstances, the Royal Military College, Duntroon, was established in 1911 for the professional training of permanent officers. After successive governments had contemplated compulsory military service, a scheme was finally implemented in 1912, in which males were to be trained in cadet units, and then in the citizen forces between the ages of 18 and 20. In the course of these two years, artillery recruits were to complete 25 days of instruction annually, of which at least 17 had to be in camp. The liability to serve continued until age 26.[14]

Military planners envisaged that by 1920 this scheme would provide a militia force of eight light horse brigades and six infantry divisions. Its field artillery would consist of 14 field artillery brigades, each of three batteries of four guns, along with separate batteries to support the light horse brigades, six howitzer batteries, and associated trains of horse drawn wagons, known as ammunition columns, for resupply. New 18-pounders were to be bought regularly to support the expansion, and sixteen 4.5-inch howitzers were ordered in 1913.[15]

By August 1914, citizen force artillerymen manned 13 garrison companies, and 27 field batteries in eight artillery brigades.[16] Constant expansion and limited training time constrained readiness. During an Imperial inspection in 1914, General Hamilton of the British Army reported favourably on the standard of driving and some of the shooting in the field artillery. However, he noted that even the better batteries had not had the opportunity to practice higher control and cooperation with the other arms, and nor had artillery brigades learnt how to manage ammunition supply because no ammunition columns had yet been formed.[17]

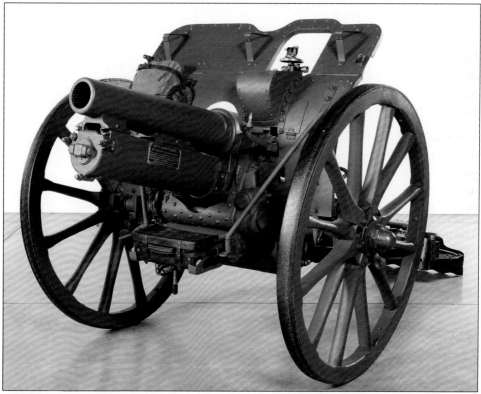

British Q.F. 4.5-inch howitzer Mk II, a breech-loading artillery piece (Courtesy AWM REL46223)

War Approaches

As it had done during colonial times, between Federation and 1914 the permanent garrison artillery continued to provide the high readiness defence against what was considered to be the most likely threat to Australia. Augmenting the permanent forces, the citizen force garrison companies and field batteries were firstly consolidated on national lines, and then expanded with compulsory training. Service in both the garrison and field branches gave many Gunners the opportunity to develop artillery skills, and allowed officers and non-commissioned officers to broaden their leadership and command experience. The advent of the 18-pounder and the 6-inch guns in the field and garrison artillery respectively provided training with modern equipment.

Technically, the garrison artillery continued its pursuit of both accuracy and consistency of fall of shot with the adoption of improved instrumentation and corrections for actual muzzle velocity. In the field artillery, the question of direct fire or indirect fire controlled by an observer remained unresolved.

By 1914, with the field force mid-way through expansion, field artillery units were not fully trained, and the howitzers that were to form part of its establishment had not arrived. Gathering war clouds signalled that the nation and its artillery would be tested before these deficiencies could be rectified.

Artillery Technology: Propellants and Calibration

Propellants are explosive compounds whose burning creates rapidly expanding gases that in turn accelerate the projectile. An ideal propellant produces neither flash nor smoke, withstands the shocks of handling and transport, remains stable in storage, leaves no residue, and does not corrode the barrel excessively.

Gunpowder, the principal propellant until the end of the 19th century, created clouds of smoke. In 1893, Britain introduced a smokeless compound of gun cotton and nitro-glycerine known as cordite, because of its cord-like shape. A modified version, cordite MD, designed to reduce barrel erosion, entered service in 1901. At the end of World War II, a third explosive was included in the mixture to make the propellant flash-less.

The heat, chemical action and pressure generated by propellant gases erode a gun's barrel. The abrasion caused by a projectile's driving band compounds the effect. Barrel wear lowers muzzle velocity and makes the projectile slightly less stable in flight, resulting in a loss of range and increased dispersion of fall of shot at the target.

For each gun type, the elevation required to achieve a specified range is determined by the use of a 'standard' muzzle velocity obtained from proof firings. In 1905, the Royal Navy and the garrison artillery began to measure actual muzzle velocity, a process known as calibration, and to compensate for the difference from the standard when producing firing data, thus improving accuracy.

The need to calibrate the heavy and field artillery arose in World War I because of the accuracy required to fire close to own troops and engage unobserved targets. Calibration became routine by 1917, and continued in subsequent conflicts through the use of periodic firings, and adjustments to muzzle velocity values calculated from wear measurements of the bore or the number of rounds fired. Since the 1960s Doppler radars have assisted in muzzle-velocity measurement.[13]

Image 1D: Cleaning Queensland cotton, a constituent of gun cotton, which is used for making cordite. Maribyrnong, January 1941 (Courtesy AWM 005024)

CHAPTER 4
To War: 1914–1915

Reports of tension in Europe began in late June 1914. Austro-Hungarian and Russian mobilisation a month later drew in Germany and France. The British Empire declared war on Germany and Austria-Hungary on 4 August 1914.[1]

Warned of imminent war six days earlier, Australia's Government offered a force of 20,000 men for overseas service. The initial challenge for the Gunners was to man the coastal forts while raising and training the artillery of the expeditionary force, and then supporting it in its first actions. Over the next 15 months, the artillery of a division would be created and committed to action at Gallipoli, providing the first experience for Australian artillerymen of modern war, while in the background further steps were taken to raise additional artillery forces.[2]

First Actions

The garrison artillery was the first to be mobilised, and a little over three hours after the declaration of war, the permanent Gunners at Port Phillip Heads fired the first Australian shot of the conflict across the bows of the German steamer *Pfalz* as she attempted to leave the bay.[3] For some months the forts were continuously manned, but after Japan allied itself with Britain and France, and the German Pacific forces were defeated, there was little chance that Australia would come under naval attack, and readiness and manning levels were gradually reduced.

In raising the expeditionary force, the military commanders of the day concluded that the generally young and inexperienced members of citizen force units would not meet the requirement. The government amended the Defence Act to allow the formation of an expeditionary body, subsequently known as the Australian Imperial Force (AIF).[4] The initial rush of recruits formed the 1st Australian Division, commanded by Major-General William Throsby Bridges, along with an additional infantry brigade, three light horse brigades and some ancillary units.

The 1st Australian Divisional Artillery

Similar to British structures of the time, the 1st Australian Division's artillery consisted of the Headquarters (HQ) Divisional Artillery, a Divisional Ammunition Column, the 1st, 2nd and 3rd Australian Field Artillery (AFA) Brigades with their ammunition columns, and nine AFA batteries each equipped with four 18 pounders. No howitzer batteries were formed, as no 4.5-inch howitzers were available.

Bridges chose Colonel J.J. Talbot Hobbs as his divisional artillery commander, titled the Commander Royal Artillery (CRA). Hobbs' three artillery brigade commanders were Lieutenant-Colonel Christian, a Boer War veteran and immediate past commander of the permanent 1st Battery RAFA, and Lieutenant-Colonels George Johnston and Charles Rosenthal, former commanders of militia batteries and brigades. The battery commanders likewise possessed permanent or militia experience. All joined a divisional structure they had not encountered previously.

Training in Egypt: 1915

En route to Europe when the Ottoman Empire joined with Germany and Austria-Hungary, the 1st Australian Division was disembarked in Egypt for training and defence duties. Here, along with the newly created New Zealand and Australia (NZ&A) Division, it was grouped into the Australian and New Zealand Army Corps (ANZAC). The NZ&A Division's artillery, commanded by Lieutenant-Colonel George Napier Johnston, consisted of the three 4-gun batteries of the 1st NZ Field Artillery Brigade, along with a battery of 4.5-inch howitzers.

The Corps Commander, Lieutenant-General Sir William Birdwood, noted the inexperience of the artillery, as did the corps' senior Gunner, Brigadier-General Charles Cunliffe-Owen. Hobbs and Napier Johnston trained their forces in accordance with the artillery manuals and notes issued by the British Expeditionary Force in France, which indicated that on the modern battlefield, direct fire was impractical, concealment was paramount, indirect laying with observers displaced from the battery was the norm, and line communications were difficult to maintain. By late March 1915, each of the Australian batteries had undertaken individual, battery and field brigade training along with collective exercises with the infantry. At a time when ammunition was restricted, they had fired 120 rounds in both day and night practices. The New Zealanders achieved similar standards.[5]

Gallipoli: 1915

While ANZAC was in training, a combined British and French fleet attempted to break through the Dardanelles to reach the Ottoman capital, Constantinople. When those attempts failed, ANZAC was earmarked for the Gallipoli campaign, and sailed in early April 1915, reinforced by the 7th Indian Mountain Artillery Brigade with its two batteries of six 10-pounder mountain guns (explosive and shrapnel shell). To open the action, General Sir Ian Hamilton, Commander of the Mediterranean Expeditionary Force, ordered the British VIII Corps to land at Cape Helles at the foot of the Gallipoli peninsula, and ANZAC to land 20 kilometres further north around Gaba Tepe.[6]

Upon landing, ANZAC could capture no more than a shallow beachhead, riven with ridges and gullies, with a frontage of approximately 3 kilometres and a depth not exceeding 1000 metres. Within a week, Hamilton placed it on the defensive. Five of ANZAC's batteries and an artillery brigade headquarters were sent to Cape Helles, leaving only two field artillery brigade headquarters and five field batteries to support the 1st Australian Division, and one field artillery brigade headquarters, two field batteries and a howitzer battery to support the NZ&A Division.

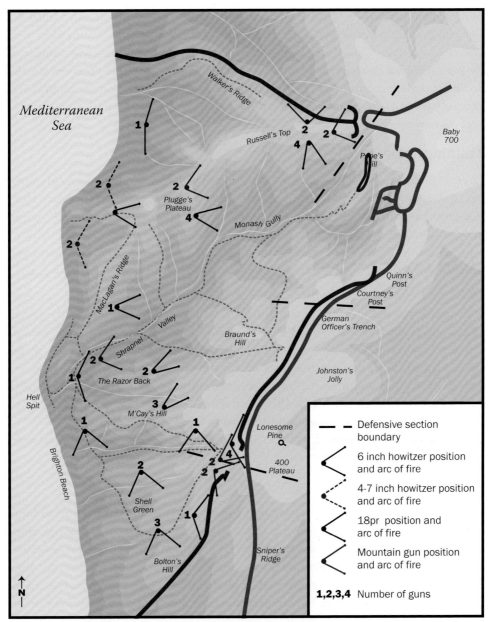

Map 4.01 Anzac Defensive Sectors and Battery Positions 25 May 1915. By 25 May, all the allotted fire units had been brought ashore and firing positions largely determined.

ANZAC's Gallipoli campaign divided into three phases. The first involved holding the line in the initial beach head, and the second an offensive in August to gain high ground to the north of that bridgehead and link up with a British landing at Suvla Bay. The final phase involved holding an extended line incorporating the newly captured territory, with the forces reinforced by two extra divisions less their artillery, one of which was the 2nd Australian Division.

Holding the Line

As shown in Map 4.01 the shallowness of the initial ANZAC beachhead and its rugged terrain meant that because of their flat trajectories the field and mountain guns had to be deployed forward on the ridge-lines, with each battery, some in split positions, having a restricted arc of fire, and each gun in a pit. The howitzers were deployed closer to the shore. Ammunition was resupplied using mules or manpower. Coverage of the front line was achieved, but only a limited number of guns could engage any one point.[7]

The terrain in the area captured after the August offensive was less rugged, allowing the batteries deployed there to stand further back. But even though more guns were landed and ANZAC's batteries returned from Cape Helles, the longer front line meant that the number of guns that could support any one point remained constrained

Three gunners of the 8th Battery with their 18-pounder Mk II in action near Walker's Ridge, Gallipoli, 1915 (Courtesy AWM A01049)

In such a small area of operations, artillery command should have been exercised at corps level, but Cunliffe-Owen was an adviser, and had no staff. Divisional command prevailed, the two artillery commanders operating cooperatively in accordance with corps directives and with communications provided by a separate artillery telephone network. Control of the fire of nominated guns was delegated to artillery brigade commanders stationed alongside the infantry commander of each defensive section. Each battery established an observation post. In terms of joint support, corps headquarters agreed that the navy would take on targets to the flanks and in depth, while the artillery handled closer missions.

Ammunition supply was restricted, but the guns provided defensive fire along the ANZAC line, and took on impromptu targets such as troop movement, observation posts and working parties. Observers 'ranged' fire onto the desired area by adjustment of fall of shot, and, for important targets, recorded bearing, range and fuse length for future use, a process known as registration. Shrapnel remained the principal 18-pounder ammunition. High explosive was available from August onwards, but not in large quantities.

Counter-battery work proved to be a major task, although observers had problems locating hostile weapons accurately when only muzzle flashes or dust raised by firing provided clues. Aerial reconnaissance was used periodically and proved beneficial, but aerial ranging of rounds onto a target commonly failed because communications broke down. The Gunners tried firing multiple batteries at hostile guns and using retaliatory fire on the Ottoman trenches, but usually only obtained a temporary effect. For their part, the Ottomans with their better observation and masked gun positions were prevented from 'making life at ANZAC very nearly intolerable' by their very limited ammunition supply.[8] Even so, they occasionally inflicted heavy damage on ANZAC's guns, and the stoicism of the detachments under fire set a standard of dedication to duty admired by their comrades.

Two gunners of the improvised Heavy Battery with a naval QF 4.7-inch gun at Gallipoli, 1915
(Courtesy AWM P08097.003)

In such rugged country, howitzers with their plunging fire were preferable to field guns, and from the outset the Gunners pressed for more. Individual 6-inchers arrived in May and June, and the landing of a 4.7-inch gun in the latter month allowed the formation of an Australian Heavy Battery with counter-battery duties. Six British 5-inch howitzer batteries arrived in late June and July, in time for the August Offensive, by which stage a few early mortars were in use with limited local effect. British 6-inch howitzer and 60-pounder batteries came ashore afterward, as did a 12-pounder anti-aircraft gun, subsequently manned by Australians.

The August Offensive

In August 1915, Hamilton decided to revitalise the campaign by capturing Suvla Bay to the north of ANZAC's beachhead, and the Sari Bair range in between. The latter task fell to the NZ&A Division, while the Australians mounted diversionary attacks at Lone Pine, the Nek and German Officers' Trench, the latter to be accompanied by the explosion of mines.[9]

In the course of the offensive, programmed artillery and naval fire supported seven attacks. In each case, batteries and ships engaged designated targets. The fire at Lone Pine suppressed the defenders sufficiently for the attackers to capture the position, but at the Nek the bombardment was ineffective, the most likely reason being insufficient coverage of flanking Ottoman machine guns.[10]

Two officers with Hotchkiss QF 12-pounder Mk I anti-aircraft gun on a carriage garrison mount, near Shrapnel Valley, Gallipoli, 1915 (Courtesy AWM C01627)

The programmed fire for three attempts on the Sari Bair heights between 7 and 9 August proved of mixed value, in some instances being positioned too far away from the attacking troops to be of use, in others leading to friendly casualties. In the largely unsuccessful attacks at Hill 60 in late August, the fire plans failed to destroy or suppress the Ottoman supporting positions and artillery, in part because there were insufficient batteries to cover the necessary targets.

Gallipoli in Retrospect

For ANZAC's Gunners, the Gallipoli campaign was a valuable introduction to war, allowing them to gain experience in providing impromptu and programmed support while setting a high standard of devotion to duty, and demonstrating the ability to adapt to unexpected circumstances and terrain. For defensive purposes, the fire support provided by the limited number of guns available along with those of the Navy and the firepower of the infantry was sufficient to hold the Ottomans in check.

As their own masters in a small bridgehead, the Gunners established reliable communications, and created a responsive command and control regime that included artillery commanders operating alongside their infantry counterparts. However, they were unable to institute an effective counter-battery system or totally reliable arrangements for support of attacks.

One of the last Australian guns on the peninsula, a QF 18-pounder, 9th Battery, 3rd Field Artillery Brigade, Gallipoli, 19 December 1915 (Courtesy AWM P00046.041)

Artillery Commanders: Brigadier-General Sir Joseph John Talbot-Hobbs, CB, KCB, KCMG

Sir Joseph John Talbot-Hobbs was one of the pre-eminent Australian Gunners of World War I. Born in London in 1864, he moved to Perth, Western Australia, in 1887 where, while serving in the citizen forces, he commanded the 1st (Western Australian) Field Battery, the Western Australian Mixed Brigade and the 22nd Infantry Brigade, while also attending various courses to further his military education at his own expense.

At the outbreak of war in 1914, Hobbs was appointed Commander, Royal Artillery for the 1st Australian Division. In this role, he wrestled with the emerging demands of trench warfare. Gallipoli was a modest introduction, as the peninsula's distinctive geography inhibited the quantity and quality of artillery support that could be provided. Hobbs ensured his artillery could support all sectors of the line, and with his counterpart in the flanking division, established command and control arrangements to provide mutual artillery support.

On the Western Front, Hobbs was exposed to the full destructive force of contemporary firepower. In deciding how best to employ his guns, Hobbs realised that close and efficient cooperation with the infantry was the key to tactical success in trench warfare. He emphasised this as his Gunners acclimatised to the Western Front, and by the time they were thrown into the maelstrom of the Somme, they had been honed to an imposing standard. 'He handled his artillery with conspicuous success', his divisional commander wrote after the battle of Pozieres, 'always ready to support the infantry generally intelligently anticipating their requirements.'

At the end of 1916, Hobbs was appointed to command the 5th Australian Division. Drawing on his combined-arms warfare experiences, he led the division with distinction for the remainder of the war. On his return to Australia he remained in the citizen forces until his retirement from the military in 1927 and was an active supporter of returned servicemen's associations and causes until his death in 1938.

Image 3B: An outdoors portrait of Major General Sir JJ Talbot Hobbs (Courtesy AWM E05007)

CHAPTER 5
The Western Front: 1916–1918

After Gallipoli, the 1st and 2nd Australian Divisions returned to Egypt, where the recently formed 2nd Division's artillery joined its parent formation. Seeking to expand the AIF, the government agreed to raise the 3rd Australian Division at home and dispatch it to Britain for training, and create the 4th and 5th Australian Divisions in Egypt by drawing on the large reinforcement pools then at hand. After expansion was achieved, the AIF's infantry divisions were to be committed to the Western Front, while its mounted troops would remain in the Middle East, supported by British artillery as required.[1]

In France and Belgium over the next three years, the Australian artillery was but one component of the much larger artillery of the British Expeditionary Force (BEF), participating in the BEF artillery's quest to nullify its German counterparts and provide the support that would ensure the success of allied attacks. For the Australians, this involved periodic reorganisation, the gradual adoption of techniques enabling fire to be opened accurately, mastering the intricacies of planning and delivering programmed fire and, in 1918, providing support to mobile operations.

Australian artillerymen commanded the divisional artilleries, and towards the end of the war, the artillery of the Australian Corps. Gunners of all ranks found themselves in the line for extended periods, supporting their own and other divisions, and setting an example of devotion to duty despite the casualties inflicted by hostile batteries and the deprivations of the battlefield.

Expansion: 1916

To create the 4th and 5th Australian Divisions in Egypt, units and individuals were transferred from the 1st and 2nd Australian Divisions, with vacancies in all four formations filled from reinforcement pools. Simultaneously, the divisional artilleries were reorganised along BEF lines to include three 18-pounder artillery brigades of four batteries, a 4.5-inch howitzer brigade with three batteries, three medium trench mortar batteries, and one heavy trench mortar battery.

The Gallipoli artillery brigade commanders rose to be divisional artillery commanders: Johnston (2nd Division), Rosenthal (4th Division) and Christian (5th Division). Behind them, experienced Gunners of all ranks stepped up a level. The training task was monumental in both scale and depth, with many of those drafted to the new batteries originally enlisted in the infantry or light horse.

LOADING A TRENCH MORTAR
OFFICIAL PHOTOGRAPH. CROWN COPYRIGHT RESERVED.   'Daily Mail' WAR POSTCARDS

Five members of an Australian artillery trench mortar battery preparing to fire their heavy trench mortar in the Chalk Pit, Pozieres, 2 August 1916 (Courtesy AWM P10028.004)

The 1st and 2nd Australian Divisions were allocated to the newly formed 1st Australian and New Zealand Army Corps (I ANZAC), and were dispatched to France in March 1916. The 4th and 5th Australian Divisions joined II ANZAC, which followed in June. At the front, the divisional artilleries underwent further reorganisation (Appendix 1, Table 2) to create, as a result of BEF experience, field artillery brigades containing three field batteries and a howitzer battery.

France: 1916

By 1916, static trench warfare on the Western Front had resulted in a growth of the artillery required for defence of Allied lines, countering the German guns, and assisting attacking infantry to assault across no-man's land through barbed wire entanglements and into the enemy trenches. Divisional artilleries were supplemented by Heavy Artillery Groups (batteries of 6, 8 and 9.2-inch howitzers and 60-pounder and 6-inch guns) allocated to corps, and even heavier artillery (9.2 and 12-inch guns and 12- and 15-inch howitzers) controlled at army level. The only Australian heavy unit was the Siege Brigade (36th Australian Heavy Artillery Group) with one 8-inch and one 9.2-inch howitzer battery, commanded by Lieutenant-Colonel WA Coxen, and manned by volunteers from the permanent artillery. With a low naval threat in Australian waters, the government allowed these members to serve abroad from September 1915. Citizen force garrison Gunners were freed for AIF service in 1916.[2]

Australian Siege Artillery Brigade in action with a BL 9.2-inch howitzer, July 1916. Brigade elements supported I ANZAC at Pozieres (Courtesy AWM EZO145)

Into Action

After landing in France, I and II ANZAC were initially allocated to a 'nursery' sector of the Second Army Front south of Armentières (see Map 5.01). In the line, the divisional artillery was divided into 'groups' of artillery brigades supporting an infantry brigade sector, with the group commander in contact with the infantry commander.[3] Batteries were deployed hidden by terrain features ('in defilade') 1500 metres or so behind the front line with a frontage of approximately 75 metres. Guns fired with barrels parallel, their fall of shot thus covering a small area.

Each battery was allocated a zone of fire and defensive barrage lines ('SOS lines'). An observer, normally the battery commander, controlled the engagement of targets. Guns were pointed (oriented) along a map bearing through the centre of their zone (the Zero Line). When opportunity targets arose, the observer ordered a switch from this line plus an estimated range gun target. Firing data for programmed targets was acquired by registration, the drawback being that the process increased the chances of the guns being located, and prejudiced surprise before an attack.

For attacks, prevailing tactics favoured preliminary bombardment and standing barrages – fire on a wide front from multiple batteries – lifting from one trench line to the next, with the intention of causing destruction. The fire plan for the XI British Corps' diversionary attack at Fromelles, in July 1916, involving the guns of the 4th and 5th Australian Divisions, followed this model. During the preliminary bombardment, certain guns and mortars were devoted to cutting the barbed wire in front of the German trenches while others barraged trenches or engaged selected depth strong-points. Unfortunately, the fire was spread too thinly to achieve the destruction envisaged by the corps commander, and his counter-battery

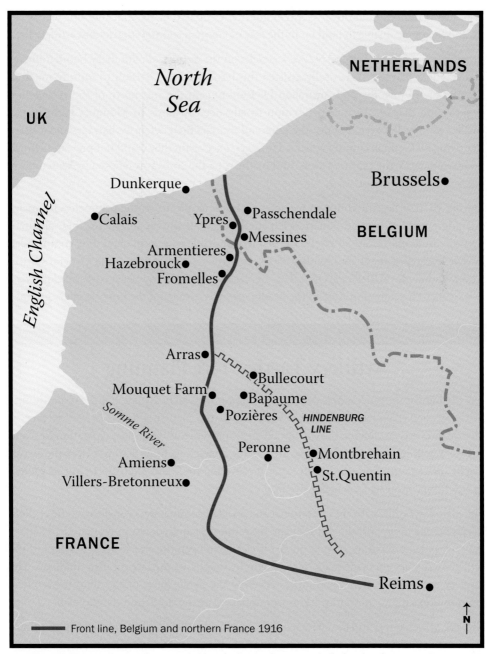

Map 5.01: The Western Front. The 1st, 2nd, 4th and 5th Australian Divisions deployed to the Western Front around Armentieres between March and June 1916. Later that year the Australians fought at Fromelles and Pozieres. In 1917 they saw action at Bullecourt, Messines and Ypres, and in 1918 principally in the area between Villers Bretonneux, Peronne and Montbrehain.

resources could not hold down German gunfire. Only two of six attacking brigades broke in, and they were unable to hold on in the face of German counter-attacks and artillery fire.[4]

Fromelles was followed by I ANZAC's attacks on the Somme. Preliminary bombardments and standing barrages successfully assisted the 1st Australian Division to capture much of Pozières on 23 July, the 2nd Australian Division to gain the area north of the village on 4 August, and the 4th Australian Division to advance eastwards to Mouquet Farm in five smaller actions. Between assaults, the guns and mortars fired defensive barrages and assisted in driving off German counter attacks. However, once again they could not prevent German bombardment of the captured areas, and by the time the corps was relieved in September it had suffered 23,000 casualties.[5]

During 1916, it became common for an army headquarters to set the parameters for major operations and for corps headquarters to plan the detail. It also became increasingly apparent that to ensure uniformity of effort, the artillery available to a corps should be commanded at that level. As a result, in October 1916, an artillery commander – the General Officer Commanding Royal Artillery (GOCRA) – replaced the artillery adviser at corps headquarters. A Brigadier-General was posted to the headquarters to command the heavy artillery groups.[6]

Artillery Tactics: Fire Planning

Fire planning is the process of providing fire support for a tactical plan. It is the responsibility of the artillery commander at the level at which the plan originates. In the defence, it incorporates targets designed to disrupt enemy arrangements (counter-preparation fire) and engage assaulting elements (defensive fire). In the attack it includes actions before the assault begins (preparatory fire), during the assault (covering fire), and after the assault to protect troops from counter-attack (defensive fire).

Fire planning begins with the operational and artillery commanders considering the artillery effects needed to support the tactical plan, the resources required, resupply and redeployment matters, and coordinating criteria, such as the time to open fire and secrecy measures. If the artillery resources are inadequate, more might be sought, or the tactical plan modified. The artillery commander then issues orders covering the deployment of the allocated artillery, ammunition supply, communications, coordinating instructions, and the fire plan.

The size of each target and the effect required governs the allocation of fire units, ammunition type and rate of fire. With their longer ranges and larger blast and splinter patterns, heavy weapons are normally allocated depth and hostile-battery targets, while the lighter field guns and mortars are used to engage areas the attackers will approach more closely. Individual target locations are normally engaged using 'concentrations', the fire of one or more gun or battery. Linear targets, or areas where target locations are unknown, called for barrages, extended lines of fire with batteries assigned to specific sections, and some batteries withheld to take on opportunity targets. During a fire plan, fire is 'lifted' onto subsequent targets in accordance with the rate of advance of the attackers.

Artillery Technology: Fixation and Orientation

Accurate maps and survey allow the precise range and direction between guns and their target to be determined. Map shooting, 'predicted fire', then becomes possible with corrections to map bearing and range to allow firstly for the difference in actual muzzle velocity from the standard contained in the weapon's firing tables, secondly for current meteorological effects on the shell in flight, and thirdly for ammunition variations from standards. If one or all of these elements are lacking, fall of shot has to be corrected onto the desired point using a process known as 'ranging' or 'adjustment of fire', which is time consuming and prejudices surprise.

Artillery survey is concerned with determining the coordinates of a specified point and the direction of grid north at that point, 'fixation' and 'orientation' respectively. Providing this data from a topographic start point aligned to the map places batteries and target acquisition devices on a common grid closely aligned with that map. This is the first step in allowing any or all of the batteries so surveyed to engage a target without ranging.

If an accurate mapping start point is not available, artillery survey can still place the batteries and observers on a common grid so that they can engage common targets effectively. Surveyed in such a fashion, they are able to engage the same target efficiently using observed fire.

In World War I, the Royal Engineers were responsible for both topographic and artillery survey. Engineer survey parties carried the latter to gun positions, leaving fixation and orientation details on a card attached to a 'bearing picket' (BP). The Gunners assumed responsibility for artillery survey in the 1920s. In conventional operations during World War II and later, artillery surveyors would typically provide a BP in each regimental area, and regimental surveyors would carry it to the gun lines.

Artillery survey methods began to change in the 1960s when gyroscopic orientation devices were issued. They were followed in the early 1980s with electro-mechanical Position and Azimuth Determining Systems (PADS) and then in the late 1980s with the use of the Global Positioning System (GPS) to provide fixation. Modern day gun sights include Inertial Navigation Systems and GPS receivers, making external survey redundant, except as a backup.

Bombardier K.L. Lutherborrow, 5th Survey Battery, taking a reading through a, theodolite, New Guinea, 22 July 1944 (Courtesy AWM 074887)

One of the lessons of 1916 was the need to more effectively counter the German artillery. Combined with the requirement to engage targets at night and even more speedily by day, this need galvanised the search for the ability to open fire accurately without ranging or registration. The search sparked efforts to improve the precision of the location (fixation) of the gun position and the orientation of the guns through better mapping and the employment of survey teams, to use aerial photography to locate targets, and to pin-point hostile batteries using intersection of bearings from surveyed flash spotting posts or sound ranging microphones. Accuracy, and the consistency of fall of shot, also involved being able to include in firing data compensation for barrel wear along with a 'correction of the moment', covering the effects of weather, differing shell and propellant types and weights, and propellant temperature.[7] A solution would not emerge fully for another 18 months.

France and Belgium: 1917

By January 1917, all five Australian infantry divisions were on the Western Front. The 3rd Australian Division under Major-General Monash was allotted to II ANZAC, and the remaining divisions to I ANZAC.

Reorganisation

The year opened with another reorganisation. Hobbs was appointed to command the 5th Australian Division. Coxen replaced him as the artillery commander of the 1st Australian Division, and Bessell-Browne rose from command of the 2nd AFA Brigade to command the 5th Division's artillery.

Across its armies, the BEF wanted to decrease the amount of time that divisional artilleries were separated from their parent formation supporting other divisions. To this end, it created a pool of independent field artillery brigades ('Army Brigades') by reducing the number of field artillery brigades in each division from four to two. The AIF artillery used this opportunity to increase the number of guns in its batteries from four to six to match British establishments, which meant it created only three (instead of ten) 'Army Brigades'. At the end of the process, the total number of Australian field artillery brigades stood at 13, and the total number of gun and howitzer batteries at 52 (see Appendix 1, Table 3).

Evolving Tactics

British artillery attack notes of March 1917 reflected the lessons of the previous year. Overpowering the German artillery became the priority task of the preliminary bombardment. Wire cutting and the destruction of defences and wire obstacles remained important, and would be assisted by recently introduced instantaneous fuses, which burst the rounds before they buried, and the fielding of 6-inch medium mortars mid-year. To facilitate the counter-bombardment effort, dedicated artillery staffs were established at corps headquarters, marking the beginning of the artillery intelligence function: the collection and collation of hostile battery data and the preparation of counter-battery plans.[8]

Artillery Commanders: Brigadier General Alfred Bessell-Browne, CB, CMG, DSO, VD

Alfred Bessell-Browne joined the Perth Volunteer Artillery in 1896, rising to sergeant in 1899. He served in two mounted infantry contingents to the Boer War, promoted to lieutenant in the first and captain in the second. The award of the DSO and a Mention in Dispatches marked Bessell-Browne already as an exceptional officer.

After the Boer War, Bessell-Browne rejoined the artillery, and commanded 37th Battery, Australian Field Artillery. He enlisted in the AIF as commander of 8th Battery, 3rd Field Artillery (FA) Brigade, and landed on Gallipoli on 4 May 1915. He commanded his battery until August, including supporting the attack at Lone Pine, and then commanded the 2nd and 3rd FA Brigades in succession. In France he initially commanded the 2nd FA Brigade before he was promoted to colonel and appointed Commander, Royal Artillery 5th Australian Division in1917.

Bessell-Browne was renowned for his courage, adaptability and innovation in deploying artillery. Appointed CMG and mentioned in dispatches for his service at Gallipoli, his service on the Western Front resulted in his appointment as CB and another nine Mentions in Dispatches. On the first night of the Battle of Pozières, he deployed one of the 2nd FA Brigade's guns to fire directly up the main street of Pozières village to provide intimate and effective fire support to the attack. Later, while commanding the 5th Divisional Artillery in the battles around Polygon Wood in September 1917, he rapidly deployed a superimposed battery to the right flank, responding skilfully to changing tactical events.

Bessell-Browne adapted quickly to the challenges of mobile warfare in 1918, continually pushing his guns up close behind the advancing infantry. In the exploitation following the attacks on the Hindenburg line in September 1918, his artillery brigades fired a creeping barrage at close to ninety degrees to the axis of advance, requiring the gun lines to be pivoted accordingly and reoriented at night, under significant time pressure – a complex modification reliant on first-rate training and precision of fire planning.

A Gunner who served at every rank to brigadier-general, Bessell-Browne's legacy to Australian artillery was his innovation and rapid application of technical and tactical solutions, based on a clear-sighted anticipation of the supported arm's fire support requirements.

Brigadier General H J Bessell-Browne with officers of the 13th Brigade, Australian Field Artillery (Courtesy AWM E03695)

Artillery Technology: Artillery Intelligence

Artillery intelligence had its genesis in the counter-battery (CB) arrangements of World War I, and in particular the establishment in 1917 of a Counter-Battery Staff Officer (CBSO) and a small office at each corps' artillery headquarters.

The CB office collated material from shelling reports, engineer flash spotting and sound ranging sections. Flash spotters obtained locations using intersected bearings to muzzle flashes from dedicated observation posts, while sound ranging teams calculated sound ranges from the different times that the sound of firing crossed a string of microphones. Aircraft provided aerial observation and, importantly, aerial photography.

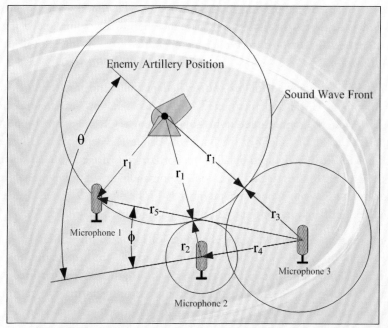

Diagram example of a Sound Ranging system in operation (Courtesy Ziggle)

The CBSO controlled the corps' counter-battery fire, predominately using heavy howitzers, taking advantage of improvements in mapping, survey, and detailed gun data calculation to engage hostile batteries without ranging. Experience showed that effective CB relied on intelligence to gather hostile battery locations, development of an engagement policy, and the dedication of guns to the role.

In World War II, artillery survey, flash spotting and sound ranging were Gunner responsibilities. CB staffs on the headquarters of the Corps Commander Medium Artillery (CCMA) collected artillery intelligence for consideration in the operational planning process. Corps orders contained a CB policy, which was implemented by the CCMA. Sound ranging remained useful, and the introduction of flash-less propellants made flash spotting less viable, and the necessity to locate mortars rose in importance, leading to the fielding of the first mortar locating radars in 1944. The analysis of shell craters was used to determine weapon calibre, type of shell and direction of fire.

After the war, survey units became 'observation' and then 'locating' units. 'Counter-bombardment' encompassed both counter-battery and counter mortar fire. The personnel involved became artillery intelligence staffs. In Australia, apart from a short-lived citizen force Observation Regiment, the Army typically created divisional locating batteries, comprising, until the 1970s, locating, survey and meteorological elements. Capabilities were expanded thereafter with the introduction of weapon (gun, mortar and rocket) locating radars, unattended ground sensors, ground surveillance radar, and, ultimately, uncrewed aerial vehicles, leading to 'locating' being now known as 'surveillance and target acquisition'.[9]

Nui Dat, South Vietnam. 1966. Radar equipment for locating and detecting enemy artillery positions, used by 131st Divisional Locating Battery, Royal Australian Artillery, 1st Australian Task Force (1ATF) (Courtesy AWM EKN/66/0064/VN)

During the attack phase, doctrinal emphasis switched from attempting destruction to suppressing or neutralising the German defences – that is, keeping the defender's head down until the attackers were almost upon him. For the field artillery this entailed creeping barrages within which brigades and batteries were allocated lanes.

'Creepers' began some 180 metres in front of the infantry and lifted in 90-metre increments at a specified interval, pausing where necessary for the infantry to consolidate intermediate objectives, and transforming beyond the final objective into a static barrage protecting consolidation on the objective. Fire was usually overhead the attackers, with the barrage lines at right angles to the line of advance. High explosive (HE) and smoke could be fired, but shrapnel was preferred because the balls went forward, were lethal and created a dust haze on impact that was useful for obscuring enemy observation. Assaulting troops were urged to 'lean on' the barrage – approach it closely – despite the risk of casualties, and were accompanied by forward observation officers (FOO), who reported back on the effectiveness of the fall of shot. Unfortunately, these observers could only communicate by telephone, ground induction (power buzzer), visual signal or pigeon, and so contact was frequently lost.

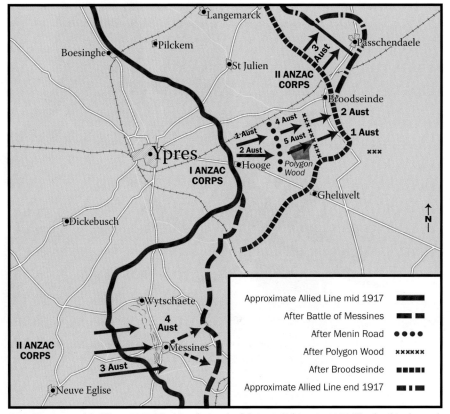

Map 5.02. Messines and 3rd Ypres 1917. The Map depicts the fighting in Belgium in 1917. The detail in the south depicts the involvement in July of II Anzac Corps in the Battle of Messines. The detail east of Ypres depicts attacks that were part of the battles of 3rd Ypres in September and October. All of these battles involved larger BEF forces, but for simplicity only the involvement of the Anzac Corps and their divisions is shown.

Field howitzers generally fired a separate 'creeper', using HE, in advance of that of the field guns. Some field howitzers joined the heavy groups in engaging depth targets and approach routes. Certain field batteries were tasked with responding to impromptu calls for fire, with their effort superimposed on the barrage in the meantime. Others were tasked to react to air observation, and provided with radio links with the aviators.

The Battles of 1917

After the German withdrawal from the Somme to the Hindenburg Line in early 1917, Australian Gunners were involved in battles at Bullecourt in April/May, in the major offensives at Messines immediately south of Ypres in June, and in the Ypres salient from July to November.

At Bullecourt, an opening quick divisional attack supported initially by tanks alone failed. It was followed by a German riposte, and the temporary loss of control of 21 Australian guns. With order restored, a second divisional attack resulted in the capture of a section of the German line, and included perhaps the first Australian use of a creeping barrage.[10]

In contrast, the Second Army's offensive at Messines (depicted in Map 5.02) was a very deliberate affair, involving 2468 guns and a month of preliminary and counter-battery fire. The 3rd Australian Division had the resources to shell over 400 targets in the days before the attack, and then advance behind an effective creeping barrage to its objectives. The 4th Australian Division received similar covering fire for its subsequent action.[11]

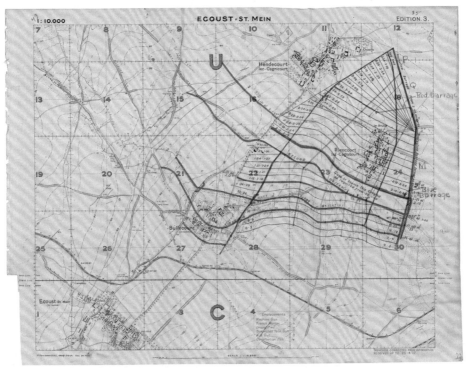

2nd Division Artillery barrage map for the Second Battle of Bullecourt, 3–15 May 1917, perhaps the first Australian employment of the creeping barrage. The Second Battle of Bullecourt was conducted by the Australian 2nd Division as part of the Battle of Arras, a larger British offensive (Courtesy AWM RCDIG1014541_36)

During the later battles in the Ypres salient, the Australian divisional artilleries initially left Second Army and joined the artillery supporting the opening attack mounted by the Fifth Army. Back in Second Army, the Australian artillery was involved in the preliminary bombardments and creeping barrages associated with the successful attacks at Menin Road (20 September), Polygon Wood (26 September) and Broodseinde (4 October). Support for subsequent attempts to take Passchendaele proved much more difficult. By then the guns had been in action for three months, hostile battery fire remained heavy, and drenching rain impeded observation and turned the battlefield to a slough, forcing the Gunners to work deep in mud, and confining movement and ammunition resupply to narrow duckboard tracks.

Ypres demanded much of the Gunners. As an example of the human cost, between 18 July and 4 November the 1st Australian Division's artillery lost 1559 killed, wounded and sick from a strength of 2648.[12]

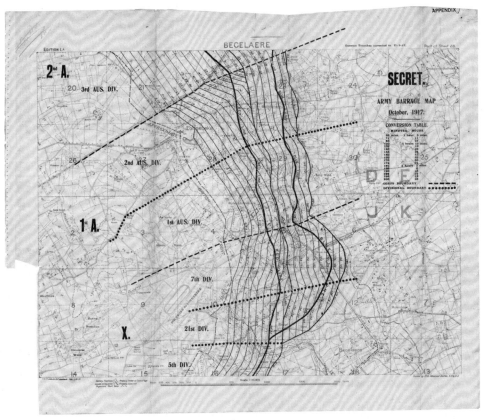

Barrage Map of I ANZAC, Battle of Broodseinde Ridge 4 October 1917. The Battle of Broodseinde Ridge included I and II ANZAC attack on the ridge as part of the Flanders offensive (Third Battle of Ypres) (Courtesy AWM RCDIG1011267)

Quo Fas Et Gloria Ducunt: Bombardier Lindsay Barrett DCM

On enlistment in the AIF Lindsay Barrett was allocated to the 13th Reinforcements of the 3rd Light Horse Regiment. Arriving in Egypt, with new units being formed for France and Belgium, the thought of the artillery appealed to the young soldier, and after further training, he was posted to 101st Howitzer Battery, part of 1st Field Artillery Brigade.

In October 1917, Barrett's battery was in action on the feature dubbed ANZAC Ridge, near Ypres in Belgium. Barrett, now a temporary bombardier, was second in command of Number 5 gun. On the morning of 26th October, the battery was firing in support of an attack. Enemy counter-battery fire was extremely heavy, but the Gunners stuck determinedly to the task.

Suddenly, an enemy round exploded between Numbers 5 and 6 guns, killing or wounding both detachments, except for Barrett. Realising that the loss of the two guns' firepower would cause a serious gap in the barrage line, Barrett took on the task of laying, loading and firing his gun singlehanded. For the next 10-15 minutes and under extremely heavy fire from enemy artillery, he did the work of an entire detachment, his efforts sustaining the effects of the barrage.

For his actions that day, Lindsay Barrett was awarded the Distinguished Conduct Medal. He later served in the militia in World War II.[13]

Group photograph of 101st Howitzer Battery, 21 May 1916 (Courtesy AWM E03605)

Towards a Change in Tactics

In 1917 tactics were characterised as 'bite and hold': take a limited objective, hold off the counter-attacks, bring up the artillery, and then repeat the process. Artillery support involved registration and lengthy preliminary bombardment, both of which prejudiced surprise. Bite and hold was successful, but it was costly in terms of manpower, ammunition and time. Towards the end of the year, advances in gunnery and air–ground cooperation offered a potentially different approach.[14]

By late 1917, guns no longer needed to register. Detailed maps and survey data at gun positions provided precise fixation and orientation. Aerial reconnaissance, air photography and advances in sound ranging and flash spotting provided accurate enemy locations. Map bearing and range to targets could be calculated precisely, compensation for gun muzzle velocity had become commonplace, meteorological data was circulated regularly, and expanded range tables for each type of gun contained data allowed batteries to calculate the correction of the moment.

Organisationally, artillery intelligence staffs at corps headquarters produced hostile battery lists, and counter-battery plans. Sufficient heavy guns were on hand to allow hostile batteries to be neutralised immediately the attack commenced, rather than engaged beforehand in an attempt at destruction.

Gunner Harold Alexander Triggs, 54 (Aust) Siege Battery (later 1st Australian Siege Battery) with BL 8-inch howitzer at Birr Cross Roads, Ypres, 26 September 1917. The battery was conducting ranging preparations prior to the Battle of Polygon Wood, 28 September 1917 (Courtesy AWM E02048)

Combining these advances with creeping barrages and employing tanks to cut the wire, preliminary bombardment could be foregone. With careful planning and stealthy deployment, attacks could be a surprise, and momentum maintained by using smoke

Artillery Commanders: Major-General Walter Adams Coxen CB, CMG, DSO

During World War I, Major-General Coxen rose to the most senior artillery position held by an Australian Gunner, that of General Officer Commanding Royal Artillery of the Australian Corps. A permanent artillery officer before the war, Coxen's accomplishments drew on his early technical training at British gunnery schools, his mathematical and organisational prowess, and his experiences in garrison and artillery instructional appointments.

Shortly after the war's outbreak, Coxen raised and commanded Australia's first heavy artillery unit, serving within the Royal Garrison Artillery, a siege brigade designated the 36th Heavy Artillery Group. In France in 1916, the group initially saw action with the British XVII Corps around Arras, and later on the Somme.

Brigadier General Walter Adams Coxen (Courtesy AWM ART02989)

In January 1917, Coxen replaced Hobbs as the Commander Royal Artillery, 1st Australian Division. He commanded the divisional artillery throughout the German withdrawal to the Hindenburg Line and the Second Battle of Bullecourt. In these actions, and in later fire plans supporting the battles of 3rd Ypres, he gained further expertise in applying increasingly refined, complex and sophisticated firepower.

After formation of the Australian Corps in November 1917, Coxen was selected to be commander of its artillery; orchestrating, along with the heavy artillery commander, the effects of all integral and allocated artillery in support of corps plans at battles such as Hamel, Amiens, and the Hindenburg Line that marked the last year of the war. Coxen's intellectual and technical capacity enabled him to provide expert advice, and exploit the recent advances made in artillery-related technologies in the application of programmed fire. Known as the "Boss Gunner', during the attack on the Hindenburg Line, Coxen coordinated the fire of the greatest number of guns ever commanded by an Australian.

After the war, General Coxen continued to serve in the permanent forces, holding several senior appointments, and retiring as Chief of the General Staff in 1931.

screens and aerial support to hinder enemy observation. The latter was provided by close air support and army-cooperation squadrons with radio links to the guns, sharing maps gridded with easily readable alphanumeric coordinates to indicate targets, and using the 'clock code' system for corrections. Attached artillery officers provided coordination, and tactical and intelligence advice.[15]

The first British operation along these lines was mounted at Cambrai in November 1917. The Germans used similar methodology on the Eastern Front in the same year. These attacks provided a blueprint for the future, although Cambrai indicated that communications using telephone were difficult to maintain once the guns had to move forward.[16]

For the Australian artillery, the opportunity to implement the new approach would lie in the operations of the Australian Corps, which, after pressure from the Australian Government, was formed in November 1917 under General Birdwood. The Australian Corps brought together the five Australian divisions. Coxen was promoted to command the Corps' artillery, and the 36th Australian Heavy Artillery Brigade was allocated in support.

The Year of Decision: 1918

In 1918, with Russia now defeated, and in an attempt to achieve strategic success before American troops arrived in numbers, Germany launched an offensive in France on 21 March aimed at the junction between British and French around Amiens. The Australian Corps was dispatched to help counter the threat, less the 1st Australian Division, which contested a second German incursion in the north around Hazebrouck.

3rd Australian Medium Trench Mortar Battery gunners in action supporting an Australian 6th Infantry Brigade raid in the vicinity of Ville-sur-Ancre, 29 May 1918 (Courtesy AWM E02429)

The Corps assisted in stabilising the situation, amongst other actions repulsing the Germans at Dernancourt (where five Australian and British artillery brigades supported the 4th Australian Division) and recapturing Villers-Bretonneux. With the German advance stalled, Australian forces embarked on a series of minor actions, in amongst which anti-aircraft machine gunners of the 53rd AFA Battery downed the German ace Captain Baron von Richthofen.[17]

Regaining the Initiative

At the end of May, when Birdwood took command of Fifth Army, Lieutenant-General Sir John Monash assumed command of the Australian Corps. Two of his five divisional commanders (Hobbs and Rosenthal) were former artillerymen. Coxen remained in command of the corps artillery.

Lieutenant-General Sir John Monash KCMG KCB VD, General Officer Commanding, Australian Corps (seated) with senior staff officers of the Australian Corps at Bertangles Chateau, 22 July 1918 (Courtesy AWM E02750)

Monash committed 16 field and 13 heavy brigades to his first divisional attack at Le Hamel on 4 July. Creeping barrages fired by field and heavy guns were complemented by a highly effective counter-battery fire plan. There was essentially no registration and no preliminary bombardment. Harassing fire before the attack was used to acclimatise the defenders to fire occurring at certain times, and to disguise what little ranging was permitted. Smoke missions with gas intermixed conditioned the defenders to don gas masks when smoke was fired, as it was in the field barrage. On the day, harassing fire was used to disguise the start of the barrage and drown the noise of tanks moving to the start lines. The battle, which included the first use of American troops under Australian command, was recognised as a model of planning and all-arms cooperation.[18]

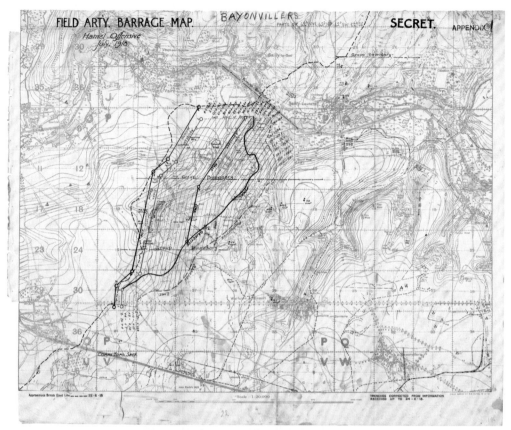

Barrage Map of 4th Division Artillery, Battle of Hamel 4 July 1918. The Battle of Hamel was conducted with the Australian 4th Division attacking the village of Hamel (Courtesy AWM RCDIG1016435)

The Battle of Amiens: August–September

A month later, on 8 August, the British 4th Army, spearheaded by the Australian and Canadian Corps, launched the allied counter-offensive, beginning with a two-phase attack around Villers-Bretonneux to capture an objective some 12 kilometres behind the German front line.[19]

In the first phase of the Australian Corps' attack, 18 field artillery brigades fired a creeping barrage, while 83 heavy howitzers fired concentrations in advance of the assault, and twice as many heavies engaged hostile batteries. The second phase was an open-warfare advance, in which field artillery brigades moved forward to engage impromptu targets, sometimes sending individual guns to accompany battalions.

In this attack and others that followed, after the German use of tanks near Villers-Bretonneux in late April 1918, some guns were specifically deployed in the anti-tank role. They were usually breech-loading converted 15-pounders manned by detachments drawn from trench mortar batteries or divisional ammunition columns.[20]

Artillery Tactics: Counter-Bombardment and the Deep Battle

In the initial years of World War I, hostile batteries could only be engaged with any effect if fall of shot could be ranged onto them. In an attempt to cover the target location, counter-battery (CB) missions might additionally include changes in line and range ('sweeping and searching'), or crossfire from dispersed batteries, or the fire from multiple batteries.

As the war progressed, air observation and photography, flash spotting and sound ranging allowed targets to be located in greater depth. The amount of heavy artillery available to engage those targets grew, and in 1917, corps CB offices were created to collate hostile battery intelligence and plan CB engagements.

CB effort first focussed on early engagement and destruction of hostile batteries. This proved disadvantageous, in that it led the enemy to provide overhead protection to gun pits, and complicate detection by creating dummy positions, firing from temporary or roving positions, or moving to alternate positions. This meant that immediately prior to an attack, accurate hostile battery location could be lost.

From late 1917, in deliberate attacks, with more accurate predicted fire and the benefits of artillery intelligence, the emphasis changed from destruction to neutralisation, achieved by silently collating enemy gun locations and engaging them at the time of the assault with the intention of disrupting their fire by the use of gas, shrapnel, high explosive or smoke. Howitzers were the preferred weapons. CB fire plans were supplemented by harassing fire on enemy artillery supply routes.

Such a methodology of deception was adopted in the lead-up to the Battle of Amiens in August 1918. The enemy was conditioned to a quiet CB pattern, the deployment of the batteries assigned to CB into their firing locations was masked, and tactics such as deliberately firing onto an old location after a hostile battery had moved were all employed.

In the conflicts that followed World War I, CB policies varied between 'active' – an approach common to the defence or mobile operations – and 'passive' – collecting information as a prelude to offensive operations.[21]

The advance continued after 8 August, often involving divisional attacks supported by creeping barrages, which increasingly incorporated smoke to screen tanks from German field-gun fire that was armour's primary threat. Mobile-warfare tactics were adopted when the Germans withdrew to the Somme bend between 25 and 29 August. Field artillery brigades were grouped with the leading infantry brigades, but found using telephone, runner and visual signalling difficult. Other field artillery brigades and heavy guns responded to calls for fire from aircraft using by now well-established radio procedures, while further heavy guns provided harassing fire in depth.

At the Somme bend, Monash faced the twin bastions of Mont St Quentin and Peronne. Their capture followed three days of quick attacks supported by standing barrages or timed concentrations of field and heavy artillery fire ahead of the advancing infantry. Thereafter the advance resumed with the mortar batteries, as they had done since mid-August, effectively using captured guns against the retreating Germans.

Final Battles: September–October

The Australian Corps' final attacks took place at the Hindenburg Line on the St Quentin Canal. The old British trenches in the area and the outpost line were captured behind a creeping barrage on 18 September. For the main attack on 29 September, with preservation of manpower an increasing concern and German morale dwindling, Fourth Army's artillery tactics reverted to those of 1917: heavy preliminary bombardments, extensive creeping barrages and counter-battery programs, the latter, in the short time available, based on judgement and air and ground observation.[22]

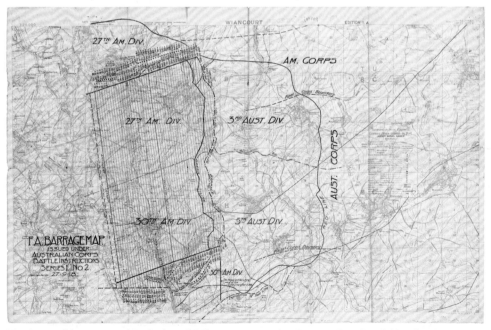

Trench map of the area around Le Catelet and Bellicourt overprinted to show time lines for a field artillery barrage on 27 September 1918 prior to the main attack on the Hindenburg Line (Courtesy AWM2022.10.1993)

Quo Fas Et Gloria Ducunt: Gunner Charles Valentine Paynter MM

Gunner Charlie Paynter originally enlisted as a member of the Light Horse before transferring to the artillery and joining 49th Battery of 13th Field Artillery Brigade.

In October 1918 he was part of a forward observation party, temporarily attached to the US 30th Infantry Division, advancing in the vicinity of the village of Montbrehain beyond the Hindenburg Line. Paynter was detailed to man a relay and transmitting station between the forward observer and the guns – little more than an unprotected hole in the ground – and subjected to the heaviest portion of the hostile artillery barrage from Zero Hour, until the advance commenced. In spite of the danger, Paynter crawled out repeatedly to repair broken communications lines. As the troops advanced, he had to run out ever further lengths of telephone line, even though he was subjected to enemy machine gun fire.

As the enemy withdrew, Paynter re-joined his observation officer. Encountering some dogged resistance, Paynter and the officer turned an abandoned German howitzer around and used it to engage the enemy at a range of 1000 yards.

Throughout the operation, Charlie Paynter showed a total disregard of the dangers around him. His citation for the award of the Military Medal noted 'His excellent conduct and devotion to duty are deserving of special recognition'.[23]

View of the Church at Montbrehain, the objective of the attack on 5 October, during which Paynter earned his MM (Courtesy AWM E03605)

For these attacks, Coxen had over 800 guns, perhaps the largest number ever controlled by an Australian officer. The divisional artillery commanders each typically controlled nine field artillery brigades. The corps' 'creeper' on 29 September covered a front of 3.5 kilometres and progressed over three and a half hours to a depth in excess of 4 kilometres, with smoke barrages on the flanks and heavy artillery fire in depth. The attacks did not go smoothly, but the objective of capturing the second Hindenburg trench line was achieved.

The artillery's capability in this set-piece engagement was matched in the more-fluid circumstances of the exploitation to the third Hindenburg trench line. Between 29 September and 2 October, two field brigades of the 5th Australian Division, each allotted to an advancing infantry brigade, pushed sections forward on nine occasions. They deployed as a whole twice, fired one combined and four individual brigade fire plans in support of local attacks – the combined plan requiring reorienting all the guns at night – and undertook impromptu and harassing missions. Over the four days they suffered 54 casualties and expended 18,551 rounds.[24]

The Australian Corps' infantry was relieved on 6 October, and its artillery was withdrawn progressively over the next month. At the Armistice on 11 November 1918, only the 36th Heavy Artillery Group was still in action, although it had fired its last rounds three days earlier.[25]

World War I in Retrospect

In World War I on the Western Front, artillery was the key to creating the conditions in which the infantry could manoeuvre, its firepower nullifying the enemy defences and thereby reducing casualties amongst the infantry and tank crews it protected.

The Australian artillery had every reason to look back on the war with solemn pride. It had expanded from three field artillery brigades to 13, created one corps and five divisional artillery headquarters, planned and participated in complex fire plans, generated highly competent artillery commanders at all echelons up to corps, and provided two of the AIF's infantry division commanders. In action its Gunners had displayed a high degree of expertise, élan and discipline. The artillery, Monash later wrote, '...undoubtedly became the paramount factor in the victories which the [Australian] Corps achieved', earning 'the confidence and gratitude of the infantry', and suppressing the German anti-tank defences[26] The Gunners suffered 14,027 casualties during the war, 58 per cent of those who had embarked as artillerymen. Although significant, this suffering was not as great as that of the infantry, for whom the figures were 166,390 and 79 per cent respectively.[27]

The Australian Gunners had been part of a successful and sophisticated British Empire artillery, a partnership recognised in May 1919 by the alliance between the Royal Artillery and the Australian artillery, through Army Order 58/1919. As part of that larger entity, the Australian artillery had benefited technically from the advances and procedures enabling indirect predicted fire, and tactically from the development of a command structure centred at corps level. This structure enabled the fire support required while sheltering the manoeuvre forces from technical detail, took best advantage of the range of the guns and their ability

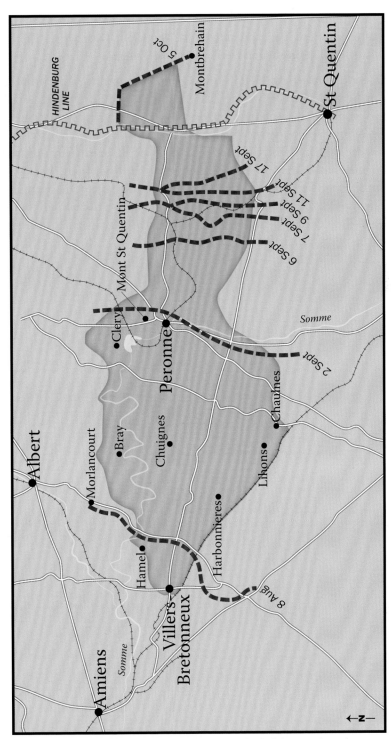

Map 5.03: The Australian Corps Advance, August-October 1918. The shaded section shows the area recovered by the Australian Corps beginning with the recapture of Villers Bretonneux in April 1918, and the seizure of Montbrehain in October 1918

to concentrate fire, and provided advice through Gunners at all levels. It was understood that the most effective fire support resulted from command of artillery at the highest level practical, with control of fire decentralised as required.

Australia's Gunners proved capable of planning and implementing close artillery support in defence and attack up to corps level. Even so, they, like other artillerymen of the era, had difficulty in providing responsive support when advancing or withdrawing, primarily because of necessary reliance on telephone communications. Furthermore, Australian units had not provided the survey, locating, and meteorological data enabling accurate predicted fire, nor operated any of the anti-aircraft guns of the BEF, nor contributed to any great degree to its heavy artillery force nor the associated counter-battery and depth battles. The war had demonstrated these capabilities would be required in a future conflict, and in such a conflict, it also remained to be seen whether the shorter-range medium and heavy mortar fire, so useful in trench warfare, would find similar utility.

CHAPTER 6
Between the Wars

With World War I at an end, Australia looked to demobilise the Australian Imperial Force and then create an Army that would allow defence of the continent within the prevailing economic constraints. The relationship with Britain remained the cornerstone of national security. Fixed defences and a field force of infantry and cavalry divisions were authorised in 1921, with permanent elements providing any high readiness capability, and citizen forces an expansion component. The artillery comprised both garrison and field elements.

During the 1920s and early 1930s the Army and its artillery was stifled by financial restrictions, over-reliance on imperial naval defence, and debate as to the Army's role. Even so, the artillery expanded somewhat through the introduction of limited medium (previously heavy) artillery, survey, locating and anti-aircraft capabilities. Further improvements occurred in the late 1930s, particularly in fixed defences and anti-aircraft artillery, but in terms of adequately manned units and the availability of modern equipment, the Army was unprepared when war broke out again in 1939.[1]

The Inter-War Army

The Australian Government consulted with senior AIF officers following World War I, and in 1921 authorised an Army establishment that allowed for a citizen force of 127,000 and a permanent cadre of 3500. Permanent officers were absorbed into a Staff Corps, and NCOs into an Instructional Corps, with responsibilities for both permanent and citizen force training. At Army Headquarters, the Directorate of Artillery was split between the Quartermaster General's Branch (design, inspection and supply of materiel), and the General Staff Branch (doctrine, organisation and training).[2]

In terms of structure (see Appendix 1, Table 4), the garrison forces comprised two Coast Artillery Brigade Headquarters, and ten (permanent) Royal Australian Garrison Artillery and 12 (citizen force) Australian Garrison Artillery batteries. The field force was organised into two light horse and four infantry divisions, with independent infantry brigades in three states providing the nucleus of a fifth division. The artillery component was four divisional artillery headquarters and 17 field artillery brigades equipped with 18-pounder guns and 4.5-inch howitzers.[3]

This structure was designed to hold an invading force until help could arrive, but it was constrained at the outset by financial stringency and the circumstance that the field force initially included neither heavier artillery nor logistic units. Further, no investment was made in modernising coast defences, obtaining the full complement of guns for the field artillery, or acquiring ammunition reserves. When the Washington Naval Agreement imposed limits on the world's navies in 1922, the government reduced the defence budget, restricting the citizen forces to 31,000 and the permanent forces to 1600. Officers and NCOs with war experience led the divisional artilleries and field brigades, but only a nucleus of each unit was manned.[4]

An Imperial Conference in 1923 confirmed that defence of the Empire rested on British maritime supremacy. With Japan a potential threat, the conference agreed to the establishment of a naval base at Singapore, with secondary stations at Sydney and Darwin.[5] A modest five-year defence program followed, with naval spending a priority. The Army was allowed to expand to 45,000. Rearmament of the coast defences was deferred, but allocations were made allowing the acquisition of sufficient 60-pounder and 6-inch howitzers to raise in 1925 two medium artillery brigades, each of two batteries, and Australia's first anti-aircraft battery of four 3-inch, 20-hundredweight (cwt) guns in 1926. These were part of the citizen force garrison artillery, as were two artillery survey companies, formed in 1925 to take over survey sound ranging and flash spotting responsibilities from the engineers. Tentative steps were also taken towards mechanical traction of the field guns, a Proof and Experimental Establishment was formed at Port Wakefield in South Australia, and the construction of an ordnance factory at Maribyrnong near Melbourne was authorised.[6]

A pair of trailer-mounted 3-inch, 20-cwt anti-aircraft guns of the 1st Anti-Aircraft Battery, Narrabeen, 1937. The gunners (left) are operating a Vickers predictor, which provided target information (Courtesy AWM P05244.003)

Throughout the 1920s, the field brigades could only achieve a moderate level of efficiency due to limited training time and the lack of horses or motorised gun tractors. Priority was given to the training of those who might lead the Army at some future mobilisation. During this decade, in Britain the Royal Artillery combined its garrison and field branches, recognising that the technical skills of both had become so similar as to make specialisation counter-productive. Australia followed suit. Permanent field and garrison Gunners were amalgamated into the Royal Australian Artillery in 1927, and at the same time coast batteries were re-designated as heavy batteries.[7] Three years later, both permanent and part-time elements adopted the same hat badge bearing the motto 'Consensus Stabiles' (Strong in Agreement). In 1936 the permanent branch was re-designated the Royal Australian Artillery Regiment and the citizen force field and garrison elements became the Royal Australian Artillery (Militia).[8]

Depression and a Changing Strategic Environment: 1929-1939

In 1929, the newly elected Government abolished compulsory training in favour of a volunteer militia. That decision, and the effect of economic depression, saw by the end of 1930, a slump in numbers enlisted to 1700 permanent force and 28,000 militia.[9]

Reviewing the strategic situation three years later, the government reaffirmed that sea power provided the principal means of defence, despite the Army's view that this approach was flawed.[10] The Army was charged with providing a divisional-level expeditionary force within three months of the outbreak of conflict. At home, it was to protect the ports from raids and minor incursions.

As Germany, Italy and Japan progressively became more warlike, the Army component of defence programs in 1933 and 1937 concentrated on the fixed defences, despite Major-General John Lavarack, a former artilleryman appointed Chief of the General Staff in 1935, advocating development of the field force.

'Titan', a floating crane unloading a 9.2inch gun off the barge and onto the beach at North Head (Courtesy AWM P02729.057)

In this period, the coast battery at Thursday Island was relocated to Darwin, and ex-naval 6-inch Mark XI guns firing 45-kilogram projectiles to 17,000 metres were installed in eight two-gun batteries around the nation, and another such battery at Port Moresby. A barracks for the 1st Heavy Brigade was established at North Head, Sydney, and two-gun batteries of 9.2-inch guns firing 172-kilogram projectiles to a range of 26,400 metres were acquired for North Head, Cape Banks, Newcastle and Rottnest Island. Their primary role was to prevent enemy ships bombarding the ports. Reports in 1938 revealed, however, that most batteries still lacked modern instruments, searchlights, armour-piercing shells and signal equipment. [11]

The defences of Darwin were strengthened in 1939 by the formation of the Darwin Mobile Force, a permanent infantry company supported by four 18-pounder and other small elements. Because the Defence Act limited those who could be permanently enlisted, members of this force, apart from the engineer component, were taken on as artillerymen.

A 3.7-inch anti-aircraft gun in the final stage of assembly at the ordnance factory in Maribyrnong, 15 May 1940 (Courtesy AWM 001597)

Artillery Technology: Anti-Aircraft Fire Control

In anti-aircraft engagements, Gunners have to determine the target's height, speed and direction along with the deflection to be applied to allow for the projectile's time of flight.

World War I Gunners used sights with deflection angles applied, so that when the sight was pointed at the target, the barrel was aimed well to its front. The first projectiles were shrapnel with powder-burning time fuses. Determining range was the key to producing an accurate fuse setting, and for this purpose the tripod-mounted optical height/range finders were used. Other instruments tracked the target and produced the vertical and horizontal deflection angles.

In the 1920s, work began on the design of predictors, mechanical computers that took inputs from optical range and height finders and calculated firing data, including allowance for wind and temperature. Data was passed electrically to repeater dials at each gun, where layers 'matched pointers' to complete the process.

During World War II, radar improved tracking, and the gradual adoption of electrical predictors produced more precise fire control. The ammunition in use was primarily high explosive with clockwork time fuses. Rapid-loading and fuze-setting devices were incorporated into gun mountings to facilitate a high rate of fire. The later introduction of proximity fuses also assisted in this regard.

Australia's 3-inch 20-cwt and 3.7-inch heavy anti-aircraft guns operated in this fashion. For protection against low-level attack, light anti-aircraft units were equipped with the 40-millimetre Bofors. This type of gun fired rapidly to provide a screen of fragments through which the aircraft would have to fly. Fire control was largely visual, though some guns were later equipped with predictors and power control.

Air defence missiles, fielded by the Australian Army from the 1970s onwards, were guided, in the case of Stinger and RBS 70 by integral heat-seeking sensors, and in the case of Rapier by radar.

Trainees of the Volunteer Defence Corps anti-aircraft searchlight school operating a Sperry gyroscope control station, Queensland, 1944 (Courtesy AWM 062578)

Anti-aircraft developments were also slanted towards the static defences, reflecting the increasing vulnerability of ports to air attack. By 1939, the 1st Anti-Aircraft Brigade had been formed, consisting of an eight-gun battery in Sydney and six-gun batteries in Darwin and Newcastle, with the militia personnel for the Darwin battery drawn from Sydney. A four-gun battery was established in Melbourne for protection of the ordnance factory. The batteries were equipped with 3-inch 20-cwt guns firing to a ceiling of 7000 metres. The ordnance factory had begun the task of producing the more-modern 3.7-inch gun, able to engage targets to a height of 9000 metres.[12]

Militia strength was raised to 35,000 in 1933, and remained at this level until 1938, when the government authorised its growth to 70,000. The following year it took steps to create from those with previous military experience Class A (under age 45) and B (age 45–60) reserves to be mobilised if required in time of war. In the field brigades the conversion of the 18-pounder and 4.2-inch howitzers to mechanical traction gained pace, but the rapid increase in unit strengths brought problems with lack of equipment and experienced trainers.[13]

War Approaches

After the financial constriction of the 1920s and the Depression, the latter half of the 1930s saw the incomplete rearmament of the coast defences and a modest increase in anti-aircraft capability, with further improvement in train. In the field force, dedicated militia volunteers, supported by the small group of permanent Gunners, kept alive the traditions and expertise gained during World War I. The gradual increase in unit strengths provided a basis for expansion, but when war broke out in September 1939, the artillery was by no means ready.

CHAPTER 7
To War Again: 1939–1941

At war initially with the Axis powers of Germany and Italy, Australia had to guard against potential naval raids and maintain a level of home defence while meeting its commitment to provide an expeditionary force (the 2nd Australian Imperial Force – 2nd AIF) and simultaneously retain the workforce required for industry, commerce and agriculture.

In the course of the next two years the Australian Government continued to upgrade the fixed defences and gradually mobilise the militia while dispatching a corps of three infantry divisions from the 2nd AIF to fight in the Middle East. Wary of Japanese intentions, it also made some pre-emptive deployments in its region.

Anti-tank and deployable anti-aircraft units were raised, and the field artillery reorganised along contemporary British Army lines. Until modern equipment became available, units made do with pre-war and even captured equipment. In action, the 2nd AIF's Gunners performed well, drawing on the experience and lessons of World War I.

Upgrading the Forts

At war's outbreak the fixed defences were mobilised, and, in an echo of 1914, Fort Nepean fired the first Australian shot of the conflict, this time across the bows of a warship not displaying the correct signals.

The fixed defences in 1940 are shown at Appendix 1, Tables 5A and B. That same year, Headquarters Fixed Defence Command was created under Brigadier J. S Whitelaw, a permanent Gunner technically trained in Britain. With his encouragement, emerging radar technology was developed and fielded. Over time, the increasing size and complexity of the static defences made it necessary to separate the management of the anti-aircraft capability from Fixed Defence Command, and in 1941 Headquarters Anti-Aircraft Command was constituted as a formation headquarters in its own right.[1]

Artillery Tactics: Air Defence Systems

Air defence is a mixture of passive and active measures. The former seeks to nullify the effectiveness of hostile air action, and the latter seeks to engage and destroy hostile air assets. Ground-Based Air Defence (GBAD) forms a sub-set of active air defence. It includes guided and unguided surface-to-air weapon systems such as anti-aircraft artillery, non-lethal means including electromagnetic systems, and integral surveillance and target acquisition assets. GBAD's persistence and all-weather capability provide its competitive advantage.

GBAD serves to protect critical assets including lines of communication, logistics and important combat elements such as counter-attack forces.

The weapon forms the principal part of the GBAD system. During World War I, weapons included standard machine guns on specialist mounts. The development of dedicated guns to counter increasing aircraft speed and altitude soon occurred. Searchlights quickly enhanced weapon systems to provide night capability and later, radar provided an all-weather capability. During World War II, radar was also used for surveillance, to alert hidden defences, and to cue and concentrate target engagement.

GBAD systems generally operate and engage hostile aircraft in specified airspace zones, known today as Missile Engagement Zones. Specific rules of engagement, known as weapon control status, regulate engagement of identified hostile targets. Interrogation by 'identification friend or foe' equipment provides an important discriminator. Early versions identified friendly aircraft by extending their 'blip' on radar displays. Modern transponders provide coded responses directly into friendly battle management systems.

A command and control element forms the Air Defence system's final component. It controls all weapon systems under command, and provides coordination with ground and air forces. During World War II, eight Anti-Air Groups operated across Australia, each controlled by an Anti-Aircraft Room.

Integrated Air and Missile Defence is the modern description of air defence. In this system, joint air, maritime and land coalition forces share target information through data links. This allows the simultaneous cueing of multiple air defence systems (surface-to-air and air-to-air) to engage hostile air threats.[2]

Gunners of 1st Section, 2nd Anti-Aircraft Battery, 2/1st Australian Anti-Aircraft Regiment, using a steam shovel to lower a cradle onto a mounting for one of their unit's 3.7-inch guns in Darwin, 1940–1941 (Courtesy AWM P02274.020)

Mobilising the Militia

The first elements of the militia field artillery to be called up were those necessary to conduct training. Units then completed 30 days training before being built in strength with enlistments from the Reserve. In January 1940 the Australian Government also reintroduced universal service, albeit for three months, after which trainees went into the Reserve unless they volunteered for militia service.

Until June 1940, the artillery retained its pre-war structure (Appendix 1, Table 6). Even with the addition of reservists, manning levels were usually short of war establishment, and enlistments into the AIF drained the units of experience. These difficulties were compounded by equipment shortages, with the field artillery still armed with Word War I weapons increasingly modified for mechanical traction. Additional units were raised when the Army transitioned from peace to war establishment in mid-1940, and two anti-aircraft and 11 anti-tank regiments were formed. However, by late 1941 these units had only approximately half the required guns, and ammunition stocks were, likewise, extremely limited.[3]

To meet increased instructional demands, the School of Artillery, which had previously been responsible for educating senior officers about artillery and providing gunnery instruction to artillery personnel, divided into a Field, Medium and Survey School at Holsworthy, and an Anti-Aircraft School at South Head. In 1941, an Anti-Tank School was created at Puckapunyal, and a School of Radiophysics (radar) at South Head. The Sydney Fire Command conducted schools for coast artillery personnel.[4]

Artillery Tactics: Anti-Tank Artillery

During and immediately after World War I, field and anti-aircraft units were tasked with anti-tank fire as a secondary role. Britain first raised dedicated anti-tank units in the late 1930s, and Australia followed suit in 1940. These units were initially armed with Ordnance QF 2-pounder (40-millimetre) guns with a fighting range of around 500 metres. The gun proved to be effective against lightly armoured Japanese tanks, but less so against German tanks. Accordingly, in 1942, it was replaced by the Ordnance QF 6-pounder (57-millimetre) with an effective range of 1600 metres. As even more heavily armoured vehicles entered service, the 6-pounder was supplemented by the Ordnance QF 17-pounder (76.2-millimetre).

These guns used direct fire, aimed by sighting telescopes. Their ammunition was commonly hardened steel shot, some types fitted with a metal cap to increase penetration. High explosive rounds were also available. In 1944, Britain perfected 'discarding-sabot' projectiles, in which a light metal casing surrounding a tungsten core fell free after leaving the muzzle, allowing the core to fly on at extremely high velocity. The 6- and 17-pounders had such rounds. Modern weapons typically use either a cone shaped high explosive that upon detonation creates a jet of molten metal to puncture the target, or plastic explosive designed to squash against the armour and induce a shock wave that peels lethal debris off the inner side of plate.

Anti-tank weapons are best sited so that their arcs interlock, with each attacking likely targets side on. Deployment in this fashion calls for centralised command rather than the allocation of guns to front-line infantry units.

Anti-tank units, re-named tank-attack units in the 1940s, remained in service until the mid-1950s, but were gradually made redundant by advances in tank armament and the development of light recoilless infantry weapons, in which the expulsion of some propellant gas to the rear balanced the recoil generated by the projectile. Back-blast made these weapons difficult to conceal, but they were universally adopted before being supplemented by modern lightweight missiles, the latest of which possess integral homing guidance.

A 2-pounder anti-tank gun being manufactured in Australia, c. 1942 (Courtesy AWM 009998)

Artillery Technology: Coast Artillery Fire Control

By the 1890s, rifled-muzzle-loading and breech-loading guns had been emplaced in Australia's colonial forts to counter potential bombardment from enemy cruisers. Lesser calibre quick-firing guns, working at close range, targeted smaller vessels attempting to penetrate the defences.

Close-range fire was essentially direct fire controlled by a battery commander. For counter-bombardment fire, a fortress section commander assigned a ship to a subordinate fire commander who assigned it to a firing group, passing to that group a deflection to the point of aim allowing for target movement, and a range, obtained from a depression range finder, adjusted for the effects of propellant performance, wind, tide height, and target travel. Advances in telephony facilitated command and control along with the transmission of data.

After 1899, the formation of the Garrison Artillery Branch in Britain brought the introduction of range-correction instruments to better determine adjustments for meteorological effects, target movement, and propellant variations. Calibration of the guns and the introduction of sights compensating for actual muzzle velocity began in 1905. Position finders also became available, capable of tracing the course of a ship, predicting its future position, passing bearing and range to that position to the guns, and ordering fire at the appropriate time. In the late 1930s, the installation of 9.2-inch and improved 6-inch guns called for longer-range target location and ranging. The system comprised two surveyed observation posts sending target bearings to a fortress plotting room, where the intersections were tracked and converted to Cartesian coordinates. These were forwarded to a battery plotting room where instruments converted the coordinates to gun bearing and range with allowances for 'correction of the moment' and ship movement. These settings were then transferred electronically to pointers at the gun sights, and the gun was traversed and elevated to match. The advent of reliable radar subsequently provided target location data even in poor visibility and at night.[5]

A 6-inch howitzer medium artillery battery commander's staff plotting range at Seymour, November 1939
(Courtesy AWM 000197)

Tactical, organisational and technical doctrine was British. Field gunnery procedures varied little from earlier practice, except batteries were now divided into 'troops'. Troop commanders acted as observers, the battery commander exercising overall command. Junior officers controlled the command posts at the gun line, where an 'artillery board' with sturdy paper 'covers' gridded at 1:25,000 was used to find bearing and range for shooting.[6]

The 2nd AIF

As with its predecessor, the 2nd AIF was raised by voluntary enlistment. By September 1940, it included Headquarters 1st Australian Corps, the 6th, 7th, 8th and 9th Australian Divisions, and Corps Troops. Brigadier-General Cyril Clowes was the Corps Commander Royal Artillery (CCRA). Major General Lavarack, former Gunner and pre-war Chief of the General Staff, commanded the 7th Australian Division. A fifth AIF Division, the 1st Armoured Division, was raised in 1941 and retained in Australia.[7]

The majority of the 2nd AIF was deployed initially to the Middle East to meet the immediate Axis threat. However, with Japan's intentions uncertain, the 8th Australian Division, less an infantry brigade and a field regiment in Darwin, was deployed to Malaya. The Torres Strait defences were strengthened; forces including coastal, anti-tank and anti-aircraft detachments were sent to Rabaul; and some fixed fortification cadres deployed to New Caledonia.

The AIF divisions organised on British lines, in which divisional artilleries comprised three field regiments and an anti-tank regiment (Appendix 1, Table 7). Field regiments, previously termed field artillery brigades, contained two batteries, each of three troops. Corps troops artillery comprised reinforcing field regiments; a survey regiment incorporating survey, flash spotting and sound ranging components; and an anti-aircraft brigade comprising three anti-aircraft regiments with associated command, signals and logistic elements.

The AIF's field artillery was also gradually re-equipped by Britain with the new 25-pounder field gun, an 88-millimetre equipment firing an 11.3-kilogram round to a maximum range of 12,253 metres. Its ammunition family included high explosive, base-ejection smoke, illumination (star), chemical, and armour-piercing projectiles. Manufacture of these guns and their ammunition in Australia bore fruit for the militia in late 1941.[8]

War in the Mediterranean: 1940–1942

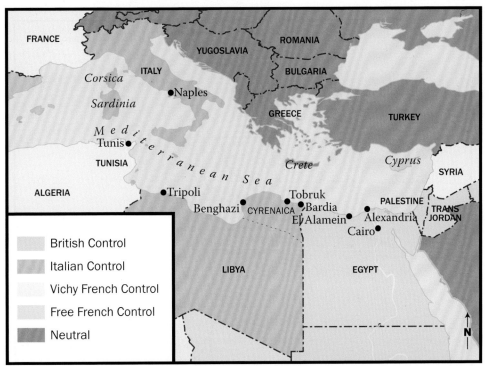

Map 7.01: The Mediterranean Theatre 1940. The 6th Australian Division was to fight in Libya (Bardia and Tobruk), Greece and Crete, the 7th Australian Division in Syria, and the 9th Australian Division in Libya (Tobruk) and Egypt (El Alamein).

Libya: 1940–41

In December 1940, the 6th Australian Division was assigned to the Western Desert Force for the advance into Libya, where it captured the fortresses of Bardia and Tobruk before advancing across Cyrenaica beyond Benghazi.[9]

In its attacks on the two fortresses, the division mounted phased operations to create a breach, expand it, and complete the capture. For his supporting fire plans, Brigadier-General Edmund Herring, the divisional artillery commander, had available four or five field regiments, two separate field batteries or elements thereof, one or two medium regiments, and survey, locating and naval gunfire support.

His programmed fire was along 1918 lines. Creeping barrages supported each phase, along with concentrations on hostile batteries and other targets. Field troops and anti-tank batteries were allotted to attacking infantry brigades for intimate support. The guns deployed covertly, were surveyed in, and provided with meteorological information. There was no registration. Battery commanders had the authority to remove certain guns from the program to engage counter-attacks, and forward observation officers at the captured positions had authority to fire a troop on opportunity targets. Communications were by telephone, with radio from divisional to regimental headquarters.[10]

Greece: April 1941

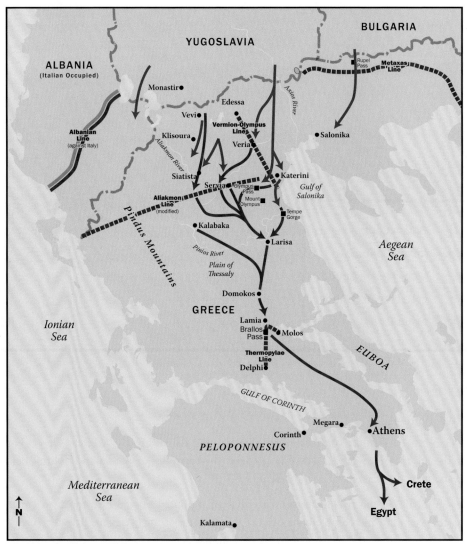

Map 7.02: The Battle for Greece, April 1941. Australian forces first occupied a defensive line in the mountain passes in the north west of Greece, the Vermion-Olympus Line, before being forced to withdraw to the Thermopylae Line, and then to evacuate.

Artillery Tactics: Deploying the Field Artillery

In conventional operations, deploying the field artillery is a complex matter. First and foremost, the weapons and locating devices have to be positioned to achieve the tasks required by the operational commander. This generally entails the identification of positions somewhat to the rear of the forward lines in defilade to enemy observation, where vegetation or structures might facilitate camouflage. Such positions allow the guns and devices to reach into the enemy area to the required depth, and at the same time, for those weapons so tasked, engage or detect targets close to the forward elements. Ideal gun positions also allow a sufficient arc of fire for multiple units to be supported without the necessity for the guns to move.

In addition to main positions, alternate, temporary and roving sites should be identified, particularly when enemy counter-battery capabilities pose a danger. There is also the need to determine locations for headquarters, wagon lines, maintenance areas, and ammunition points.

Terrain, vegetation, navigability and road networks are important factors in positioning the artillery. Its sites must allow for deployment, redeployment and resupply without prejudicing security. They must also allow for reliable intercommunication, and to gain maximum effect, must be mutually surveyed, although in recent years the difficulties involved in this have been to large degree overcome by inertial navigation and satellite-based systems.

Artillery commanders advise the staffs on the technical aspects of artillery deployment, and, depending on command arrangements, may be responsible for controlling the movement of artillery resources. The choreography of deployment becomes more difficult in mobile operations, requiring consideration of the use of step-up positions and hides.

In low-level conflict, deployment is generally much simpler because fewer guns are involved and enemy counter-battery capabilities are limited. Guns generally deploy with the units they are directly supporting, and adopt positions offering the ability to fire throughout 6400 mils (i.e. 360 degrees).

Batteries and regiments effect deployment through the use of reconnaissance groups to prepare the allocated positions for the arrival of the gun group or locating device. Artillery command, liaison and observation elements typically deploy with the affiliated operational/ tactical headquarters.

In March 1941, the 6th Australian Division in Cyrenaica was relieved by the 9th Australian Division and sent to join I Australian Corps for the hastily arranged defence of Greece. The artillery for this campaign included eight field regiments and two anti-tank regiments drawn from the 6th Australian Division, 2nd New Zealand Division and the British 1st Armoured Brigade Group. Corps and Force artillery added two medium regiments, a survey regiment, and one light and one heavy anti-aircraft regiment.[11]

In early April, the Corps deployed to the mountain passes in the north-east of Greece. The distance between the passes meant artillery command had to be decentralised, with no more than two field regiments covering any one pass, along with anti-tank batteries. Over the next month, the Gunners resisted stoically, but German air and armoured superiority forced a steady withdrawal to the shorter line from Thermopylae to the Gulf of Corinth. Here, around Brallos Pass, the Australians again delayed the German advance on the left, before withdrawing, destroying their guns, and embarking for Egypt or Crete.

An Australian 25-pounder Mk I (18/25-pounder) field gun and a No 27 Mk I Limber being towed by an LP No 3 or 3A artillery tractor through the Verroia Pass, Greece, April 1941 (Courtesy AWM P04680.001)

In the fighting, the artillery's highest casualties occurred in the 2/1st Anti-Tank Regiment, whose 2-pounder guns proved ineffective against German tanks. As the artillery commander, Clowes lamented the inability to develop sufficient weight of fire on the German approach routes because of a lack of reinforcing field regiments. He also noted the greater strength and range of the German medium artillery, which, combined with limited allied air reconnaissance and the constant movement once withdrawal began, made counter-battery work difficult. The few anti-aircraft and anti-tank units were overwhelmed, and the necessity to use field guns in an anti-tank role detracted from their primary purpose. The time taken to lay and retrieve telephone line during the withdrawal, and its significant maintenance impost, was also a significant drawback.

Tobruk: April – September 1941

At the same time as attacking Greece, the Germans advanced into Cyrenaica, forcing the 9th Australian Division and other British forces to withdraw to Tobruk in April 1941. Tasked with the port's defence, Major-General Morshead, General Officer Commanding 9th Division, could call on four Australian infantry brigades and a British armoured brigade. Morshead's own division's artillery was still being equipped, and so the garrison was supported by four British field regiments, two anti-tank regiments, and two anti-aircraft regiments.[12]

Australian gunners of the 3rd Anti-Tank Regiment, Tobruk, behind one of their 2-pounder anti-tank guns, 8 September 1941 (Courtesy AWM 020762)

Among the latter, the 2/8th Light Anti-Aircraft (LAA) Battery, equipped with captured Italian weapons, was the lone Australian sub-unit. During the siege it claimed 14 kills, 14 probables and damage to 60 other aircraft. One of the two anti-tank regiments, the 2/3rd was also Australian. Equipped initially with Bofors 37-millimetre guns and later with 2-pounder anti-tank guns, it also assumed command of the infantry anti-tank companies using captured Italian weapons. These and Italian field guns were pressed into service as 'bush artillery' in both the anti-tank and field role, so called as some pieces were manned by non-Gunners, and some lacked sights.

Quo Fas Et Gloria Ducunt: Bombardier Edward James Courtney MM

As the Italian Army garrisons fell to the Commonwealth forces in the early stages of the desert campaign, so did large quantities of arms, ammunition and equipment. Although some equipment was of dubious quality, it was still functional and, in the right hands, lethal.

In the defence of Tobruk, Gunner Edward Courtney was assigned to a captured 20-millimetre Breda anti-aircraft gun. On ANZAC Day 1941, during an attack by 40 enemy aircraft, the Breda manned by Courtney and his detachment had a stoppage. The detachment was ordered to take cover, but Courtney remained at his post. Despite heavy machine gun fire and nearby bomb blasts he was able to clear the stoppage and effectively resume firing.

On 7 May, Courtney's detachment was among the Australian Gunners tasked to provide anti-aircraft protection to a troop of 60-pounder guns. While being attacked by enemy dive bombers and escorting fighters, his Breda jammed once more. Even though enemy aircraft were strafing the position, Courtney continued to work on clearing the stoppage and bring the gun back into action.

Bombardier Edward James Courtney was awarded the Military Medal for 'Bravery and devotion to duty in an anti-aircraft detachment whilst under heavy dive bombing and machine gun fire'. He went on to fight at El Alamein, and in New Guinea.[13]

BDR Edward James Courtney in the gun seat of a captured Italian Breda 20mm cannon (Courtesy AWM 020589)

Morshead grouped his field regiments under command of the infantry brigades, perhaps because the 30-kilometre front was too large to be covered from a central location. Nevertheless, multiple batteries could engage each area of the front. The field guns provided defensive fire and support to patrols and raids. They had a direct fire role in anti-tank defence, taking on vehicles that had penetrated the front line while the infantry disposed of their infantry support. One commentator observed that the necessity for the British artillery and the Australian infantry to establish mutual trust hastened the evolution of affiliation, whereby particular batteries and battalions commonly worked together.[14]

At the beginning of May, one of the 9th Australian Division's field regiments, the 2/12th, arrived, ultimately manning a troop of 60-pounders, two troops of 4.5-inch howitzers, a troop of 25-pounder for a period, and three troops of captured equipment. When flash spotting and sound ranging sections along with a counter-battery staff deployed in June, the 60-pounder troop was used for counter-battery work, while the other troops supported the infantry garrison by providing harassing and defensive fire, and took on opportunity targets, commonly using temporary positions. The regiment contributed to the successful defence of Tobruk until it was withdrawn in September/October 1941, along with the majority of Australian units.[15]

Crete: April–May 1941

At the end of the unsuccessful campaign in Greece, the 19th Infantry Brigade and 2/2nd and 2/3rd Field Regiments were among the Australian units evacuated to Crete. Here they joined the 2/7th LAA Battery, redeployed from Egypt.[16]

For the defence of the island, New Zealand infantry were assigned to Maleme and Suda Bay on the north-west coast, the 19th Brigade was based at Georgioupoli-Retimo 20 miles to the east, and a British brigade at Heraklion 40 miles further to the east again. The 2/7th LAA Battery initially deployed sections at Maleme and Suda Bay with the remainder of the battery at Heraklion. The only field guns available to the defenders were captured Italian weapons, some without fire control instruments and sights. The Australian quota armed two troops in each of the 5th and 6th Batteries, 2/3rd Field Regiment. The 2/2nd Field Regiment temporarily became infantry.

When the airborne invasion began on 20 May 1941, the 6th Battery's guns at Retimo assisted the infantry in holding the position until the defenders surrendered nine days later. At Heraklion, the 2/7th LAA Battery provided support until the garrison was evacuated. The 5th Battery's guns were drawn into the defence of Maleme. When that position was lost, they supported the withdrawal across the mountains to the south coast, where they assisted in the defence of the evacuation zone before the majority of battery members went into captivity. The Gunners had done what they could on Crete, a New Zealand historian describing their support as 'a splendid achievement'.[17]

Syria: June–July

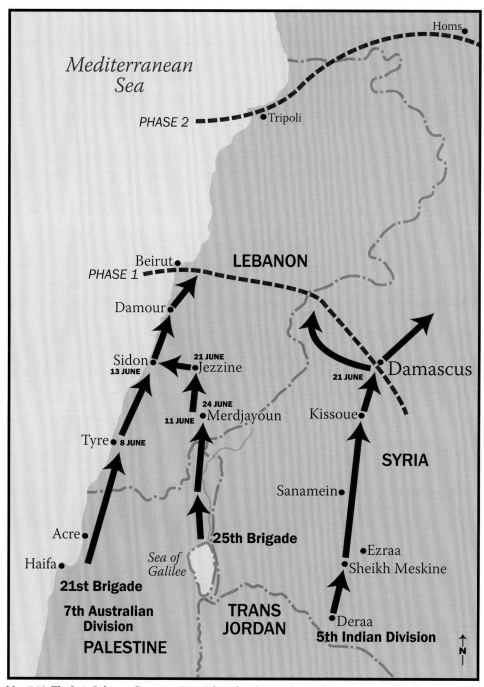

Map 7.03: The Syria Lebanon Campaign, June–July 1941. The map depicts the two axes on which the 7th Australian Division advance to Damour, and the accompanying advance of the 5th Indian Division on Damascus.

While the fighting in Tobruk and Crete was in progress, other elements of the 2nd AIF's artillery were deployed to protect Allied bases and to skirmish with Axis troops on the Egyptian border with Libya. However, they were not involved in the tactics whereby individual batteries were sent out with armoured columns, known as 'jock' columns, to harass the enemy.

When the Allies decided in June 1941 to invade Syria to prevent its Vichy French government aiding the Germans, the task fell to I Australian Corps, under Lieutenant-General Lavarack, and the 7th Australian Division. Brigadier-General Frank Berryman was the divisional artillery commander, and the formation was supported by its three field regiments, hastily equipped with 25-pounder, the 2/2nd Anti-Tank Regiment, along with a British medium regiment, LAA battery, and survey regiment.[18]

On 8 June 1941, the 7th Australian Division commenced its advance towards Beirut, an infantry brigade with a field regiment, an anti-tank battery, and a LAA section under command on the coastal road through Sidon and Damour, and a similar force on the inland road through Merdjayoun and Jezzine.

The Gunners provided impromptu and harassing fire, and creeping barrages and programmed concentrations to fix Vichy defenders while the infantry manoeuvred. The guns on the coast road twice engaged Vichy warships. Single guns and gun sections were often deployed forward in anti-tank or direct-fire roles.

An Australian Ford Marmon-Herrington artillery tractor, model LP3 or LP3A, towing a trailer, ammunition No. 27 MKI and a 25-pounder gun, Nazareth, June 1941 (Courtesy AWM 008724)

Berryman travelled along the inland route separate from divisional headquarters. When a Vichy counter-attack took Merdjayoun, Lavarack assigned him provisional command of the force tasked with its recapture. In the subsequent fighting, Lieutenant Roden Cutler, a forward observer, was awarded the Victoria Cross, the only Australian Gunner to be so recognised.

Artillery Commanders: Lieutenant General Sir Frank Horton Berryman, KCVO, CB, CBE, DSO

Sir Frank Berryman was one of Australia's leading artillery officers of his generation, although he is more renowned as the Australian Army's preeminent staff officer of the Pacific War. One of the first RMC Duntroon graduates, Berryman was among several staff cadets that elected for an artillery commission on their early graduation in 1915. After some brief training, he began his service in the 4th Field Artillery Brigade, and subsequently commanded both the 18th and 14th Batteries successively. He was awarded the Distinguished Service Order, and ended the war as Brigade Major of 7th Infantry Brigade.

Studio portrait of Major Frank Horton Berryman, DSO, 4th Australian Field Artillery Brigade (Courtesy AWM P02543.001)

In the interwar period, Berryman attended Royal Artillery College in Woolwich and Staff College at Camberley. At the start of World War II, he was appointed the senior staff officer (GS01) in the 6th Division, and was responsible for planning the operations at Bardia and Tobruk, extensively employing the division's supporting artillery. Thereafter he was appointed Commander, Royal Artillery (CRA) 7th Division.

It was as CRA that Berryman had his most direct impact on Australian artillery. He trained his regiments hard, insisting that they emphasise operating over open sights against enemy tanks, the use of alternate positions, and operating independently.

Berryman insisted on independent action, drive and determination among his Gunners, which was reflected in the artillery's outstanding performance in the Syria-Lebanon campaign. During these operations, Berryman's tactical reputation was such that he was assigned command of Berryforce, an independent composite formation tasked with checking the Vichy French counter-attack at Merdjayoun.

At the conclusion of the Syria-Lebanon campaign, Berryman was appointed the senior staff officer of I Australian Corps. He fulfilled several staff roles at corps level and above for the remainder of the war, also commanding II Australian Corps in the final stage of the Huon Peninsula campaign in New Guinea, and I Corps for a brief period in Australia. His reputation as a meticulous staff officer and operational planner, combined with his broad military experience, saw him conclude the war as the Chief of Staff of Advanced Land Headquarters.

Quo Fas Et Gloria Ducunt: Lieutenant Sir Roden Cutler VC, AK, KCMG, KCVO, CBE

Arthur Roden Cutler remains one of the most distinguished of Australian gunners, and the recipient of Australia's highest award for gallantry – the Victoria Cross.

In May 1940, Cutler transferred from the citizen's militia to the Second AIF, commissioning into the 2/5th Field Regiment, part of the 7th Australian Division. In 1941, Cutler served with the 2/5th in the Syria-Lebanon Campaign, fighting against Vichy French forces, including the tough, experienced French Foreign Legion units.

During the period between 19 June and 6 July, Cutler's regiment was involved in the Battle of Merdjayoun. Cutler's exploits over two weeks included repairing a vital field telephone communications line under heavy fire, repulsing enemy tank-attacks with an anti-tank rifle, setting up an outpost to bring artillery fire onto a road used by the enemy, and – employing a 25-pounder field gun – demolishing an anti-tank gun and post that was threatening the Australian advance.

Later, Cutler was seriously wounded during the Battle of Damour, losing a leg as a result. He was awarded the Victoria Cross for his actions in the Merdjayoun-Damour area, and was medically discharged in 1942. His subsequent civilian career included being the State Governor of New South Wales. An extract from Lieutenant Arthur Roden Cutler's Victoria Cross Citation reads: 'For most conspicuous and sustained gallantry during the Syrian Campaign and for outstanding bravery during the bitter fighting at Merdjayoun when this artillery officer became a byword amongst the forward troops with whom he worked.'[19]

Lieutenant Arthur Roden Cutler, VC (Courtesy AWM 012274)

Command of the artillery was centralised for the attack on Damour on 6 July. Sixty guns were assembled and surveyed. Sound ranging and flash spotting groups were deployed, but with limited success because of the rugged terrain and prevailing wind. Preliminary fire and a counter-battery program preceded six hours of timed barrages. The town was taken, and six days later Vichy forces capitulated.

In his report on the fighting, Berryman expressed general satisfaction with the artillery's performance. As others had advised, he recommended that field regiments should have three batteries so that one could be affiliated with each battalion in an infantry brigade, and a reorganisation along those lines occurred later in the year.

Berryman also pointed out that the lack of opportunity to calibrate the 25-pounders before the operation, stale meteorological data, and inadequate maps made predicted fire inaccurate. He stressed the importance of the infantry taking ground that allowed good artillery observation, and reported that operations had demanded large amounts of telephone cable, with observation posts typically being five kilometres or more from the batteries. Radios had been tried, but the sets were not man-portable.

El Alamein: July – October 1942

With Japan's entry into the war in December 1941, the majority of I Australian Corps returned to Australia. The 9th Australian Division remained, and in mid-1942 was ordered to Egypt, where in July it mounted two hard-fought brigade attacks and subsequent defensive actions to assist in halting the German advance near El Alamein, to the west of Alexandria. In late October it then participated in the major Eighth Army attack under General Montgomery, the second and more famous battle of Alamein.[20]

Twenty-five-pounder guns of the 2/8th Field Regiment in action on the coastal section near El Alamein, 12 July 1942 (Courtesy AWM 024515)

The July brigade actions were supported by the divisional artillery typically reinforced by a medium troop and field battery. Anti-tank elements moved forward with the infantry to guard against counter-attack, while anti-aircraft batteries protected the gun positions.

The Second Battle of El Alamein in October 1942 was similar in scale and methodology to the attack at Amiens on 8 August 1918. The 9th Division was one of four attacking divisions in XXX Corps, and the covering fire for its initial advance was provided by four field regiments, and, at designated times, four medium batteries. Because the enemy locations had largely been accurately plotted, and because all the components allowing accurate predicted fire were in place, the divisional artillery commander, Brigadier-General Ramsay, provided covering fire in the form of timed concentrations.

The fire plan assisted the division to achieve its objectives, but a subsequent armoured breakout failed to eventuate. Amended plans required three further Australian attacks for which Ramsay produced the fire plans, the first supported by seven field and two medium regiments, and the latter two by 13 field and three medium regiments, the largest number of guns controlled by an Australian in the war. These attacks included the use of barrages as exact enemy locations were less well known.

To protect the captured objectives from counter-attacks, observers were pushed forward along with anti-tank guns. On-call defensive fire tasks were planned, marked on map traces, and passed to the artillery of supporting divisions. Centralised control allowed the massing of fire, the concentration from divisional artillery and a medium regiment proving sufficient to break up the strongest counter-attack. Comprehensive harassing and counter-battery programs allowed the enemy no rest.

Gunners (reinforcements) of 3rd Anti-Tank Regiment firing a 6-pounder anti-tank gun at practice near the lagoon at El Alamein, 8 August 1942 (Courtesy AWM 024797)

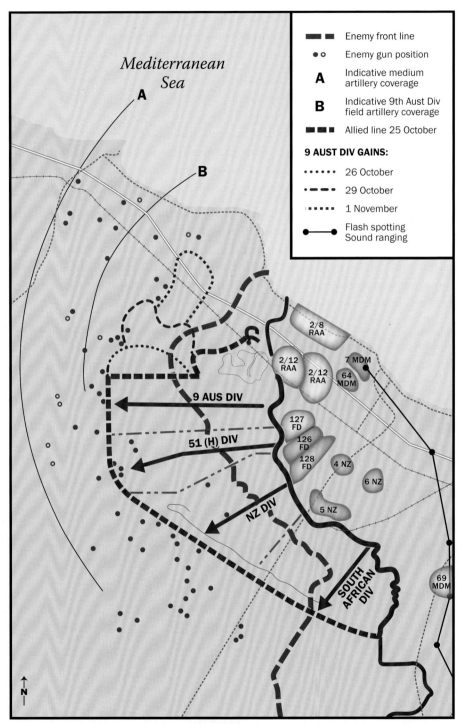

Map 7.04: The Attack at El Alamein, October 1942. The map shows the axes of advance of the attacking divisions for the initial attack on 23 October. It includes the regimental gun areas, the location of sound ranging and flash spotting capabilities, the location of hostile batteries, and representative arcs for the medium and Australian field artillery. The vectors of subsequent attacks by the 9th Australian Division are also shown

Artillery Commanders: Major-General Sir Alan Hollick Ramsay, CB, CBE, DSO, ED

Sir Alan Ramsay was one of Australia's leading Gunners in World War II and controlled the largest concentration of guns by any Australian in that conflict. He learnt his tradecraft as a Gunner and NCO on the gun lines of the 4th Field Artillery Brigade on the Western Front during World War I.

Between the wars, Ramsay continued to serve in the citizens' forces, and by 1939 was an acting colonel and Commander Royal Artillery (CRA) of the 4th Division. With the outbreak of World War II, Ramsay accepted a demotion to raise the 2/2nd Field Artillery Regiment. Within a year, he was promoted to brigadier and deployed as Commander, Royal Artillery, of the 9th Australian Division.

Ramsay trained the 9th Division's field artillery, anti-tank and light anti-aircraft regiments relentlessly, developing the skills required to provide fast, accurate and flexible fires to support the division. An aggressive Gunner, Ramsay always looked for opportunities to strike the Axis forces.

Ramsay commanded the 9th Division's artillery throughout its operations in North Africa, notably at El Alamein. At one stage during the Second Battle of El Alamein, Ramsay controlled 360 guns, and the 9th Division's guns alone fired over 200,000 rounds. Ramsay's meticulous planning, his development of the divisional artillery's technical procedures and the training of his artillery staff, set high standards within the Eighth Army, whose commander, General Montgomery would later circulate some of Ramsay's divisional fire plans throughout the Eighth Army and British staff colleges as an exemplar of their type. Under Ramsay's direction, the 9th Division Gunners were regarded as among the best in North Africa.

In February 1943, Ramsay returned to Australia and was appointed to command the II Corps Artillery in New Guinea. He was promoted to Major General in 1944, taking command of 5th Infantry Division in New Britain until the end of hostilities, except for two months spent commanding the 11th Division on Bougainville.

Brigadier A.H. Ramsay examining a map for artillery planning purposes (Courtesy AWM 02407)

In the El Alamein battles, the anti-tank gunners suffered most heavily, losing 36 guns in the October actions, but knocking out 24 tanks. The new 6-pounder gun performed well. Ramsay's view was that although these guns might move forward with the infantry, as soon as practical they should revert to regimental command so that a coordinated defence could be established. He had little to say about LAA as allied air superiority prevailed. Nevertheless, guns were pushed forward to provide protection at minefield gaps, and in the initial October attack LAA tracer was used to mark the axis of advance.

A Promising Beginning

Between its raising and its withdrawal from the Middle East, the artillery of the 2nd AIF endured a period where modern armaments were not always available and obsolete or captured weapons had to be pressed into service, and where Allied forces were committed in disadvantageous circumstances. Nevertheless, it maintained the traditions of the original AIF, displaying efficiency, devotion to duty, flexibility and initiative.

The 2nd AIF's Gunners demonstrated proficiency in defence (Tobruk) and attack (Bardia, Damour, Alamein) and in the more fluid circumstances of Greece and Syria. In doing so they handled field artillery so as to apply the maximum amount of firepower that circumstances allowed. However, their dependence on field telephones remained a significant drawback in mobile operations, and hampered the ability to concentrate massed impromptu fire.

While operations in the Middle East were in progress, in Australia the coastal and anti-aircraft artillery of the fixed defences were mobilised and grew in organisation and capability. The militia field artillery was partially mobilised, but as Japan entered the war in 1941, it was prevented from being operationally capable by shortages of equipment and ammunition, and by lack of training.

CHAPTER 8
The Pacific War: 1941–1942

When Japan finally entered the war on 7 December 1941, Australia was at a disadvantage. Until the 2nd AIF could return from the Middle East, and until American troops could arrive, all that could be done was to resist as best as possible in Malaya, Singapore and the islands to the north, and take urgent action to increase the readiness of the militia.

Accordingly, the militia was fully mobilised, and command arrangements were reorganised along Allied lines. In the meantime, Australian forces suffered a number of defeats before Japanese attempts to capture Port Moresby were thwarted, and the north coast of Papua recaptured.

Experience in this fighting revealed that jungle warfare would impose significant constraints on the artillery and call for different approaches than hitherto required.

Japan invaded Malaya at the same time it attacked Pearl Harbour and the Philippines. The subsequent advance on Singapore coincided with moves into Papua, New Guinea and the Netherlands East Indies. The small Australian garrisons, including in some cases coastal, anti-aircraft and anti-tank components, resisted as best they could, but Rabaul, Ambon and Timor all fell in February 1942. Australia's two main northern garrisons at Port Moresby and Darwin, with their stronger anti-aircraft and fixed defences, were bombed on 15 and 19 February respectively, the first of many subsequent air raids.[1]

Malaya and Singapore: 1942

Australia's contribution to the land defence of Singapore was the 8th Australian Division, less an infantry brigade. Its artillery comprised two field regiments, which had been recently equipped with 25-pounder, and an anti-tank regiment equipped with 2-pounders. The division did not see action until mid-January 1942, by which time Allied forces had been forced back to Johore, adjacent to Singapore Island.

Here the division was split, an infantry brigade supported by a field regiment and anti-tank batteries to defend each of the western and eastern approaches without anti-aircraft protection. On these approaches, terrain and vegetation facilitated Japanese infiltration, hampered observation, inhibited communications, and restricted movement to roads.[3]

Command of the Australian batteries was necessarily dispersed in order to cover multiple roads in the west. Some local concentrations were fired, destruction was wrought on occasions by anti-tank guns and by 25-pounders using direct fire out of necessity, but massed artillery fire was impractical. The Japanese momentum could not be halted, and the Allies were forced to withdraw.

Quo Fas Et Gloria Ducunt: Gunner Wilbert Thomas 'Darkie' Hudson, MM

Wilbert Hudson enlisted in the Militia Forces on 5 April 1940 and was posted to the 2nd Heavy Anti-Aircraft Battery, which was deployed to Darwin in November 1941 as part of the town's defences. A combination of the harsh tropical sun of the Northern Territory and his normally dark olive complexion, meant that Hudson was soon given the nickname of 'Darkie' by his mates.

Based at Berrimah, Hudson was showering when the first air raid sirens sounded just before 10.00 hours on Thursday 19 February 1942. He had no time to dress and ran to his 'battle station' dressed in nothing more than his helmet, boots and a towel around his waist.

The angle of approach by the attacking aircraft meant that 'Darkie' and his number two could not effectively engage with their Lewis light machine gun. They immediately redeployed into the open paddock and set up with 'Darkie' doing the firing and the gun supported on the shoulder of his mate. As an enemy Zero bored in on the pair, they stood their ground and poured a steady stream of fire into the fighter, sending it spiralling off in flames. During the action 'Darkie' realised that he'd unfortunately lost his towel and his modesty.

For his courage and determination that day, Gunner Wilbert 'Darkie' Hudson was awarded with the Military Medal, one of the first resulting from action on Australian soil. His citation stated that 'he handled his Lewis Gun with great skill and tenacity'.[2]

Gunner Wilbert Thomas 'Darkie' Hudson MM (Courtesy AWM P02539.001)

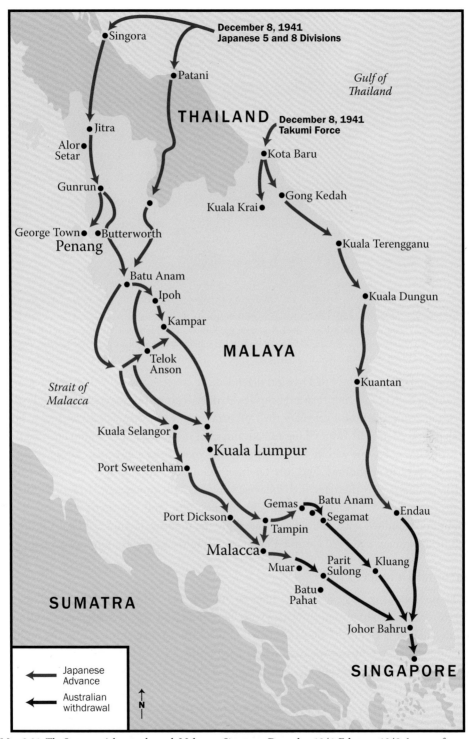

Map 8.01: The Japanese Advance through Malaya to Singapore December 1941-February 1942. Japanese forces took just 70 days to defeat the British Empire forces in Malaya and Singapore, including the Australian 8th Division. Singapore surrendered on 15 February 1942.

A 2-pounder anti-tank gun of the 4th Anti-Tank Regiment, 8th Australian Division, 2nd AIF in action at a road block at Bakri on the Muar-Parit Sulong Road, Malaya, 18 January 1942. In the background is a destroyed Japanese Type 95 Ha-Go Medium Tank (Courtesy AWM 011302)

On Singapore Island, the 8th Division defended the western sector with a field regiment supporting each of the three forward brigades. Artillery command was centralised, but when the Japanese attacked on 8 February their preparatory fire cut the artillery telephone lines, precluding the Gunners from taking full advantage of massed fire. The regiments fired their defensive fire tasks, but within a day Japanese lodgements and subsequent advances forced the defenders to withdraw. The 8th Division's Gunners stubbornly provided defensive and harassing fire in the days that followed, but constant movement, lack of battlefield information, loss of guns, disrupted communications, and an increasing scarcity of ammunition, limited what could be achieved. By the time the fortress fell on 15 February, each field regiment had fired around 45,000 rounds in the previous month of action.

National Defence: 1942

At home, following the call-up of cadres in August, the militia was fully mobilised by December 1941. Three months later, with Singapore and the Netherlands East Indies having fallen, US General Douglas MacArthur arrived in Australia to take up the position of Commander-in-Chief of the South-West Pacific Area (SWPA). The Australian, General Thomas Blamey, became Commander-in-Chief of the Australian Army, and through Land Headquarters (LHQ) commanded the Allied Land Forces. Major-General J S Whitelaw was appointed the Major-General Royal Artillery at LHQ, the adviser on all artillery matters and the Inspector of Coast and Anti-Aircraft Defences.[4]

By mid-1942, Australia had mobilised two army headquarters, three corps headquarters, and 13 divisions. In all, the artillery comprised 33 field regiments, 12 anti-tank regiments,

37 coast batteries and over 80 anti-aircraft batteries, the largest organisation ever to serve on full-time duty. (Appendix 1, Tables 8 and 9). With the exception of some anti-aircraft units and a field regiment committed early to operations in northern Australia and New Guinea, the militia artillery at this stage was principally involved in training.

Conflict reached Sydney in late May 1942, when Japanese midget submarines entered Sydney Harbour, but achieved little success. A week later larger Japanese submarines shelled Rose Bay and then Newcastle, breaking off before the Sydney fixed defences could obtain an accurate fix, and once the Newcastle defences returned fire.[5] Thereafter, Fixed Defence Command continued to work with local scientific bodies to improve its radar and plotting capabilities. To provide mobile coastal defence, a decision was made to raise batteries, armed with US 155-mm M1917 towed guns, along with searchlights, and fire control equipment. Nineteen such batteries, designated by letter, eventuated.

Members of 'T' Australian Heavy Battery, Magnetic Battery, standing next to a 155mm M1917/1918 gun as it is fired. 1944, Magnetic Island, Australia (Courtesy AWM P02729.033)

Women in Artillery Roles: 1942

To assist in staffing the fixed defences, members of the Australian Women's Army Service (AWAS) were posted to coast and anti-aircraft home defence units from mid-1942 onwards. By December 1942 their numbers totalled 3600. Precluded from serving on the guns, they worked in command and observation posts, and operated instruments and searchlights.[6]

Gunner Hopper and another member of the Australian Women's Army Service operating the telescope identification instrument at 400 Heavy Anti-Aircraft Gun Station, Melbourne, 18 May 1943 (Courtesy AWM 051884)

Halting the Japanese Advance: August 1942

The first priority in the SWPA was to halt the Japanese advance, a task assisted by the naval victories in the Coral Sea and at Midway in May and June 1942. When the former precluded a seaborne assault on Port Moresby, the Japanese turned to achieving that aim by an advance from Buna/Gona in the north over the Kokoda track, and another from the east through Milne Bay,[7]

The attack on Milne Bay commenced on 25 August 1942. Major-General Cyril Clowes, formerly the artillery commander of I Australian Corps, commanded the defences. He had three anti-aircraft batteries at his disposal, but only one field and one anti-tank battery, the mobility of all these sub-units hampered by mud and jungle.

The decisive action took place at Number 3 Airstrip on 31 August, well within range of the guns, whose defensive fire helped repel three assaults by the relatively small Japanese force. Next day, Clowes successfully counter-attacked, with 3.7-inch anti-aircraft guns firing in the ground role once the Japanese withdrew beyond 25-pounder range.

At about the same time as the Milne Bay action, the Japanese advance across the Kokoda Track had reached Ioribaiwa, some 40 kilometres from Port Moresby. Acknowledging that the defenders had previously been without artillery support, two 25-pounder of the militia

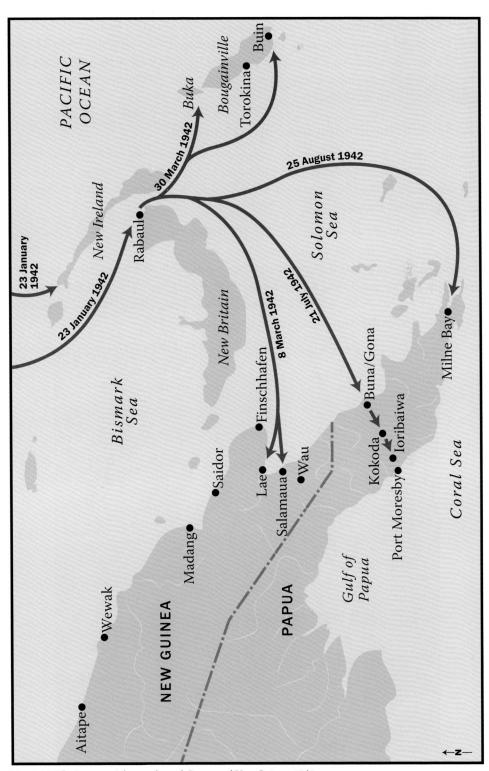

Map 8.02: The Japanese Advance through Papua and New Guinea, 1942.

14th Field Regiment were hauled with great difficulty to a position from which Ioribaiwa could be engaged at maximum range. Facing increased resistance and with stretched supply lines, the Japanese withdrew. While terrain precluded the field artillery from following, Port Moresby's anti-aircraft guns continued to see action, with the Japanese conducting their eighth air raid on 16 September.

The Battle of the Beachheads: North Papua 1942

The Japanese retired from Kokoda to Buna, Gona and Sanananda on the north coast of Papua, where between November 1942 and January 1943 the 32nd American Division and the 7th Australian Division, after a series of hard fought brigade actions, captured Buna and the remaining two villages.[8]

Artillery was brought forward by air and sea. Transport difficulties limited the initial deployment to two sections of the newly formed 1st Mountain Battery (four 3.7-inch howitzers), and three troops of 25-pounder, 12 guns in all, from two different field regiments. Under sporadic air attack and hostile battery and ground fire, these guns supported the Allied attacks in November and early December, before being joined by more 25-pounder and four 4.5-inch howitzers for the final actions in January 1943.

Smoke and flash of a 3.7-inch howitzer as it shells Japanese positions at Buna, Papua, 5 December 1942 (Courtesy AWM 013983)

The area of operations posed serious challenges. Guns were few, mobility was restricted, and ammunition limited. Topographic maps lacked the detail required for predicted fire. In jungle interspersed with swamp, patches of kunai grass and coconut groves, observation and target location were difficult, with observers at times resorting to observations posts in trees. The enemy fought from bunkers with overhead protection. Engagements occurred at close range.

The Gunners provided concentrations on targets identified by aerial and ground reconnaissance, and harassing fire. The difficult going made programmed fire in support of attacks impractical, so concentrations were fired on enemy positions, lifting under the control of observers accompanying the attackers. To assist with the engagement of common targets and in the absence of survey until late in the operation, the batteries improvised a grid using back bearings and ranges derived from aerial registration. Aerial ranging on depth targets was common, while ground observers used smoke rounds to improve identification of fall of shot, or crept high explosive rounds onto close targets, judging the position of the exploding projectiles from compass bearing and sound. Direct fire was used wherever practical to destroy bunkers.

The fighting identified that in jungle warfare more observers were required, and more signallers to maintain cable communications. Batteries were vulnerable to ground attack, and had to take greater protective precautions.

With the beachheads area captured, an Australian brigade was deployed to Wau in central New Guinea, to prevent the Japanese advancing inland from Lae and Salamaua. A troop of 25-pounder and two light anti-aircraft guns were flown in to assist with securing the position. The Allies now had the initiative, and at national level thoughts turned to gradually reducing the forces that had been mobilised, retaining only those required for future operations, and reorganising them for operations in a tropical environment.

CHAPTER 9
Taking the Offensive: 1943-1944

The Japanese defeats in Papua, along with those in Guadalcanal and on the Bismarck Sea in early 1943, signalled that any direct threat to Australia had passed. Later that year the Allies began their counter-offensive in New Guinea and the Solomon Islands, with Australian troops allocated the task of capturing Salamaua, Lae and the Huon Peninsula on New Guinea's north coast, thereby seizing ground for the construction of bases and staging facilities for future operations. Based on the experiences of jungle warfare to date, the artillery involved in these battles was restructured and to a certain degree re-equipped, but continued to face challenges imposed by the terrain.[1]

At home in 1943 and 1944, the government sought the release of military manpower for industry and agriculture. Accordingly, Land Headquarters reshaped its forces, gradually reducing the fixed defences and the number of militia units.

Reorganisation

In jungle fighting in 1942, attacks above brigade level had been rare, mobility was restricted, and logistics were reliant on air and sea transport. Standard infantry divisions were too cumbersome, and with this in mind, five infantry divisions in II Australian Corps and New Guinea Force (Appendix 1, Table 10) were converted to a 'jungle' organisation, in which the artillery comprised one field regiment and one light anti-aircraft (LAA) battery. Other field, medium, light and heavy anti-aircraft, tank-attack – 'anti-tank' was re-designated 'tank-attack' at this time to imbue a more positive spirit – and survey units were held in pools for allocation to meet specific requirements. Remaining formations and units on the Army order of battle were either progressively disbanded or had their strengths reduced.[2]

While the 25-pounder remained the basic weapon of the field artillery, efforts were made to supplement it with a more mobile capability. Some Gunners favoured the wider employment of the 3.7-inch mountain guns, but authorities settled on the Australian-designed 'Short' 25-pounder. With its barrel shortened and other parts removed, it weighed 500 kilograms less than the standard gun, and could be broken down into 14 parts for transport. One battery in each jungle regiment was to be issued with the gun, despite criticism during trials of its stability, its more dispersed fall of shot, and its lack of range compared with its parent.[3]

A 'short' 25-pounder gun of the 2/5th Field Regiment hitched to a jeep and ready for the road in Port Moresby, 15 November 1943. (Courtesy AWM 059988)

Jungle divisions were light infantry formations, fighting in a close-quarter environment. Artillery support was essentially provided on the basis of a battery per infantry brigade. The perceived operational environment did not accommodate the deployment of large numbers of guns or guns of heavier calibre, meaning that depth support fell to the Air Force or, close to the coast, the Navy. In doctrine and training, Australian Gunners could follow techniques evolving contemporaneously in Europe and the Middle East for fire planning and impromptu target engagement at divisional level and above, but in action, practical considerations demanded concentration on accurate, intimate support at lower levels, and on inter-service cooperation.[4]

Salamaua: July – September 1943

The plan for the first phase of the year's campaigning was for an advance on Salamaua to divert Japanese attention from Lae, which would then be taken in a pincer attack, one claw emanating from the aerial seizure of Nadzab inland, the other from a beach landing. The 3rd Australian Division and elements of the US 41st Division began the advance on Salamaua in July 1943. The Australians set out from Wau in the interior on two brigade axes, while the Americans attacked with a single brigade along the coast from Nassau Bay. After two months of fighting, Salamaua fell on 13 September.[5]

Australian artillery support consisted of a mountain section comprising two 3.7-inch howitzers inland, and a field battery of eight 25-pounders, brought forward by barge, at the coast. The construction and lesser weight of the mountain guns allowed movement along the restricted jungle trails, while the field guns essentially remained static covering an arc of the battlefield. The Americans deployed at the coast two artillery battalions of 12 pieces,

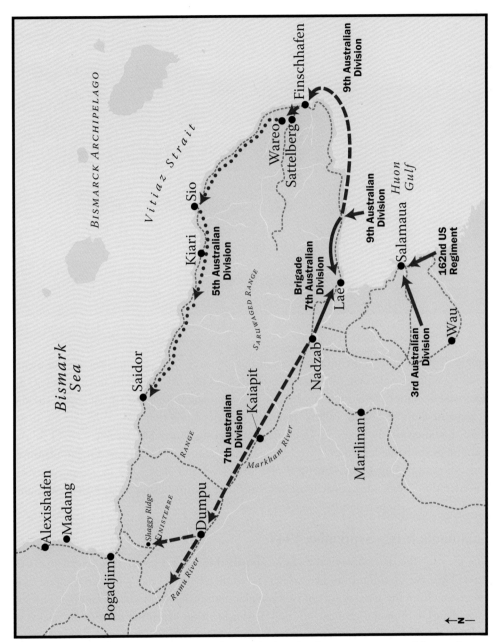

Map 9.01: Australian New Guinea Operations 1943. In 1943, Australian forces set out to capture Salamaua, Lae, Finschhafen and the Huon Peninsula, in that order. The captured ground would then be a base for further operations.

one with 75- millimetre and the other with 105-millimetre howitzers. An Australian and an American LAA battery were deployed to defend the supply port and the gun positions, and for the last few days of the fighting two 155-millimetre guns manned by 2nd AIF Gunners provided some depth and counter-battery fire. Coordination was vested in an ad hoc headquarters headed by an American officer with Australian staff.

Japanese defensive positions on knolls and razor-backed ridge tops were the principal artillery targets. Close targets were ranged by observers with the forward infantry using smoke or creeping rounds onto the target by sound. Observation posts were also established in each brigade area and on prominent features. These posts mainly controlled harassing or counter-battery fire as the vegetation-cloaked enemy movement and opportunity targets were few. Air Force spotters were employed for targets in depth.

Infantry commanders typically called for heavy bombardment of enemy positions once located. Observers had to take account of the line of fire, the height of the trees, and the width of the ridge. It was found that instantaneously fused high explosive stripped away the vegetation, and delay fuses could then be used to damage defensive bunkers and allow the infantry, assaulting hard on the heels of the artillery fire, to approach more closely.

Such tactics placed an emphasis on accuracy and the ability to concentrate fire from multiple fire units. To these ends, the guns were surveyed onto the same map grid, important targets were registered, and 'datum points' were engaged to derive meteorological corrections. Command posts and observers learnt to cope with the fact that smoke ranged differently from high explosive, and that the rounds with fuses capped for delay did not range in accordance with the firing tables.

The fighting demonstrated the need for close liaison with the infantry, and for extra observers in each battery along with additional signallers to man both the static and mobile observation posts. Communications proved difficult, telephone lines being unreliable and vulnerable, and the radios available too heavy for mobile operations. With the Japanese able to infiltrate through the close country, batteries also had to take greater responsibility for their own protection.

Lae: September 1943

The battle for Lae began shortly before Salamaua was captured. Inland, on 5 September, American paratroopers, accompanied by an Australian short 25-pounder section, seized an airhead at Nadzab 30 kilometres from Lae, from whence an air-landed infantry brigade and field battery, both from the 7th Australian Division, advanced on the town. Simultaneously, the 9th Australian Division conducted an amphibious landing some 40 kilometres to the east of the town, and then advanced along the coast. It had its own field regiment and LAA battery, and to assist with the advance and the security of the beachhead was supplemented by an additional field regiment, a field battery, a 155 millimetre gun section, an LAA regiment, a tank-attack battery, a survey section, a RAAF meteorological flight, and observers from the 1st Naval Bombardment Group.[6]

The parachuting of the short 25-pounder at Nadzab was the first time the Australian artillery had carried out such a manoeuvre. It was an innovative action, mounted with little training. In the event, only one gun could be assembled immediately after the drop, and its support was not required.[7]

The 7th Australian Division's brigade was able to make steady progress along a track towards Lae, while the 9th Division advanced through jungle and along the coast, its progress impeded by rivers and bad weather. In both cases, observers travelled with the forward battalions, engaging targets as required. Some of the 9th Australian Division's guns were brought forward on makeshift roads, others on barges. The 155s were landed late in the advance on a beach closer to the objective.

By 16 September both divisions were ready to attack Lae, which had been subjected to air and naval bombardment for some time. The 9th Division's artillery, which had fired ten battery fire plans, seven observed missions and 21 harassing fire serials during the advance, assembled 22 guns to support the division's attack, but the fire plan, which included fire from the 155s, ceased after 30 minutes when the 7th Division discovered that the defenders had withdrawn.

The 7th Division's artillery did not record any lessons from the action. Brigadier STW Goodwin, commanding the 9th Division's artillery, reported that the operation had reinforced the value of concentrated artillery fire. The mapping, survey and meteorological data available meant the guns had been able to use predicted fire, and RAAF air observation had been important. He stressed the need in jungle fighting for additional observers to accompany the infantry, and identified the major problems as being the inability to use guns because of failures in line communications, the unsuitability of the bulky radios of the day, and the lack of gun tractors suited to the conditions. He also noted the importance of LAA. The Division experienced 25 air raids on the beachhead and the advancing force between the landing and 16 September.

The Huon Peninsula.

With Lae and Salamaua captured, allied attention turned to securing the Huon Peninsula. The 9th Australian Division was tasked with capturing Finschhafen, and the 7th Australian Division with advancing up the Markham and Ramu River valleys and blocking Japanese access across the Finisterre Range into the Allied rear area.[9]

The action at Finschhafen began on 22 September with the assault landing of an infantry brigade. The town was captured on 2 October, and further elements of the 9th Australian Division then came forward just in time to repel a counter-attack by a Japanese division. Afterwards, the force was increased again to capture the outlying high ground around Sattelberg and Wareo, so guaranteeing the security of the area, and facilitating the subsequent advance along the north coast of the peninsula towards Sio.

Up until the Japanese counter-attack was defeated, the only artillery support available was the field regiment and two LAA batteries that had accompanied the initial landing. They

Quo Fas Et Gloria Ducunt: Lieutenant John N Pearson MC

It was to be an undoubted 'first' for the RAA – executing a combat parachute insertion at Nadzab of two guns, 192 rounds of ammunition and detachments into battle. The 2/4th Field Regiment volunteered two of its eight 'short' 25-pounders to be disassembled and parachuted in, accompanied by four officers and 30 other ranks, under the command of Lieutenant Johnny Pearson. A number of the contingent had undertaken some rudimentary parachute training, but for some, their first jump would be the operational sortie.

Prior inspection of the guns found serious flaws, and six were cannibalised to build two complete guns fit for the task. These guns were then proofed by firing 20 rounds. One failed, necessitating significant work overnight to make it serviceable.

Once in the air, the order for action stations would have come all too quickly for Pearson to stand in the aircraft doorway, awaiting the tap on the shoulder and that first step into history.

Arriving on the ground, Pearson assembled his men. Miraculously only one man was injured, sustaining a broken collarbone. The Gunners searched for the gun parts in the high kunai grass, and laboured until they had found one complete set of components. The gun was quickly assembled and made ready to fire, though the call never came.

Pearson later served with distinction at Shaggy Ridge, earning a Military Cross, when he and his party moved with the lead infantry element, through enemy rifle and mountain gun fire and maintained continuous and 'dangerously close' fire on the enemy. A month before war's end, Pearson was killed in action at Balikpapan, Borneo, again operating with the leading infantry.[8]

Image 4F: Lieutenant JN Pearson (right) (Courtesy AWM 030139/08)

managed to provide the necessary defensive fire despite one of the field batteries and an anti-aircraft battery being attacked. However, it was clear that a greater level of support would be required for the forthcoming Australian attacks, even though the Japanese would be subject to aerial bombardment. A second field regiment, a mountain gun section, another LAA battery, a section of 155-millimetre guns and a tank-attack battery were brought in, the latter element primarily to provide coastal defence.

When the Australian offensive commenced, the brigade advancing on Sattelberg was able to call on the fire of two batteries and a mountain section, while the other brigades generally had a battery in support. Heavy concentrations preceded an assault. There was little need for counter-battery fire as the Japanese typically deployed their guns and heavy weapons individually on high ground and fired at short range. Observation posts were manned to identify and neutralise them, while other observers travelled with the infantry to control fire. RAAF spotters, reporting through battery command posts, were also used. The field artillery played a key role at Finschhafen, as did the anti-aircraft elements, who reported some 15 air raids in November, one of these killing Brigadier Goodwin, the divisional artillery commander.

Inland, the 7th Australian Division advanced along the Ramu River to Dumpu, from whence it slowly pushed two brigades into the Finisterre Ranges in the direction of Shaggy Ridge and the Kankiryo Pass. Support was provided by an LAA battery, and two batteries of the 2/4th Field Regiment. The CRA 7th Division did not deploy, perhaps because the division essentially had a containment role, and only one gun regiment was employed, the commander of which acted as artillery adviser at divisional headquarters.

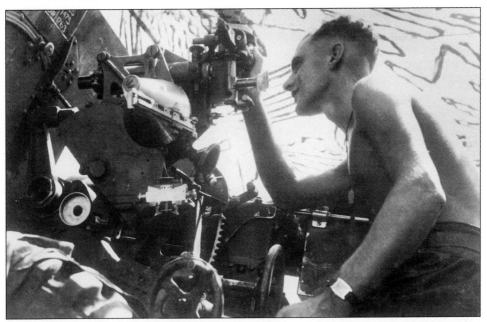

Bombardier GD O'Neill of the 54th Battery, 2/4th Australian Field Regiment laying a gun at Ramu Valley, New Guinea, 23 October 1943 (Courtesy AWM 059039)

For much of the time each battery supported a brigade, but survey was available and efforts were made to ensure both batteries could engage registered targets across the whole front, thus increasing the ability to mass fire. The significant action here occurred in mid-January 1944 when both batteries provided heavy concentrations controlled by observers moving with the infantry to assist the capture of Shaggy Ridge and the nearby pass. The observers in these successful attacks were able to maintain continuous communication using a combination of line and radio.

Subsequently, follow-on Australian forces, supported by a mountain gun section, were able to cross the Finisterre Ranges and reach the north coast of the peninsula, ultimately joining other elements advancing along that coast from Finschhafen, with their supporting field batteries barged forward successively. The seizure of Madang in April 1944 completed the operation.

Coast and Anti-Aircraft Artillery Reductions

With each progressive Allied success, the demise of the Japanese air and naval threat allowed reductions to be made in resources devoted to coast and air defence in the rear areas. In New Guinea in late 1943, these resources comprised the fixed defences at Port Moresby, 12 coastal 'letter' batteries, and the anti-aircraft elements at Appendix 1, Table 11. At the same time, in Australia, there were 121 coast defence guns of all calibres, and 567 anti-aircraft guns. They were supported by 115 coast searchlights and 312 anti-aircraft searchlights, 34 long-range radars, and 17 coast defence radars.[10]

Throughout 1943 and 1944, the coast batteries were gradually withdrawn from service or manned at diminished levels, such that by early 1945 all of the 9.2-inch guns and three-quarters of the 6-inch guns were in 'care and maintenance', and 16 of the 19 155-millimetre 'letter batteries' had been disbanded.

Gunners cleaning a 9.2-inch gun at North Head Battery, Sydney Fortress Area, 20 January 1944 (Courtesy AWM 063461)

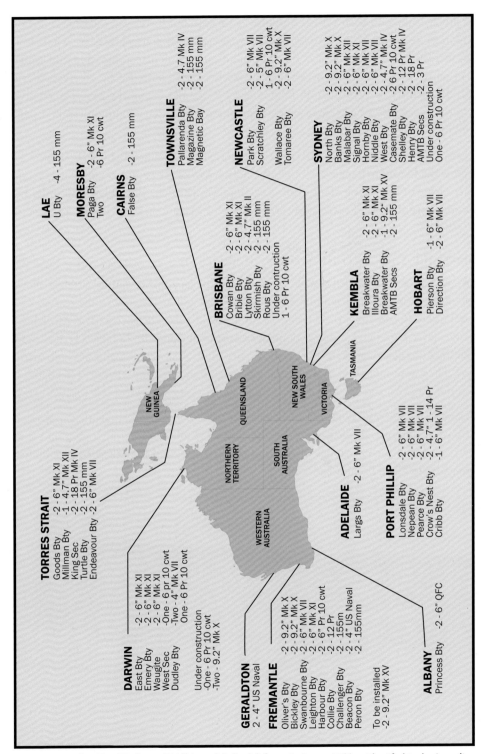

LAE
U Bty   -4 - 155 mm

MORESBY
Paga Bty   -2 - 6" Mk XI
Two   -6 Pr 10 cwt

CAIRNS
False Bty   -2 - 155 mm

TOWNSVILLE
Pallarenda Bty   -2 - 4.7' Mk IV
Magazine Bty   -2 - 155 mm
Magnetic Bay   -2 - 155 mm

NEWCASTLE
Park Bty   -2 - 6" Mk VII
Scratchley Bty   -2 - 5" Mk VII
   1 - 6 Pr 10 cwt
Wallace Bty   -2 - 9.2" Mk X
Tomaree Bty   -2 - 6" Mk VII

SYDNEY
North Bty   -2 - 9.2" Mk X
Banks Bty   -2 - 9.2" Mk X
Malabar Bty   -2 - 6" Mk VII
Signal Bty   -2 - 6" Mk XII
Hornby Bty   -2 - 6" Mk VII
Niddle Bty   -2 - 6" Mk XI
West Bty   -2 - 4.7" Mk IV
Casemate Bty   -2 6 Pr 10 cwt
Shelley Bty   -2 - 12 Pr Mk IV
Henry Bty   -2 - 18 Pr
AMTB Secs   -2 - 3 Pr
Under construction
One - 6 Pr 10 cwt

BRISBANE
Cowan Bty   -2 - 6" Mk XI
Bribie Bty   -2 - 6" Mk XI
Lytton Bty   -2 - 4.7" Mk II
Skirmish Bty   -2 - 155 mm
Rous Bty   -2 - 155 mm
Under contruction
1 - 6 Pr 10 cwt

KEMBLA
Breakwater Bty   -2 - 6" Mk XI
Illoura Bty   -2 - 6" Mk XI
Breakwater Bty   -1 - 9.2" Mk XV
AMTB Secs   -2 - 155 mm

HOBART
Pierson Bty   -1 - 6" Mk VII
Direction Bty   -2 - 6" Mk VII

TASMANIA

NEW GUINEA

NEW SOUTH WALES

QUEENSLAND

NORTHERN TERRITORY

SOUTH AUSTRALIA

VICTORIA

WESTERN AUSTRALIA

TORRES STRAIT
Goods Bty   -2 - 6" Mk XI
Millman Bty   -1 - 4.7" Mk XII
King Sec   -2 - 18 Pr Mk IV
Turtle Bty   -2 - 155 mm
Endeavour Bty   -2 - 6" Mk VII

DARWIN
East Bty   -2 - 6" Mk XI
Emery Bty   -2 - 6" Mk XI
Waugite   -2 - 6" Mk XI
West Sec   -One - 6 pr 10 cwt
Dudley Bty   -Two - 4" Mk VII
   One - 6 Pr 10 cwt
Under construction
-One - 6 Pr 10 cwt
-Two - 9.2" Mk X

GERALDTON
2 - 4" US Naval

FREMANTLE
Oliver's Bty   -2 - 9.2" Mk X
Bickley Bty   -2 - 9.2" Mk X
Swanbourne Bty   -2 - 6" Mk VII
Leighton Bty   -2 - 6" Mk XI
Harbour Bty   -2 - 6" Pr 10 cwt
Collie Bty   -2 - 12 Pr
Challenger Bty   -2 - 155m
Beacon Bty   -2 - 4" US Naval
Peron Bty   -2 - 155mm
To be installed
-2 - 9.2" Mk XV

ALBANY
Princess Bty   -2 - 6" QFC

ADELAIDE
Largs   -2 - 6" Mk VII

PORT PHILLIP
Lonsdale Bty   -2 - 6" Mk VII
Nepean Bty   -2 - 6" Mk VII
Pearce Bty   -2 - 6" Mk VII
Crow's Nest Bty   -2 - 4.7" 1 - 14 Pr
Cribb Bty   -1 - 6" Mk VII

Map 9.02: Australian Fixed Defences 1944. Australia's fixed defences in August 1944, as identified in the Australian Military Forces, 'The Australian War Effort', 31 August 1944, AWM 54, item 243/2/1.

Similarly, of the 34 coast and anti-aircraft searchlight batteries taken over by the artillery in 1943, only 12 remained in January 1945, and the number of servicewomen with the guns diminished accordingly.

Reduction of the static anti-aircraft defences began in January 1944, with lower manning and readiness levels progressing sequentially from south to north. By December of that year, all remaining batteries and groups except those in Sydney and Western Australia had been disbanded, along with seven mobile anti-aircraft regiments, leaving only seven composite anti-aircraft regiments (HAA and LAA sub-units) and an LAA regiment in service. By July 1945 only three composite anti-aircraft regiments, one HAA battery and one LAA battery on operations remained. All other units were under orders to disband.

Preparing for the Final Campaigns

In 1943 and early 1944, field and anti-aircraft artillery units were an integral part of the operational forces, and played a material part the outcome of battles in the littoral. The Gunners became adept at deploying by sea, air and land, and amassed a wealth of experience in the technical aspects of providing accurate fire support along with liaison and observation in tropical environments, and in cooperation with the Air Force and Navy. Their experience in generating fire superiority caused them to recognise, as evident at Finschhafen, that the light scales of the jungle division were inadequate for future campaigning against stronger Japanese forces. Line and nascent radio communications remained problem areas, mobility required more powerful gun tractors, and standard 25-pounder guns were preferred to the short version, whose muzzle-blast, slower rate of fire, lesser range, susceptibility to mechanical failure, and larger impact zone attracted criticism.

In a wider context, as the war moved further from Australian shores the number of artillery units was reduced, offering the opportunity to return manpower to the civilian economy, and also to restructure forces for the final campaigns. Artillery in the base areas was in decline. The focus for 1945 would be the artillery in the field formations.

CHAPTER 10

The Final Battles: 1944-1945

During the last year of the war, two corps headquarters and six divisions conducted six separate actions: one each in Bougainville, New Britain and northern New Guinea; and three around North Borneo. Those formations contained a more generous scale of artillery than under the jungle division regime, leading Horner to note in his history of the Australian artillery that in July 1945 that there were more artillery units and sub-units in action at any other single time of the war.[1]

As in the previous three years, the fighting consisted of tropical warfare advances against stubbornly defended positions with the guns providing support using what were by then well-developed techniques. In the absence of air and tank threats, anti-aircraft and tank-attack elements were commonly switched to other roles.

Reorganisation and Tasking

At the end of 1944, the artillery structure was as shown at Appendix 1, Table 12. With the exception of the artillery of the 5th Australian Division, the divisions of I and II Australian Corps now contained two or three field regiments, and the three AIF divisions had regained a tank-attack regiment. The increased allocations reflected that fire superiority was by now central to the way the Army chose to fight in order to reduce difficult Japanese defences and minimise casualties.

With the Americans focussing on the Philippines, the Australian First Army was tasked to take over in Bougainville, New Britain and northern New Guinea and conduct limited offensive operations. Meanwhile, I Australian Corps was to carry the Allied advance into northern Borneo.[2] These tasks were of small strategic value, yet involved hard fighting against well-developed Japanese positions.

First Army Operations

First Army controlled three widely dispersed operations in which the Gunners faced challenges provided by Japanese resistance as well as terrain and thick vegetation.[3]

Bougainville

First Army allotted Bougainville to II Australian Corps, which commanded the reinforced 3rd Australian Division. From its base area at Torokina on the west coast of the island, the Division was to press the Japanese back to the Buka Passage in the north, and move on the Japanese headquarters at Buin in the south. Its artillery – which originally comprised two

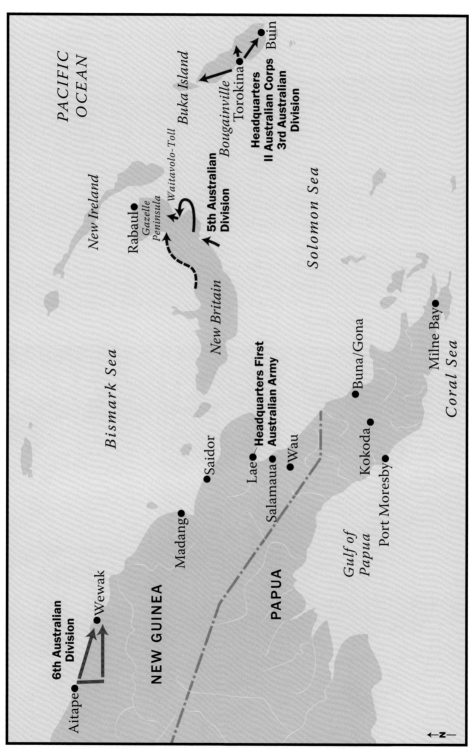

Map 10.01: First Army Operations 1944-5. In 1944-5, the Australian First Army undertook three widely dispersed operations against remnant Japanese forces

field regiments, a mountain battery and a survey battery – was later joined by another field regiment and a 155-millimetre battery. A static LAA battery and a heavy anti-aircraft HAA troop were located in the base area.[4]

3rd Australian Division advanced one battalion, with fire support from a battery, across the centre of the island creating an observation and patrol base overlooking the east coast. It advanced by barge an infantry brigade supported typically by two batteries, a survey troop, and later a section of 3.7-inch HAA guns in the ground role, along the north-west coast towards the Buka Passage. In the principal action, three infantry brigades advanced southwards in succession, along the rudimentary Torokina to Buin road, facing increasing Japanese resistance at the rivers cutting across the line of march. Actions here were supported by two field regiments, survey and meteorological troops, the 155-millimetre guns, air reconnaissance, air observation post (Air OP), and bombing raids.

Air OP was a nascent capability supplementing long-standing artillery reconnaissance support (known as ArtyR) provided by RAAF Army Cooperation squadrons. Using light aircraft stationed close to the front with RAAF pilots and artillery observers, it sought to diminish the longer response times and lack of pilot familiarity with artillery observation of fire procedures inherent to ArtyR.

Battery of mountain guns open up on the Japanese at Tsimba Area, Bougainville Island, Solomon Islands, 2 February 1945 (Courtesy AWM 018053)

New Britain

On New Britain, the 5th Australian Division, supported by a field regiment and a survey battery, was tasked with confining the Japanese to the Gazelle Peninsula in the north-east of the island. In March 1945, the Division, supported by regimental concentrations and counter-mortar tasks landed close to, and then captured the Waitavalo-Tol heights at the neck of the peninsula, which was vital ground for its containment task. Thereafter, the artillery provided harassing and defensive fire.

Aitape-Wewak

On New Guinea's north coast, the 6th Australian Division, supported by three field regiments, a tank-attack regiment and a survey battery, took over from the Americans at Aitape before advancing on Wewak.

Two infantry brigades advancing in turn moved along the coast, captured Wewak, and subsequently drove into the mountains south east of the town. They were supported by aerial bombardment, naval gunfire, two field regiments, six 75-millimetre pack howitzers, a 155-millimetre gun section, Air OP, and survey elements. The Division's third brigade advanced in parallel on the far side of the coastal mountain range, supported by a battery of 4.2-inch mortars and later a troop of 25-pounder and a section of 75-millimetre pack howitzers.

Gunners of the 2/1st Tank Attack Regiment digging a pit for the trail while mounting a 75-millimetre pack howitzer on the back of a truck to attain high elevation at Boiken Area, Aitape-Wewak Sector, 28 April 1945 (Courtesy AWM 091318)

Artillery Employment

Artillery employment in all three operations involved a mixture of defensive and harassing fire, impromptu support for patrols, and heavy preparatory fire followed by covering fire for attacks.[5]

Facing neither air nor tank threat, artillery commanders used anti-aircraft and tank-attack units for coastal defence, to man weapons such as 4.2-inch mortars and 75-millimetre howitzers, to provide additional observation parties, and in some instances to act as infantry. These out of role deployments demonstrated the versatility of Gunners across the artillery branches.

Multiple modes of transport were used to redeploy batteries and resupply ammunition: air, barge and road at Wewak; barge and road in Bougainville. Ground mobility was inhibited by the state of the roads and a lack of regimental transport, in particular suitable lorries and tracked tractors.

During the advances, artillery regimental commanders positioned themselves at the advancing infantry brigade's headquarters, while batteries assigned officers to battalion headquarters. Observation posts were established if the terrain allowed, but, more frequently, artillery observers travelled with infantry companies or patrols, seeking ground clearance to fire through the officers at battalion when front lines were uncertain.

In close terrain, ranging followed the jungle practice of using sound or smoke. The 3rd Division's artillery also explored ranging with inert rounds to avoid the danger of tree bursts or to conceal the location of critical targets, such as close defensive fire tasks. In close terrain, observers sometimes also fired missions simply to deduce their position by relation to the fall of shot.

As the formations advanced, survey elements worked to place the gun positions and observation posts on the same topographic grid so that the fire of multiple units could be more readily concentrated. On Bougainville, the survey battery also provided meteorological data. Radio and cable communications existed down to the gun lines, but further forward, despite its shortcomings, cable was more reliable.

All formations noted that the gunnery procedures in the manuals were sound, simply needing adjustment for tropical conditions. For his part, the artillery commander of the 3rd Division considered that quick fire planning at regimental and battery level needed improvement, and that cooperation would have been better had the artillery and infantry trained together before the operation began.

Preparatory fire support for attacks typically involved heavy aerial and artillery bombardment and, where practical, incorporation of naval gunfire. On Bougainville, subsequent covering fire during generally took the form of a series of linear concentrations controlled by the observer with the infantry. The majority of the divisional artillery supported the 6th Division's attack at Wewak, and the war diaries show that in the more open terrain divisional-level targets were circulated, allowing for impromptu or programmed engagement as required.

In terms of target acquisition, ground observation was supplemented by ArtyR and Air OP. Further, both the 3rd and 6th Australian Divisions established ad-hoc counter-battery offices to collect artillery intelligence and coordinate responses.

I Australian Corps: Borneo

I Australian Corps conducted three landings in and round North Borneo: at Tarakan by 26th Infantry Brigade in May 1945 (Oboe 1), at Labuan and Brunei by the 9th Australian Division in June (Oboe 6), and at Balikpapan by the 7th Australian Division in July (Oboe 2). All involved significant fire support to minimise casualties.[6]

Tarakan

In addition to aerial bombardment, the landing at Tarakan was supported by the fire of three cruisers and six destroyers coordinated by the Naval Bombardment Group, and a gun battery positioned on a nearby island. The assaulting infantry brigade's artillery initially comprised a field regiment and composite anti-aircraft regiment.[7]

Ashore, observation officers accompanied each battalion, and Air OP was available. As advances on the small island closed on enemy defences in its centre, communications were established that allowed observers to fire any troop, so that targets could be engaged with the safest line of fire. Defended localities were attacked methodically by bombing, naval gunfire, and artillery and mortar fire. Where positions on ridgelines made attack with indirect fire difficult, direct fire was employed using combinations of tanks and field, HAA and tank-attack guns. For the assault on enemy positions, battalion-level fire plans were prepared by battery commanders, the serials generally being engaged 'on-call', as the close and rugged terrain made determining the required duration of fire difficult.

Gun detachments 1 and 2 of Corps Troop, 2/7th Field Regiment during the fighting for Tarakan Hill and oilfields, shelling targets beyond the airstrip, 2 May 1945 (Courtesy AWM 089402)

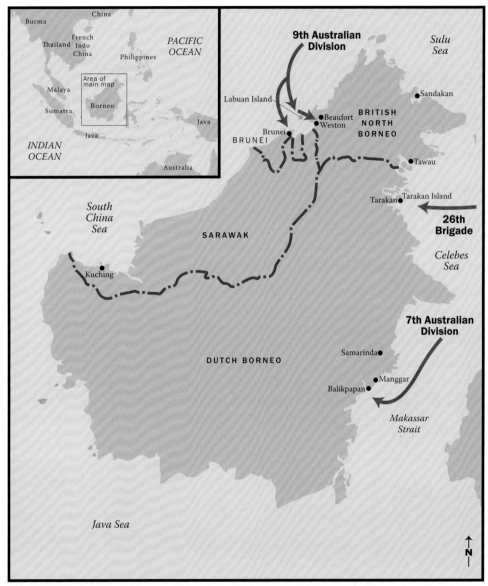

Map 10.02: Borneo, 1944-45. The map outlines the three Australian landings in Borneo

Labuan and Brunei

At Brunei Bay, the attackers advanced on two axes. The 24th Brigade captured Labuan Island, after which it crossed to the mainland and exploited to Beaufort and beyond. Its artillery support was provided by a field regiment, an LAA troop and, later, 3.7-inch HAA guns in the ground role along with tank-attack Gunners manning mortars and pack howitzers.[8]

On the second axis, the 20th Brigade, supported by a field regiment and LAA elements, landed on Brunei Bluff and Maura Island, and, with little opposition, captured Brunei township before exploiting to the south-west. In both landings efforts were made to ensure early access to organic indirect fire, in 24th Brigade by including some 25-pounder and 4.2-inch mortars in the first wave, and in 20th Brigade by floating 75-millimetre pack howitzers ashore in waterproof containers.

The heaviest resistance was encountered on Labuan Island where the defenders withdrew into 'the pocket' – a thickly vegetated ridge. The Japanese position resisted initial infantry assault and was only captured after five days of air, naval and artillery bombardment.

Balikpapan

For the landing at Balikpapan, the 7th Division fielded its three field, composite anti-aircraft and tank-attack regiments, along with a survey battery. In view of estimated Japanese strength, a medium regiment was called forward to Morotai, but in the event its support was not required.[9]

The division landed on 1 July 1945 after heavy air and naval bombardment. Some 4.2-inch mortars and 6-pounder guns were sent ashore to provide initial support, and, once ashore, a field regiment supported each of the two assault infantry brigades. As with Tarakan and Brunei, fire arranged through the Naval Bombardment Group was also available.

Once the beachhead was secured, one infantry brigade advanced on the oil refinery and port area, and the other advanced along the coast to the airfield at Manggar. The third brigade, landed later, advanced inland. The Divisional Commander, Major-General Milford, an artilleryman, enjoined his brigadiers to use as much firepower as possible. Manggar was only secured after a particularly strong defensive position containing coast and field guns was reduced using direct tank-attack and field gun fire along with air and naval bombardment. With the town and airfield secured and defended by anti-aircraft elements, the advances ceased in late July with the Japanese pushed back far enough to maintain security of the area by patrolling.

In these actions the field artillery provided impromptu concentrations and direct fire, programmed fire to support a subsidiary landing opposite the town, defensive fire, extensive harassing fire, and counter-battery fire. On the coast the terrain allowed the use of occasional observation posts, but in the close country of the inland route observers travelling with the infantry were employed. The battery of 4.2-inch mortars was used to good effect in this area. Aerial observation provided by ArtyR and Air OP detachments was a valuable adjunct, the artillery commonly marking targets with smoke to assist air strikes. All regiments communicated by cable and radio, one noting that because the artillery prioritised information transfer so that fire could be applied safely, Gunner headquarters often had tactical information before their infantry counterparts.

Gunners of the 8th Battery, 2/4th Australian Field Regiment in action at the landing at Balikpapan engaging Japanese positions 6000 yards away, early July 1945 (Courtesy AWM 019437)

The Conflict Ends

For the campaigns fought in the littoral areas of Papua, New Guinea, Bougainville and North Borneo from 1942 onwards, Australia was able to mass the firepower that assured victory and lessened the casualties amongst its comrades in arms. Artillery was a key component, and for the Gunners, success against a determined enemy was the culmination of four hard years in which innovation and the adaptation of gunnery techniques enabled them to achieve fire superiority in the tropical environment in close cooperation with the Air Force and the Navy. In physically debilitating conditions, they carried out their tasks with skill and devotion to duty.

At war's end, the Australian artillery could look back once more on its contribution with pride. It had raised a technically adept arm out of one that had withered between the wars. It had provided support in a greater number of theatres than in World War I, raised a larger number of units, and fielded a greater diversity of equipment. Women had been successfully employed in the static defences. Thirty-four brigadiers had filled artillery appointments, and, amongst other senior appointments, the Gunners had provided an Army Commander

(Lavarack), two corps commanders (Herring and Berryman), and two of the five divisional commanders in the final campaigns (Ramsay and Milford). Between 120,000 and 150,000 had served in the artillery, of whom 2297, additional to those who perished as prisoners-of-war, died from other than natural causes.[10]

In the Fixed Defence and Anti-Aircraft Commands, although many of the units did not see action, Gunners had conscientiously performed their role, incorporated searchlights, embraced emerging technologies such as radar, experimented with electronic computation of firing data for coast guns, and developed headquarters and processes operating jointly with the Navy and Air Force.[11]

In each theatre of war, the field Gunners had understood the importance of accuracy, striven to use predicted fire, and sought the ability to concentrate the fire of multiple batteries. Operations demonstrated the necessity for close liaison between the Gunners and the infantry at all levels, and the usefulness of observers travelling with forward elements, although communication by line was a consistent problem, and radio remained an unreliable replacement.

The war reinforced the requirement for the artillery to be able to counter hostile guns and mortars, a task made more difficult in tropical conditions. As in World War I, air observation played an important role and saw the introduction of airborne artillery observers in the Air OP capability.

In all the campaigns of the war, and particularly in tropical operations from 1941 onwards, Australian Gunners typically employed their guns and coordinated fire support at infantry division level and below. At war's end, both they and their fellow manoeuvre-arm commanders lacked the experience obtained in North Africa and Europe with the application in conventional operations of massed indirect-fire and the employment of heavier calibre weapons in the depth battle. The compensation was a greater understanding of joint operations and joint fire support brought about by the littoral amphibious operations in the latter years of the conflict.

CHAPTER 11

Forming the Post-War Army

At the end of World War II, to provide the full-time forces to enforce the Japanese surrender and cover the demobilisation of the 2nd AIF, the Australian Government established an 'Interim Army', which was in turn displaced by the post-war Army in 1947. Legislation for the latter force included provision, as in the past, for citizen force and permanent elements. However, in contrast to previous structures, the permanent force was based around a combat brigade of all arms and services. The Australian Regular Army (ARA) was born.

National defence strategy continued to be based on a security relationship with an external partner – initially Britain, but later the USA – plus collective security through the United Nations (UN). Soviet Russia posed a general threat, and the possibility of global conflict induced the government in 1950 to reintroduce compulsory military service, resulting in a large citizen force artillery by the middle of the decade. However, from that point the greater probability of limited regional conflicts arising at short notice led to a policy of forward defence and a switch from conventional warfare. Consequent restructuring and military modernisation saw a significant demise in the overall size of the artillery and a reduction in its overall capabilities, but a small increase in its ARA element.[1]

A New Army

Australia's immediate imperative after the Japanese surrender in August 1945 was to return its forces and materiel from the South West Pacific, while demobilising as soon as practicable and maintaining the capability to enforce the surrender. As part of the latter commitment, the Army formed the 34th Infantry Brigade Group to join the British Commonwealth Occupation Forces in Japan. Combat was not expected, and so the group contained only one field battery. It was designated A Field Battery in 1946, because one of the sub-units from which it was raised, 2nd Mountain Battery, traced its heritage to A Battery of the NSW Permanent Artillery. After assisting with disarmament and reconstruction, A Battery returned to Australia with the majority of the brigade group in 1948.[2]

The Interim Army that provided the coverage for the immediate post war tasks gave way in 1947 to a 19,000 strong permanent army, based around an infantry brigade group. This was the first time that permanent infantry and armoured forces had been raised. A Citizen Military Force (CMF) of 50,000, organised as two infantry divisions and supporting troops, constituted an expansion base for more-substantial conflict.[3]

The artillery component of the ARA and CMF is shown at Appendix 1, Tables 13 and 14. The structure reflected an expectation of conventional rather than tropical operations.

Within it, the Directorate of Artillery provided advice to the staff and technical control of the artillery, and the separate wartime artillery schools were combined into a central school at North Head, Manly. A coast artillery element remained, but was manned on a very limited basis. In September 1949, the Royal Australian Artillery Regiment and the Royal Australian Artillery (Militia) were amalgamated to become the Royal Australian Artillery (RAA), and the motto *Quo Fas et Gloria Ducunt* was adopted.

Field and anti-aircraft units were equipped with wartime weapons, while medium and tank-attack regiments were armed respectively with the 5.5-inch gun and the 17-pounder anti-tank gun, both of which had been introduced into service towards the end of the war. A feature of the new organisation was that one battery of 22nd Field Regiment, part of a CMF armoured brigade group, was issued with an Australian-developed self-propelled gun: the 'Yeramba', a 25-pounder ordnance mounted on the chassis of a General Grant tank, the first appearance of such a capability in the Australian artillery. While this was a notable step forward, conversely no Air Observation Post (Air OP) flights were raised, although agreement was reached that selected Gunner officers could be trained for the role.

P SP Battery, 22nd Field Regiment formed up on parade, Puckapunyal, c. 1956. The 'X' on the Grant tank denotes it as the battery commander's OP vehicle (Courtesy RAAHC)

Korea: 1950–1953

When North Korea attacked South Korea in 1950 and the UN sought forces to restore the situation. Australia contributed the 3rd Battalion, Royal Australian Regiment (3RAR), to a British Commonwealth infantry brigade group. New Zealand provided an artillery field regiment, with individual Australian Gunners seconded periodically to its ranks. Five Australian Gunner officers flew with a British Air OP flight. Other Australian artillerymen served as Ground Liaison Officers with Navy or Air Force elements, or volunteered to serve with 3RAR, on British headquarters, or with British artillery units. On the expansion of the Australian commitment to two battalions in 1952, a shortage of platoon commanders resulted in many junior Gunner officers being employed in the role.[4]

Quo Fas Et Gloria Ducunt:
Captain John Robert Salmon, CBE

A graduate of the Royal Military College Duntroon's Class of 1946, John Salmon was posted initially to A Field Battery and deployed on post-war duties in Japan, as part of the British Commonwealth Occupation Forces. Following several staff postings, he was attached to 16th Field Regiment, Royal New Zealand Artillery, as a troop commander, for active service in Korea.

In December 1952, Salmon was a forward observation officer, with B Company, 1 RAR. The company was planning an action, dubbed 'Operation Fauna', to capture prisoners for unit identification and to destroy enemy bunkers to prevent the enemy defensive line advancing. Surprise was all-important, and artillery fire was only authorised if it was compromised. Fire Plan 'Capstan' was prepared, to cover the company's withdrawal.

Negotiating an Allied minefield through a pre-arranged lane, the company approached the Chinese position through the snow and ice. Suddenly shouts and shots from the trenches indicated that the company had been compromised. Salmon initiated 'Capstan' to have rounds fall on pre-adjusted targets, before being severely wounded by two enemy hand grenades. B Company headquarters was unknowingly lying on an underground bunker.

With his signaller and assistant under each shoulder, Salmon guided the company back to the minefield lane under the cover of 'Capstan's' effective fire. In the Australian lines he was evacuated to a field hospital where 17 grenade fragments were removed, but five remained. Afterwards, Salmon returned to Australia and continued a distinguished 38-year career as a Gunner and staff officer, before retiring as a Brigadier, and having been made a Commander of the Order of the British Empire.[5]

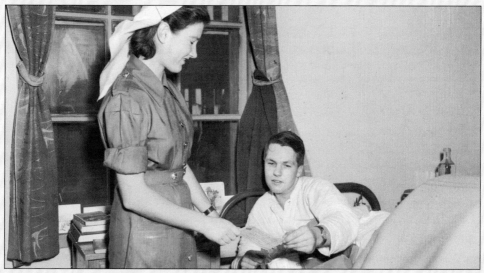

25 December 1952. Nurse CC O'Connor assists a recuperating Captain John Robert Salmon (Courtesy AWM 148282)

Powerful Part-Time Forces

Concerned by the communist takeover of China, the Cold War between the Communist bloc and the West, in 1950 the Government introduced a national service scheme, whereby 18-year-old males undertook 98 days of full-time training before completing a further 78 days in CMF units over the succeeding three years. Over 30,000 trainees were enlisted in each of the first six years of the scheme.[6]

Although the national servicemen were not required to serve overseas, the Government's intention was to prepare the CMF to become an expeditionary force should war break out.[7] By 1953 the influx had boosted the strength of the CMF to 80,000. Most units were close to full strength, wartime weapons and ammunition were readily available, and officers and NCO with war experience ensured a reasonable standard of proficiency. The artillery structure (Appendix 1, Table 15) grew large enough to include Army Groups Royal Artillery (AGRA) – descendants of World War I's Heavy Artillery Groups – commanding artillery units outside the divisional establishments. Reflecting wartime lessons, light regiments and an amphibious-observation capability also appeared on the order of battle, but tank-attack units were absent, as responsibility for combating enemy armour transferred to the Armoured Corps in 1952.[8]

A Citizen's Army Force (CMF) poster that states, 'Spare time for Australia's defence in the Citizen Army' (Courtesy AWM ARTV09284)

Towards Forward Defence

This was the CMF artillery at its most powerful, but looming changes foreshadowed a decline. One factor was that by the mid-1950s, jet aircraft had made heavy anti-aircraft guns obsolete. An active HAA regiment remained in service, along with provision for other anti-aircraft units in the Order of Battle, until, in the 1960s, the Air Force assumed responsibility for air defence above 4600 metres, for which it was equipped with Bloodhound missiles. The Army assumed responsibility for low-level air defence using improved Bofors 40-millimetre guns. CMF anti-aircraft units were gradually disbanded.[9]

A second and more pervasive factor was that as the 1950s progressed, insurgency in Malaya, and the partition of Vietnam, caused the Government to become increasingly concerned by the threat of communist aggression in South-East Asia. Early in the decade Australia joined with New Zealand and Britain in a defence agreement concerning Malaya, and it also signed the ANZUS Treaty with America and New Zealand. In 1954, Australia joined the South East Asia Treaty Organisation, and the next year agreed to participate in establishing a British Commonwealth tri-Service Far East Strategic Reserve (FESR) in Malaya.[10]

The Army contribution to the FESR was an infantry battalion to join the 28th Commonwealth Infantry Brigade, and a battery to form part of the supporting field regiment. The 105th Field Battery (eight 25-pounders) was raised and dispatched for the purpose to Butterworth.

The four guns of B Troop, 105 Field Battery, Royal Australian Artillery, let fly a barrage of 25-pounder shells against communist terrorists, Malaya, 1 January 1957 (Courtesy AWM HOB/56/0287/MC)

Map 11.01: Malayan Emergency, 1948-1960. The red square shows the location of the Central Committee of the Malayan Communist Party, and the yellow stars the location of the Malayan and Races Liberation Army regiments. Australian forces operated out of Butterworth. (Map courtesy www.britishempire.co.uk)

The Australian elements inevitably became involved in combating local communist insurgency during the Malayan Emergency. Three Australian field batteries served on rotation before the Emergency ended in 1960, supporting patrolling battalions and providing harassing fire onto suspected terrorist bases or locations. Tactical engagements were largely fleeting, making responsiveness a key factor. Fire was usually predicted, but could also be controlled by air or ground observers. Individual troop deployments were common, and communication was by radio. The dispersed nature of the operations along with the limited capabilities of the terrorists meant there was no need to concentrate artillery support. Gunners also conducted local patrols, manned checkpoints, and undertook internal security duties.[11]

Reorganisation: 1957–1959

A defence review in 1956 confirmed that under its international agreements, Australia would be required to participate in limited wars and counter-insurgency campaigns, for which Regular forces available at short notice were required. It recommended restructuring the CMF for a follow-on role. In response, in 1957 the Government increased the size of the ARA by a battalion group and announced the CMF's three divisions would have a ceiling of 50,000, about half their war establishment. It also signalled an intention to standardise on American equipment, reflecting a growing security alliance.[12]

In the ARA, 1st Field Regiment changed from its 1949 organisation – one field, one heavy anti-aircraft (HAA) and one locating battery – to one comprising two field batteries of 25-pounder (101st and 105th) and a light battery equipped with 4.2-inch mortars (102nd). The previous locating battery became 101st Field Battery, 102nd Battery was raised from scratch, and the HAA battery disbanded, contributing personnel to the newly raised independent 111th LAA Battery and an anti-aircraft element at the School of Artillery. Sixteen Air OP Flight was raised by the Air Force to train Army pilots. Standardisation meant in due course the 25-pounder would be replaced with American 105-millimetre M2A2 howitzers, which fired a 15-kilogram projectile to a maximum range of 11,270 metres. While its range was slightly less than the 25-pounder, the M2A2 fired a heavier projectile, and could fire at elevations above 800 mils (45 degrees), an advantage in close country.

In 1959, the shift in emphasis to forces capable of short-notice involvement in limited war alongside major allies led the government to suspend the national service scheme, partly to assist the ARA in manning its units by reducing the number of cadre in the CMF, partly because the conscripts were not bound to serve overseas, and partly to divert funding to the permanent forces.

The effect on the CMF artillery was dramatic. By 1960, the Headquarters Corps Artillery, the AGRA Headquarters, 20th Locating Regiment, the light field regiments, anti-aircraft control and reporting capabilities, the movement light searchlight units, and the self-propelled field regiment had all been disbanded.[13] The number of medium and LAA regiments had been reduced, with the two surviving medium regiments (one unmanned) located in Victoria, and the surviving LAA regiments in NSW.

These changes affected the artillery's overall capability. The CMF structure in theory still permitted artillery operations at divisional level, but unit manning and training levels made their practice outside of command post exercises difficult. The single ARA field regiment was increasingly focused on the commitment of a battery to Malaya and the prospect of wider involvement in the area. Accordingly, the RAA's capability to support conventional warfare was diminished. Tight economic times raised questions as to what further changes might lie in store

CHAPTER 12
Forward Defence: 1955–1972

The forward defence policy of protecting national interests in Australia's region by short-notice participation in limited wars and counter-insurgency campaigns lasted until 1972. It entailed artillery support to conflicts in Malaya, North Borneo and Vietnam, support which was principally provided by field and locating elements, and limited to infantry brigade or task force level.

Restructuring preceded the operational commitments as the Army sought to position itself to operate with major allies. The resultant changes strengthened the Australian Regular Army (ARA) artillery in terms of units and its position as the repository of technical expertise, but weakened the Citizen Military Forces (CMF) units, manpower and morale. The period also saw the end of the coast artillery era.

National service was reintroduced in 1964, on this occasion to assist the ARA. It proved a boon to Australia's involvement in the Vietnam War, in which the artillery played a key role. By the time the conflict ended, Australia's Gunners had become expert in providing close support in low to mid-intensity conflict, but the artillery's capacity to provide fire support and coordination beyond this had deteriorated.

The Pentropic Division: 1960–1963

Sparked by financial considerations and the policy requirement to work alongside the US Army, in 1960 the Australian Army created a divisional structure designed to be air portable and capable of fighting in a limited war in South East Asia.[1]

Like the US 'Pentomic' Division design that it emulated, the Australian 'Pentropic' Division was based on five battle groups, each comprising a five-company infantry battalion, a field regiment, an engineer squadron and other combat and support elements. It also contained an armoured regiment, a locating battery in divisional troops, and a single Task Force (TF) Headquarters, which could, if necessary, command multiple battle groups. Combat Support Groups contained medium artillery and LAA regiments for reinforcement purposes, along with a gun-locating capability.

From an artillery perspective, the Pentropic organisation retained a divisional artillery headquarters and strengthened the divisional artillery by increasing the number of organic field regiments. Also at this time, there were plans to include surface-to-surface and surface-to-air guided weapons batteries in the Combat Support Groups. In the event, however, none were purchased.

The Army formed the 1st Pentropic Division with two ARA and three CMF battalions, and the 3rd Pentropic Division with five CMF battalions. The CMF 2nd Division commanded Lines of Communications units. The artillery component of these divisions is at Appendix 1, Table 16.

Field regiments in the Pentropic divisions had two batteries, each equipped with either eight 105-millimetre M2A2 howitzers, or eight 105-millimetre L5 pack howitzers. The latter was an Italian gun firing the same ammunition as the M2A2. It had a shorter range (10,000 metres) and was less robust, but it was potentially more mobile, being lighter and capable of being disassembled for transport, and thus potentially preferable in tropical service. The divisional locating battery had a survey troop, a radar troop equipped with first-generation AN/KPQ-1 mortar-locating radars, and five counter-bombardment (artillery intelligence) sections.

Early M2A2 105-millimetre howitzer manufactured in 1959, on display in the Australian War Memorial. The M2A2 was a general purpose, towed, light field artillery weapon, which consisted of a barrel, recoil mechanism and carriage (Courtesy AWM REL26769)

For the ARA, the Pentropic organisation meant raising a second field regiment, the 4th Field Regiment. It was in this period as well that the 16th Army Light Aircraft Squadron was raised at Amberley, with the existing 16th Air OP Flight as its nucleus. However, for the CMF the result was devastating. Thirty-one infantry battalions were condensed into eight Pentropic battalions, demolishing many traditional community links. Seven artillery regiments were either disbanded or amalgamated.

A Change of Title and the End of an Era: 1962

Unrelated to the introduction of the Pentropic division, but in alignment with the other British Commonwealth artilleries, on 19 September 1962, the Australian artillery was re-titled 'The Royal Regiment of Australian Artillery'. At the same time, Her Majesty, Queen Elizabeth II, The Queen of Australia, became the Regiment's Captain-General.[2]

In the same year, Australian defence chiefs concluded that missiles and air power had made coast artillery defences redundant and closed the fixed defences. The last regular unit had disbanded ten years previously, ending a permanent coast artillery presence first begun in 1871. Now the three remaining part-time batteries marched out of the forts they had occupied for nearly a century, and converted to anti-aircraft units. The guns were sold for scrap.[3] An era had ended.

The Tropical Warfare Division: 1963

In 1963, for a number of reasons, not least that the US Army had abandoned the Pentomic organisation, the Australian Army adopted a revised divisional structure on more traditional lines. The Tropical Warfare Division included ten infantry battalions, a cavalry regiment, three field regiments, a divisional locating battery, an aviation regiment, and allocations of engineers, signals and other support units. It had three TF Headquarters under which units could be grouped for operations or training.[4]

Each field regiment had three six-gun batteries, and the divisional locating battery contained a survey troop, a mortar-locating radar troop, and three artillery intelligence sections. This organisation required the raising of a third ARA field regiment, 12th Field Regiment, along with three additional field batteries and a second LAA battery. 131st Divisional Locating Battery became an ARA unit. CMF artillery units differed little from those in the Pentropic structure.

The six-gun battery of the revised division followed British practice, which had, in fact, prevailed in the Australian batteries sent to Malaya since 1960. Its adoption capped a number of evolutions in field gunnery throughout the 1950s.[5] Command terminology remained unaltered, but control terminology was expanded to include 'In Direct Support', 'In Support' or 'At Priority Call'. Batteries allocated 'In Direct Support' provided observers and the battery commander's party to the nominated unit, and fired for that unit, within ammunition authorisations, without further reference. Batteries responded to calls for fire from units to which they were allotted 'In Support' if practical. 'Priority Call' tasks superseded the other two, but the allocation was reserved for special commitments.

Target-grid procedure was introduced, observers henceforth normally adjusting fire along the line observer-target using a single gun, rather than along the line battery-target using a section, as had applied previously. Zero Lines and pivot guns were superseded in 1957 by the orientation of the guns on a centre-of-arc, and prediction from the battery centre. Measurement of sighting angles in mils rather than degrees and minutes, and metric distance measurement was adopted in 1960. That same year the Plotter Fire Control Field Branch

Artillery (Light) replaced the artillery board as the means of computing bearing and distance in battery command posts.

To facilitate the manning of the ARA, in 1964 the Government introduced a selective national service scheme, under which 20-year-old draftees, selected by a ballot of birth dates, served for two years. Service overseas was voluntary. An option allowed potential draftees to secure exemption from full time service by enlisting in the CMF for six years, but the CMF suffered in the following period from a loss of individuals to full-time duty and minimal ARA cadre support. Legislation was changed to allow the call out of the CMF, but no such action was taken when operational commitments arose. The purpose of the CMF remained unclear, hampering recruitment.

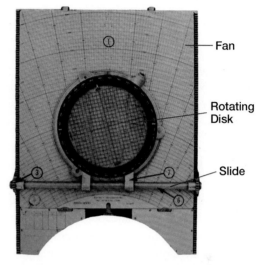

Plotter Fire Control Field Branch Artillery (Light), 1960s. Lightweight plotters were used by Australian batteries in Borneo and by Australian and New Zealand batteries in Vietnam (Courtesy Nigel Evans, Tripod)

Konfrontasi: 1964–66

It was at this time that Indonesia embarked on confrontation (*Konfrontasi*) with newly created Malaysia. Hostile activities included incursions into the Malaysian mainland and provinces in North Borneo. Australian agreed its Far East Strategic Reserve (FESR) elements could be used in actions on the mainland, and in June 1964 deployed the 111th LAA Battery to protect the air base at Butterworth.[6]

Initially, individuals serving in the FESR, but not units, were permitted to serve in North Borneo. That policy changed in April 1965, and 102nd Field Battery, equipped with six L5 pack howitzers, was positioned near Kuching with a British L5 Section and two 4.2-inch mortars also under its command. The enhanced battery supported three British battalions, with the battery commander at the headquarters of one, and a captain at the headquarters of each of the others. In addition, the battery manned three static observation posts using NCO observers, and provided two observer parties for deployment as required.

Its guns were spread across five bases, moving between them to support different operations. At each company base there was a small command post in addition to the gun detachment(s). Bases responded to calls for fire from patrols and provided nightly harassing fire. Including its administrative position, the battery area comprised a triangle some 64 kilometres wide and 48 kilometres deep. Its operations demonstrated there was a role for artillery in this limited form of warfare, gunnery techniques remained sound, and that radio communications could be made to work in difficult country over considerable distances.

Artillery Commanders: Major Arthur McDermott

Major Arthur McDermott commanded the first Australian anti-aircraft battery to be deployed on operations after World War II. On graduation from Duntroon into the artillery in 1951, McDermott was immediately seconded for duty as a platoon commander with the infantry in Korea. Afterwards, he served as adjutant of two CMF heavy anti-aircraft regiments, and then with a regular gun battery, before attending Staff College in the UK.

After his return to Australia in 1964, McDermott was appointed battery commander of 111th LAA Battery at Holsworthy. Confrontation between Malaysia and Indonesia prompted the Government to provide ground-based air defence of the air base at Butterworth, Malaysia, and within a month of taking command, McDermott was tasked to deploy the battery. Inside four weeks the sub-unit grew to war establishment, completed pre-embarkation requirements, undertook a reconnaissance, and finalised preparations for sailing. McDermott continued battery training during the voyage, and at Butterworth he established an inner and outer ring of 40-millimetre guns, a control and reporting unit in conjunction with the RAAF, and early warning posts on Penang Island.

He completed his tour in late 1964. Eight months later he was made the 2IC of 1st Field Regiment, the first gun regiment to be deployed to Vietnam. In country, he played a key role in establishing the unit at Nui Dat and overseeing logistic matters, including the supply of ammunition during the battle at Long Tan. When the regimental commander returned to Australia early, McDermott temporarily administered command. Subsequently, he served in logistic and air staff appointments at HQ 1st Division before retiring in 1975.

Gunners of the 102nd Field Battery prepare to fire their 105-millimetre L5 pack howitzer in support of Gurkha troops in North Borneo, 1965 (Courtesy AWM CUN/65/0853A/MC)

Vietnam: 1962–72

Australia's military commitment in South Vietnam began slightly earlier than its involvement in Confrontation. First to deploy, in 1962, was the Australian Army Training Team Vietnam. From June 1964 onwards its members, who included individual Gunners, accompanied South Vietnamese army units into combat, and a former artillery officer, Major Peter Badcoe, was awarded the Victoria Cross posthumously in 1967.[7]

In 1965 Australia increased its commitment, with the 1st Battalion, Royal Australian Regiment (1RAR), and 105th Field Battery, equipped with six L5 howitzers, joining the 173rd US Airborne Brigade. In March 1966, the battery and two American counterparts fired for over four hours repelling an attack on an American battalion by two Viet Cong (VC) regiments, the American commander afterwards stating he had never seen finer shooting. Twenty-five years later, the Army authorised 105th Field battery, as part of the 1RAR Group, to wear the US Meritorious Unit Citation awarded to 173rd Airborne Brigade.[8]

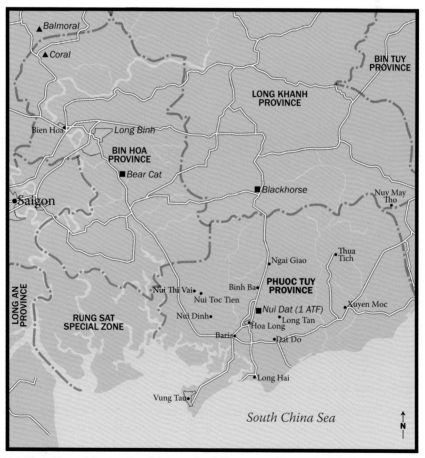

Map 12.01: Phuoc Tuy and Surrounding Provinces, South Vietnam, 1966-1971. From 1966 to 1971 the 1st Australian Task Force was based at Nui Dat in Phuoc Tuy Province, where it was supported (in rotation) by the 1st, 4th and 12th Field regiments. Occasionally, Task force units were deployed to neighbouring provinces. Fire Support Patrol Base Coral, for example, was located in Bien Hoa Province.

In March 1966, Australia increased its commitment to a task force, which was given responsibility for Phuoc Tuy Province in cooperation with the Army of the Republic of Vietnam.[9] The 1st Australian Task Force (1 ATF) was supported by a field regiment (rotating annually) and a detachment of 131st Divisional Locating Battery (individual rotations). It was also allotted operational control of a battery of US 155-millimetre M109 self-propelled howitzers.

1st Field Regiment, commanded by Lieutenant Colonel RMC Cubis, was the first gun regiment to deploy. It brought 103rd Field Battery, and took the already-deployed 105th Battery and 161st Battery RNZA under command upon arrival. Batteries were initially equipped with L5 pack howitzers, but from May 1967 onwards, switched to the more-robust M2A2. 131st Battery surveyors provided survey to gun positions across the province while American sources circulated regular meteorological messages and batteries undertook periodic calibration or checks of fall of shot to maintain the accuracy of fire. In the 1 ATF base, the batteries held defensive fire and hostile battery target lists prepared by the regimental headquarters.

Gunners from 108th Field Battery work feverishly to free their M2A2 howitzer from the mud during Operation Paddington, the massive Allied offensive in Phuoc Tuy Province, July 1967 (Courtesy AWM COL/67/0548/VN)

In addition to providing survey, the 131st Battery detachment, operating AN-KPQ 1 radars and, later, sound ranging equipment, provided mortar and rocket-location coverage for the TF base. Towards the end of the Australian involvement, it deployed strings of ground sensors, providing data that led to several successful ambushes. Broader surveillance through signals intelligence and American airborne detection devices yielded information that was used in operational planning and the targeting of harassing fire.

No LAA sub-units were deployed, but personnel from 16th LAA Regiment assisted in manning guns on the landing craft of 32nd Small Ships Squadron while on operations in South Vietnamese waters. Members of 67 Ground Liaison Section were embedded in the Air Force helicopter and Caribou squadrons supporting the Task Force.

The operating environment was complex, requiring coordination of artillery fire with allied forces, civilian authorities, air movements, and aerial and naval gunfire support. As a coordinating body, and to facilitate air and ground clearance to fire, the artillery established a Fire Support Coordination Centre (FSCC), which included the Artillery Tactical (Arty Tac) Headquarters, the regimental command post, the locating command post, US Air Force and Navy liaison officers, and the Air Warning Control Centre.

Large wall maps of the Task Force Operations (left) and Artillery Tactical (Arty Tac) Headquarters (right) at the 1 Australian Task Force (1ATF) base, 8 September 1969 (Courtesy AWM P05764.003)

Rules of engagement played a significant role. In conjunction with provincial authorities, no-fire zones were established around civilian population centres. Outside of these, except in support of a contact, guns could not fire without ground clearance from the headquarters controlling the location in which the target appeared, and without air clearance from the FSCC.

Long Tan

In the late afternoon of 18 August 1966, very early in 1 ATF's deployment, the value of artillery was clearly demonstrated when D Company 6RAR contacted a much larger North Vietnamese Army force to the east of Nui Dat. The three batteries of the regiment fired in support for three hours, with breaks only for an ineffective airstrike and a helicopter drop

Artillery Commanders: Lieutenant Colonel RMC Cubis, MVO

Lieutenant Colonel Cubis was the commander of the first artillery regiment committed to South Vietnam. Unfortunately, as the result of an inability to forge a cohesive working relationship at Task Force Headquarters, he was not able to complete his tour of duty, underlining for Gunners the importance of working cooperatively to create mutual understanding, without compromising principles.

In his early career, Cubis served in Korea as staff officer within Headquarters 1st Commonwealth Division, and 14th Regiment, Royal Artillery, and had qualified on the UK Long Gunnery Course. In June 1966, he deployed to South Vietnam as Commanding Officer of 1st Field Regiment, comprising the incoming 103rd Battery, and the already-deployed 105th Battery and 161st Battery (Royal New Zealand Artillery). Cubis assumed command at the newly-established 1st Australian Task Force (1 ATF) base at Nui Dat.

As 1ATF settled in, Cubis became concerned by what he saw as inadequate understanding in the Task Force of the role of artillery. He felt excluded from operational planning, was concerned that the siting of gun batteries on the base perimeter risked compromising the regiment's primary mission of providing fire support if the base was attacked, and considered disproportionate demands were being placed on his regiment to meet other priorities.

Despite these tensions, the batteries forged strong relationships with their affiliated battalions, and the regiment's fire support coordination centre at Task Force Headquarters proved effective and efficient. The part played by the artillery under Cubis' command during the Battle of Long Tan exemplified the importance and capability of the arm.

Matters, however, came to a head in November 1966 when, during a battery fire mission, Cubis became concerned with troop safety and ultimately terminated the mission without consulting the originating observer or his battery commander. Cubis' intervention was raised along the infantry command channels, leading to a situation where, standing by his judgement, he refused the Task Force Commander's order to resume the mission. With the relationship with his superior finally broken, Lieutenant Colonel Cubis, who had been considering his options for some time, tendered his resignation, and was relieved of his command.

Captain R M C Cubis, conducts a briefing in the Commonwealth Division, Korea (Courtesy IWM BF 10768)

of small-arms ammunition to the beleaguered company. Firing at six rounds per gun per minute at the most intense period, the field guns provided intimate defensive fire while the 155s engaged targets in depth, the guns together expending 3500 rounds in gathering darkness and driving rain.[10]

Only the artillery could have provided such continuous close support for the time required. It was clearly the decisive factor in the battle, assisted by the circumstance that all batteries were in range, all the elements for accurate fire were in place, the batteries were well supplied with ammunition, and radio nets remained operable.

Securing Phuoc Tuy

With the knowledge that infantry supported by artillery could contend with larger opposing forces, the majority of operations to secure the province consisted of patrolling in temporary battalion areas of operation. A direct support field battery was located at the battalion fire support and patrol base (FSPB) with the battery commander at the battalion headquarters. Initially, establishments only provided three observer parties, but the number was soon increased to four to allow one for each infantry company.[11]

At battalion headquarters the battery commander coordinated fire support. Communication was by radio. On patrol, company headquarters and the artillery observer generally travelled with one platoon; the observer's assistant, a bombardier, at another; and often a mortar fire controller (MFC) at the third. All could direct fire and coordinate it when necessary with other fire support such as helicopter gunships.

Mapping of the areas of operation was adequate, but accurate navigation in close country by compass bearing and pacing had its difficulties. The guns provided protective and cut-off fire when contact occurred, covering fire for local assaults, defensive fire for static or night locations, and harassing fire. For safety, the first round of a non-contact engagement was typically placed 1000 metres from the observer's location, and walked in by sound. As in previous jungle conflicts, observers had to be aware of tree height in the target area, and special (danger close) procedures were put in place when bringing fire close to the infantry.

Batteries deployed by road or helicopter. In the TF base and in FSPB the command post was dug in with overhead protection, the guns were encircled by earthen bunds, and the ammunition and detachment shelters were also under overhead protection. The battery's portion of the perimeter was shielded by earthwork 'bunds', with barbed wire entanglements to the front, overseen by one or two machine gun posts. Guns were manned in shifts.

As 1 ATF gained ascendancy, battalions patrolled further from Nui Dat, and later it was not uncommon for sections to be deployed outside the battalion FSPB to extend the area of coverage. In the course of a tour, a battery could deploy as an entity or by section or sub-section on numerous occasions. As an example, on its second tour, 105th Battery elements deployed or redeployed on 31 occasions, and fired 76,000 rounds.[13]

Quo Fas Et Gloria Ducunt: Lance Bombardier Peter 'Blue' Maher, MM

Lance Bombardier Peter 'Blue' Maher, 12th Field Regiment and his signaller Gunner Bayne 'Gus' Kelly, were attached to 5 Platoon, B Company, 3 RAR during a three-day battalion operation north of Phuoc Tuy Province. Towards last light on 6 June, 5 Platoon located a large occupied bunker complex. The platoon was directed to withdraw to a night defensive position pending an attack the next morning.

At first light on 7 June 1971, Blue adjusted covering fire onto the bunkers prior to 5 Platoon's assault. However, the infantry soon came under heavy fire from a range of 15 metres and took a number of casualties. Asked, years later, about his reaction at this point, he replied, 'We just focussed on our job [of bringing in fire support] and had faith in the infantry.' Blue engaged the bunkers again with fire 'very close' to 5 Platoon from A and 104th Field Batteries, as well as from US 155-millimetre guns.

Later that morning, the remainder of B Company closed up to reinforce the platoon. When the Company's forward observation officer was mortally wounded, Blue again found himself coordinating artillery as close as 100 metres, pausing to allow RAAF Bushranger and US Cobra gunship strikes. At this time, an RAAF Iroquois resupply helicopter was shot down, and burst into flames.

Later, D Company 3 RAR and Centurion tanks from 1st Armoured Regiment joined the fray that afternoon, sweeping through the bunker complex. A total of 47 bunkers were uncovered. Lance Bombardier Maher was awarded the Military Medal for his steadfast coordination of sustained and accurate indirect fire and gunship support over almost 24 hours.[12]

Soldiers from 5 Platoon, B Company, 3RAR at Nui Dat a fortnight after the fierce action in Long Khanh province (Courtesy AWM P05146.001)

A 105-millimetre howitzer of A Battery 12th Field Regt photographed through the cargo inspection hatch of a US Chinook helicopter at 2000 feet, returning to Nui Dat, South Vietnam, May 1971 (Courtesy AWM PJE/71/0271/VN)

FSPB Coral: 1968

Occasionally, operations took place outside Phuoc Tuy Province in support of wider allied actions. In one example, following the North Vietnamese Tet Offensive in 1968, 1 ATF units were deployed to the Long Kanh and then Bien Hoa Provinces on the eastern approaches to Saigon. 12th Field Regiment and other elements were ordered to create a base to be known as FSPB Coral on 12 May, but a confused and disrupted deployment found the 102nd and 161st batteries in isolated positions and unable to complete their defensive arrangements before last light. In the early hours of 13 May, a North Vietnamese Army battalion attacked through the 102nd battery position and the adjacent mortar platoon of 1RAR.[14]

One gun and the mortars were overrun, and another gun damaged. However, the attacker's penetration was limited by dogged defence, direct fire from the forward guns including the firing of 'Splintex' rounds with their shotgun-like effect, and fire support from other batteries and gunships. The enemy withdrew at first light, but not before, whilst defending itself, 102nd battery fired three section missions in support of the infantry. Fighting in the area continued for some time, and included an unsuccessful attack on FSPB Balmoral a fortnight later, during which the guns at Coral provided defensive fire.

Artillery Tactics: Gun Position Defence

Artillery gun positions are priority targets, and threats to the guns vary by theatre of war and operation. Counter-battery, air attack and direct assault have all been encountered. Australian guns were attacked from the ground at Noreuil in World War I, at Salamaua in the World War II, at Coral in Vietnam, and at Budwan in Afghanistan. They were attacked from the air in Greece, Crete and New Guinea.

In low-level operations where the adversary has had a limited counter-battery and air capabilities, gun positions have tended to be more static and protected by local defence works. If necessary, guns employ direct fire techniques, using HE or near-muzzle-burst anti-personnel rounds, and anti-armour projectiles

In conventional operations movement, camouflage and deception mitigate the risk of attack. Artillery tactics are underpinned by a continual time-and-space appreciation for deploying the guns, requiring the allocation of sufficient battle space for artillery units to manoeuvre to take advantage of the protection provided by terrain and vegetation. Intelligence on enemy artillery, ground and air threat is vital.

The guns reveal their location once fire missions commence. While usually not critical in low-level operations, such exposure can be lethal in higher intensity conflict. As a consequence, alternative positions are pre-planned, and techniques such as predicted fire and single guns firing from temporary positions are employed, to avoid 'unmasking' main gun positions. Covered positions ('hides') may be used between deployments. Armoured self-propelled guns and howitzers with independent communications and firing data computation provide options for greater dispersal, while still being able to concentrate fire. 'Shoot-and-Scoot' is normal practice.

Regardless of the nature or level of threat, Gunners normally do not anticipate support from other arms for gun position defence. Batteries are armed with personal and crew-served weapons. Gunners also routinely prepare defensive fire-plans to be fired in support of their positions by neighbouring batteries. Ready-reaction parties are detailed to conduct counter-attacks. Sentries and patrols beyond the perimeter of gun positions provide additional warning and protection. There are never enough Gunners, and there is little rest on a static gun position.

Gunners of No. 6 detachment, 102nd Field Battery standing by their smoke-blackened M2A2 after the first early morning assault by NVA on FSB Coral, 13 May 1968 (Courtesy AWM P02950.002)

On the 40th anniversary of its defensive action, for the professionalism, dedication and courage of its members while in extreme danger, 102nd Field Battery was awarded the Honour Title 'Coral'. Ten years later, it and the other Gunner units of 1 ATF (Forward) at the time were among those awarded a Meritorious Unit Citation for Gallantry.

The End of Forward Defence

It was fitting that Gunners were on operational service in 1971, the year the Australian artillery recorded a century of continuous permanent service. The centenary was marked by the retirement of the King's Banner, and the presentation of the Banner of Her Majesty Queen Elizabeth II. Gunners from A Battery returned temporarily from South Vietnam to participate in the ceremony. In September of that same year, at Nui Le, three guns of the 104th Battery re-emphasised the value of artillery when, firing at extreme range, they prevented D Company, 4RAR/NZ being overrun.

However, with involvement in Vietnam increasingly unpopular, the vast majority of Australian troops were withdrawn in 1971, signalling an end to an era of regional operational deployments. Nonetheless, Australia maintained a battalion and a battery in Singapore and a LAA battery at Butterworth for a period, under the Five Power Defence Arrangements with Malaysia.

Artillery had played an important role in Australia's forward defence posture, albeit on a much lesser scale than in the world wars. Responsive fire support, regardless of time of day and weather, had protected the ground troops. With close air support, helicopter gunships, naval gunfire and aerial surveillance available to complement the artillery, fire support coordination at task force and battalion level had become a Gunner task, and had been handled well.

Throughout the era only the regular field artillery provided operational support, becoming the repository of artillery technical expertise and recent operational experience. The CMF artillery suffered from the lack of a clear role and from recruitment problems. How the balance between the permanent and part-time forces might be struck was a key question for post-conflict consideration, along with the issue of whether the Army's focus should remain on counter-insurgency or shift to a higher level of conflict.

CHAPTER 13
Continental Defence: 1972–1999

Australia's withdrawal from Vietnam coincided with Britain's reduction of its commitments 'East of Suez' and the adoption by the USA of the Guam Doctrine, under which America's allies were expected to be more self-reliant. Australia's defence policy was still based around the ANZUS Alliance and UN collective security policy, but over the next quarter century focus turned to defence of continental Australia. This period saw the development of a joint command and control system, increasing Australian Defence Force (ADF) presence in the north, and an emphasis on protection against credible low-level threats, all within the context of constrained defence budgets. The governance of Defence also changed. In 1975, the three Services lost their individual Ministers, and were grouped under the Defence Minister. A Chief of the Defence Force Staff and a defence force headquarters were created, and Army Headquarters was retitled as Army Office.

Restructuring was constant within the Army, commencing with the Citizen Military Forces (CMF) becoming the Army Reserve (ARES). Over time, ADF operational planning concentrated on mobile, dispersed operations against irregular adversaries on the Australian mainland. In this context, the increased combat power of infantry and light armour and the advent of armed helicopters called into question the requirement for artillery. A capability was retained, but with no apparent need for divisional-level fire coordination or the application of artillery in depth. Divisional artillery headquarters were disbanded, and the number of artillery units reduced. Australia's post-Vietnam strategic introspectiveness dispelled any impetus for significant artillery modernisation in this period.

Combined, these factors would lead to a waning of Australian artillery capability. The surviving Australian Regular Army (ARA) artillery units maintained their ability to provide accurate battery and regimental fire, developed procedures to use precision-guided munitions, and retained the ability to integrate joint fires on behalf of the supported arm commander. Alongside, the less well-resourced ARES units worked to maintain baseline battery-level competency.

A New Army Structure: 1970s

Following the Vietnam War, the Army changed from geographic to functionally based commands, and divided into headquarters tasked with generating forces, and those with employing forces. Consequently, artillery regiments and batteries became part of Field Force Command. Along with other corps schools, the School of Artillery joined Training

Command, as did the CMF regional training groups. Army's proof and experimental function became part of Logistics Command. The Directorate of Artillery remained at Army Headquarters, guiding acquisitions, policy, doctrine, and postings. [1]

At the tactical level, the demise of 'Forward Defence' as a strategic posture was reflected in the contracting of field artillery structures. The regular artillery initially comprised four gun regiments (1st, 4th, 8th, and 12th), nine gun batteries (A and 101st to 108th Batteries) and a locating battery (131st). Post-Vietnam reductions soon led to the amalgamation of the 8th and 12th Regiments, and the disbandment of the 104th and 106th Batteries. Anti-Aircraft Artillery was retitled Air Defence in 1974, and the capability condensed to one regiment (16th) of two batteries (110th, 111th).

The CMF, whose artillery strength had ebbed to 48 per cent of establishments, was subjected to a fundamental review that changed its role from the Army's expansion force to being the reserve component of the force-in-being. Renamed the Army Reserve, only units manned above 70 per cent of establishment were retained. [2] At this point, the reserve artillery comprised two divisional artillery headquarters, four field regiments, a medium regiment, three independent batteries, two divisional locating batteries and a light anti-aircraft battery. Appendix 1, Table 17 details the composition of the artillery in 1976.

A Revised Defence Policy: 1976

The 1976 Defence White Paper, *Australian Defence,* provided the initial post-Vietnam defence policy. It concluded that future defence activities were 'more likely to be in our own neighbourhood…and they would be conducted as joint operations by the (Australian Defence Force) ADF'. It also spoke of a need for self-reliance and the ability to deal with 'selected shorter-term contingencies'. [3]

To meet this guidance, the Army sought to develop a 'core force', capable of handling local situations and expanding to meet a major threat. It retained its divisional structures as a means of providing experience for commanders and staffs, and trained for conventional warfare in a potentially hostile air environment against a Soviet-era threat, conceiving that a force prepared for such operations would be capable of handling a lower-level contingency if necessary. [4]

For Gunners, the technical aspects of providing fire support remained the same as in Vietnam and Malaysia, but training emphasised the principle of exercising artillery command at the highest practical level, and delegating control of fire as required. Formation-level exercises were held throughout the 1970s – some involving Navy, Air Force and allied elements – including some in which the field regiments of the 1st Division fired divisional missions. [5]

As it had from the 1950s, the School of Artillery instructed regular recruits and specialists, provided development courses for officers and senior NCOs both regular and reserve, and maintained contemporary artillery doctrine, which increasingly reflected the standardisation agreements between the American, British, Canadian and Australia artilleries, a process Australia had joined in 1962. The Army continued its policy of sending selected RAA officers and NCOs to Britain, Canada and the USA to train as gunnery instructors, and began an exchange of instructors with the British and American artillery schools.

The period also witnessed acknowledgement of more than a century of Australian artillery service when, in 1977, Her Majesty Queen Elizabeth II dedicated the Royal Australian Artillery National Memorial on Mount Pleasant in Canberra.

A number of artillery equipment projects that had begun earlier came to fruition in the 1970s and into the 1980s, in part offsetting the contraction of the RAA's force structure. 16th Air Defence Regiment was re-armed with one battery of 'Redeye' shoulder-fired, heat-seeking missiles for very-low-level air defence, and one battery of 'Rapier' missiles with associated radar to provide for low-level air defence, both heralding the RAA's belated entry into the missile age.[6]

Gunners from 110 Battery, 16th Air Defence Regiment take part in a training shoot at Beecroft, near Nowra, NSW, October 1980 (Courtesy Defence Image Gallery SYDA_80_300_05.jpg)

On the field artillery side, the long-serving medium (5.5-inch) and field (M2A2, L5, and 25-pounder) guns were gradually phased out of regular service in favour of the American-designed 155-millimetre M198 towed howitzer (introduced 1983) and the 105-millimetre L118/L119 Hamel gun, an Australian-built version of the British light gun (introduced 1988).[7] Importantly, this re-equipment completed the alignment of the RAA's calibres with contemporary US and NATO standards. The M2A2 remained in reserve service as it was a simpler gun to deploy and maintain in the training time available.

Computerised calculation of firing data using various platforms was introduced into battery and locating command posts in the 1970s. In the 1980s, observers were issued with laser range finders, and position-and-azimuth-determining systems using inertial navigation were fielded to assist with survey of the guns. The AN/KPQ1 mortar-locating radar was replaced by the more capable American AN/TPQ36 weapon-locating radar, and new sound ranging, meteorological and muzzle-velocity measuring equipment was issued.[8]

8th/12th Medium Regiment, Battery Command Post operating the Field Artillery Computer Equipment (FACE), Exercise Intrepid Gunner, Beecroft Naval Range, 1981 (Courtesy Defence Image Gallery SYDA_81_113_01.jpg)

These acquisitions provided the basis for accurate and responsive target acquisition and engagement, but the sustainability of the artillery capability was significantly constrained by limited domestic ammunition production, and relatively small holdings of the more modern ammunition types that began to enter service to provide greater range through improved design, rocket assistance, or terminal guidance.

Moves to Increase Readiness

In 1979, the regular Army's 1st Division reorganised with a view to developing a force to operate on lighter scales in the tropical north, while retaining a range of skills for expansion. The 3rd Brigade (formerly 3rd Task Force) in Townsville became a short-notice, air-mobile Operational Deployment Force. The brigade's manoeuvre units were supported by the two batteries of 4th Field Regiment equipped with L5 pack howitzers for carriage by Iroquois and Chinook helicopters, or transport aircraft.[9]

The 1st Brigade at Holsworthy became a mechanised brigade and, although technically directly supported by 5th/11th Field Regiment in Brisbane, developed local informal relationships with the co-located 8th/12th Medium Regiment. In 1983, 3RAR, supported by A Field Battery, began collective training as a parachute battalion group.[10]

The 6th Brigade in Brisbane and the brigades of the reserve's 2nd and 3rd Divisions remained light infantry formations, drawing their fire support from 1st Field Regiment and the reserve regiments and batteries respectively. Following the Soviet invasion of Afghanistan in 1979, 104th Battery was re-raised with both a reserve and regular component, and the reserve 113th Battery converted from anti-aircraft to field artillery in 1986.

Headquarters Field Force Artillery adopted the 'Army Training and Evaluation Program' (ARTEP) in the early 1980s, as the assessment mechanism for collective performance. The ARTEP was used to assess the professional and technical standards of regular regiments and batteries annually, and reserve regiments and batteries biennially. ARTEPs remained the cornerstone of artillery training into the early 2000s, with reserve battery results providing the basis of the annual award of the long-established Mount Schanck Trophy, and ARA battery results leading to the award of the 'Coral' trophy.[11]

The 'Defence of Australia' Period: 1987–1998

The Dibb Review of defence capabilities in 1986, and the ensuing 1987 White Paper, *The Defence of Australia*, narrowed strategic focus and force preparedness to the defence of continental Australia. [12] The Navy and Air Force were tasked with denying the maritime approaches to Australia, while the Army was to provide mobile forces capable of rapid deployment across northern Australia to deal with credible low-level penetration of the sea-air gap, and to protect the naval and air bases. Such strategic thinking was to prevail for the next decade-and-a-half. The end of the Cold War and the absence of an overt regional threat reinforced the view that defence forces capable of expansion to undertake conventional war fighting were not required. The fall of the Berlin Wall and Soviet power in 1989 further weakened arguments for a more potent Defence Force that was capable of conventional warfare involving substantial joint fires and artillery support.

Further reorganisation ensued, with the emphasis now on joint operations. Following the establishment of Headquarters Australian Defence Force under the Chief of the Defence Force, Field Force Command became Land Command, a joint component command. Its structure provided for: northern surveillance through Regional Force Surveillance Units; a Ready Deployment Force of an infantry brigade supported by a field artillery regiment; a mixed regular/reserve manoeuvre force in the 1st Division based on two regular and two reserve brigades with integral artillery support; a reserve follow-on force centred on the two infantry brigades of the 2nd Division and their artillery, with vital asset protection assigned to the remaining reserve formations; and a logistics support force. In the resulting restructure, 102nd Field Battery was disbanded in 1987.

Under the new command arrangements, Commander, Land Command Artillery advised on offensive fire support, and exercised technical control of the Land Command's artillery. Land Command Artillery's only direct command was 16th Air Defence Regiment. Although the capability represented by this regiment compared modestly to contemporary artillery forces, it was at the time considered a sufficient force element to establish air defence procedures, and to meet any low-level conflict needs.

In December 1989, the Directorate of Artillery moved from Canberra to join the School of Artillery at North Head, creating the Artillery Centre.[13] Exercise Kangaroo 89, conducted across the north of Australia, demonstrated that artillery support at brigade level remained useful.[14] However, other interpretations held that in highly mobile operations against a widely dispersed and lightly equipped enemy, artillery was the least relevant of the combat arms. Threats could be countered effectively by infantry and light-armoured forces alone, and in the absence of an air threat the Air Force could deal with targets in depth.

The 1987 White Paper identified the need to modernise equipment in all three services, and to fund the establishment of defence facilities in the west and north, including the move of 1st Brigade to Darwin. It projected an annual increase in the defence budget that did not eventuate.[15] Each Service suffered as funding instead tightened, and the Army suffered disproportionately as Navy and Air Force enhancements to cover the sea-air gap took priority.[16]

These restructures overlapped with the softening of Australia's economy in the early 1990s, leading to further contraction in RAA force structure. Commonwealth budgetary pressures led to a Force Structure Review in 1991, which sought to generate the same combat power from smaller establishments, and to reduce the size of headquarters and base units. A parallel review triggered the introduction of the Ready Reserve Scheme, in which part-time soldiers completed a year's training full-time, and then four years of part-time service.

As a result of these reviews, Headquarters 1st Division assumed an additional role as the Deployable Joint Force Headquarters, and commanded two regular Army brigades, with the third becoming a ready reserve formation. 1st Field Regiment was converted to a ready reserve/general reserve unit with a regular cadre. Headquarters 2nd Division, commanding seven infantry brigades was tasked with developing doctrine for conventional operations. Headquarters 3rd Division was disbanded.[17] The artillery integral to the revised structure is at Appendix 1, Table 18.

The ensuing 1994 White Paper, *Defending Australia,* continued the strategic thinking of its predecessors, and this, combined with declining defence budgets and falling defence force strengths, had a deleterious effect on all areas of the ADF and Army especially.[18] By 1995 the RAA was at its smallest-ever order of battle. Any degree of short-term readiness was limited to the regular or integrated regular/reserve/ready reserve units. Between them, the reserve gun regiments fielded only 11 field batteries and one medium battery, with many below full strength.

Ready Reserve gunners of 1st Field Regiment conduct a live fire exercise with 105-millimetre Hamel Guns, February 1992 (Courtesy Defence Image Gallery SYDA_91_014_04.jpg)

In the regular force, the artillery's medium batteries were assigned direct support roles with tactical manoeuvre units. This and a coincident reduction in divisional artillery staff meant that the Gunners ceased to perform general support functions such as counter-battery/mortar and depth engagement, and provided little beyond formation-level close support. Nevertheless, the higher-readiness regular Gunner units possessed up-to-date equipment, were mobile, well-trained, could deliver fire accurately, and participated in annual joint and multi-regiment live-firing exercises.

An advanced air defence simulator was acquired in 1994, and that same year a limited amount of laser-guided American 155-millimetre M712 Copperhead ammunition was purchased.[19] Combined with improvements in fire control computerisation and target designation by observers, these precision-guided munitions foreshadowed an ability to accurately apply fire from distributed gun positions, engaging targets effectively with minimal collateral damage and minimum ammunition expenditure, and with increased survivability resulting from more dispersed firing locations.

Artillery Technology: Precision Guided and Extended Range Munitions

The pursuit of target reach and effect is central to artillery. The research fields of precision guidance and extended ranges for munitions are therefore continually fertile areas for capability development.

Precision-guided munitions (PGM) technology has revolutionised artillery, as the factors affecting a projectile's flight can now be compensated for *during* flight, rather than predicted *prior* to launch.

At its simplest, precision-guidance technology comprises an element that can fixate a target's true location, a means of communicating those coordinates to the projectile, and a projectile that is capable of adjusting its trajectory during a decisive segment of its flight. The 'fix' element can be determined either by computation or observation, or combination of both. More recent developments allow this fixation to be updated continually, permitting engagement of moving targets. The communication link is invariably digital using radio, laser or other electromagnetic means. Flight control surfaces integral to the projectile – usually in the form of *canard* (nose-fitted) winglets – ensure the desired target effect.

Precision-guidance technology permits field artillery to prosecute destruction missions with single-round efficiency. The trade-off is the size of the effective payload, and – ultimately – unit cost. Considering the pay-offs for successful target effects, PGMs are now indispensable items in modern artillery arsenals.

Extended-range (ER) technology allows greater reach through either increasing flight efficiency or using on-board powered thrust. Aerodynamic efficiency can be achieved through projectile shape, including decreasing trailing turbulence through 'base-bleed' designs. Alternatively, positive lift is introduced through fitting winglets, often teamed with PGM technology.

Extending projectile range through on-board powered thrust is less dependent on flight performance, and limited principally by design trade-offs between payload and thrust. Thrust is usually delivered by simple solid-fuel rocket motors. While thrust from a set quantity of fuel can be calculated, powered range extension adds complexity and probable error to ballistic predictions.

ER and PGM technology is frequently combined to offset mutual disadvantages. However, combining both leads invariably to significant increases in overall projectile size and mass, which in turn increases unit cost, and logistic and maintenance overheads. Hence, the continued application of ballistic science to improve precision and range in cheaper, simpler and less problematic 'unguided' projectiles remains appealing. Unguided artillery projectiles will, therefore, remain a practical complement to PGMs and powered ER munitions for the foreseeable future.

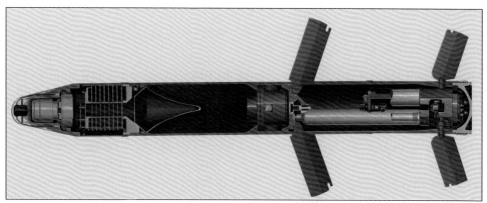

Cross-section of M712 Copperhead 155-millimetre cannon-launched guided projectile (CLGP) ammunition (Courtesy Lockheed Martin Corporation)

However, the ability to sustain the precision artillery capability was low. Stocks of such 'smart' rounds were very small, and forging facilities for the domestic production of conventional 155-millimetre ammunition had by now been foregone. So too had the acquisition of longer-range 105-millimetre British-manufactured 'Abbott' ammunition for the Hamel gun. This decision was partly due to the higher unit cost of these rounds, and partly because the nations in the America-Britain-Canada-Australia (ABCA) standardisation agreement were anticipating adopting a standardised 155-millimetre calibre for field artillery, as that calibre offered the greatest scope to accommodate ongoing developments in both range and precision guidance.

During the 1990s, constant restructuring, declining defence budgets, and the continuing search for efficiency reduced the size of the ARA from 31,143 in 1991 to 23,906 in 1999.[20] With increasing restrictions on Sydney's firing ranges, in 1997 the School of Artillery moved from North Head, Sydney, to Puckapunyal, Victoria, where it became part of the Combined Arms Training Centre. 53rd Independent Battery was raised to provide the School's integral fire support.

That same year saw the disbandment of Corps Directorates, with their functions taken over by Army Headquarters personnel, operations and materiel staffs. A senior serving former RAA officer was appointed as the Honorary Head of Regiment as a secondary duty, to oversee Regimental trade, ceremonial and heritage matters.[21] Funding reductions also severely limited artillery-related overseas exchanges, attachments and training, including the practice of sending officers and warrant officers to qualify in gunnery and locating streams. At the same time, RAA drivers, quartermaster staff and clerks in regiments and batteries were replaced by Transport and Ordnance Corps personnel.

Restructuring the Army: 1996–1998

By 1996, pressures were such that a study was commissioned into the 'Army in the 21st Century' (A21). Challenges increased when an incoming Government discontinued the Ready Reserve Scheme and, unwilling to raise defence expenditure, instituted the Defence

Efficiency Review, designed to improve the 'teeth-to-tail' ratio by further outsourcing non-combat support, health and maintenance.[22] The Army's organisational response would have significant implications for the RAA.

The A21 study led to a plan for Restructuring the Army (RTA), predicated on projecting small combat forces specifically designed for – rather than adapted to – countering widespread, low-level but lethal threats on the Australian mainland.[23] In the light of financial and manpower restrictions and with little need seen for massed artillery fire, the plan had a considerable impact on Land Command's artillery. Headquarters 1st Division Artillery was disbanded in 1997, and Headquarters 2nd Division Artillery followed within three years. 2nd/15th Field Regiment and 10th Medium Regiment combined to form 2nd/10th Medium Regiment. In 1998, 5th/11th Field Regiment and the independent 13th Field Battery were integrated into 1st Field Regiment, which thereafter comprised two ARA and two ARES gun batteries.[24]

With divisional artillery headquarters disbanded, field and medium regiments were grouped under full command of a manoeuvre brigade headquarters, as opposed to being habitually allocated in support to those formations on operations. 131st Divisional Locating Battery joined with the 1st Divisional Intelligence Company to trial the concept of a Reconnaissance, Intelligence, Surveillance and Target Acquisition (RISTA) Regiment.

Another trial was then instituted examining further reorganisation under which gun batteries with organic weapon-locating, meteorological and survey troops, as well as light armoured cavalry elements, would form Fire Support Companies to be integrated into motorised infantry battalions that also included engineer, reconnaissance and surveillance assets. Trials of the motorised battalion component of the RTA concept saw the integration of 101st Battery into 6RAR.[25] The resulting organisation was reminiscent of the Pentropic Division structures in the 1960s, and the British Eighth Army's 'jock' columns of World War II.

At this time, the increasingly joint and 'task-organised' nature of artillery employment and other fire support measures brought about changes in fire support terminology. The term 'offensive support' – encompassing naval gunfire, fire from ground-based weapons other than small arms, and offensive air support – replaced 'fire support'. Fire Support Coordination Centres became Joint Offensive Support Coordination Centres (JOSCCs), and the Forward Observer parties became known as Joint Offensive Support Teams (JOST), reflecting their wider access to joint, non-artillery fire support. By this stage too, the British artillery command and control terminology adopted in the 1950s had been replaced, as a result of standardisation agreements, with US/NATO terminology.

The RTA trials concluded at the end of the decade. At the conclusion of the RISTA trial, 131st Divisional Locating Battery was retitled 131st Surveillance and Target Acquisition Battery, and artillery development staff commenced studies into its future employment of Uncrewed Aerial Vehicles (UAVs).[26]

The motorised battalion trial, rather than supporting the embedding of batteries into infantry units, indicated that artillery regiments with integral surveillance and target acquisition systems should exist at brigade level, and be able to allot sub-units in support of battle groups as required. This conclusion was based on two key observations. First, from a resource perspective, the cost and complexity of having fire support companies organic to each motorised battalion was too great to sustain at unit level in terms of principal and complete equipment schedules and commensurate repair parts. Second, the motorised battalion structure was inflexible when a range of scenarios was considered. Comprising only two manoeuvre sub-units, it was incapable of mounting battalion-scale offensive action against a conventionally configured enemy, and unable to scale up to major war-fighting operations. These findings underscored the enduring relevance of the artillery principles of cooperation, concentration, economy of effort, and sustainment.

The RTA trials and associated studies had a positive outcome in that they identified the need to acquire medium range surface-to-air missiles to replace Rapier, and wheeled self-propelled guns and armoured mortar carriers with the mobility to support the manoeuvre forces.[27] As an offshoot of the RTA process, efforts were also made to revitalise the Army Reserve by increasing recruiting, retention and availability; raising individual and collective competency; providing greater access to modern equipment; and improving administrative support.[28] The 4th Brigade was given four years to become an operationally viable formation capable of protective operations in defence of Australia. The Revitalisation of the Reserve trial saw an influx of cadre staff and resources into the 2nd/10th Medium Regiment well above typical levels. Due to a range of factors, the trial was discontinued, but not before many Victorian Gunners deployed into northern Australia for the first time, training alongside regular Army counterparts as part of well-resourced and well-supported joint live-fire exercises.[29]

International Peacekeeping: 1990s

Throughout the post-Vietnam period, somewhat in divergence from its strategic focus on continental defence although consistent with its stance on collective security, Australia responded to approaches by the United Nations (UN) and other international bodies to provide forces for peacekeeping. This was not new, as Australia's involvement in peacekeeping under Chapter Six of the UN Charter dated from the UN's earliest days, and even before the UN, peace enforcement of a different nature had seen deployment of a gun battery for precautionary purposes with the British Occupation Commonwealth Force in Japan.

After the Vietnam War, the Army's contribution to peacekeeping usually consisted of individual observers, some of whom were Gunners, in places like Israel, Syria, and Kashmir. Larger contributions were made outside the UN to the Commonwealth Monitoring Force in Zimbabwe in 1979–80, and the Multinational Force and Observers in the Sinai, but again, these were individual rather than unit postings.[30] Deployment under Chapter Six conditions, the low threat environment limited the employment of these Gunners to command, staff, liaison, communications and non-lethal targeting roles.

What differed in the 1990s was the increasing number of missions and the occasional incidence of peace enforcement – that is, the establishment of order by armed force under

Chapter Seven of the UN Charter, as had been done in Korea in the 1950s. The Iraqi invasion of Kuwait led to the Gulf War of 1990–91 (Operations Desert Shield and Desert Storm) where international armed force was authorised to restore Kuwait's independence under a UN Chapter Seven peace enforcement resolution. Australia's contribution was primarily naval. The Army's only involvement, outside of individual augmentations and special forces, was that between September 1990 and June 1991, 16th Air Defence Regiment deployed RBS-70 missile launchers and command elements aboard HMA Ships *Success* and *Westralia* to assist in protecting them from close air and small surface threats. This was not a standard role for ground-based air defence elements, with challenges encountered in integrating into wider maritime air defence command and control.[31]

HMAS *Success* at battle stations, Arabian Gulf, 11 January 1991 (Courtesy RAN Success_II_11_Jan1991.jpg)

The First Gulf War was followed by a number of smaller peacekeeping missions, mostly under Chapter Six of the UN Charter. For these missions, the Army typically provided observers or specialists such as medical staff, signallers, engineers, and command elements in the case of the United Nations Transitional Authority in Cambodia, and that of Bougainville.[32] Even with the elevated ground threat during missions such as Rwanda, Somalia and the former Yugoslavia, Australian peacekeepers relied on neutrality and a low profile to counter any potential 'threat to force'. The same approach was adopted later in subsequent regional peacekeeping deployments.

Australia's participation in the UN-sanctioned but American-led Task Force to Somalia in 1992–3 offered the potential for greater artillery involvement, as the purpose of the mission was to impose sufficient order to allow movement towards a political settlement. In the event, Australia committed an infantry battalion group, with its artillery component drawn from the command, liaison and observation group of 107th Battery. Without the need to coordinate allied fire support, the Gunners formed the contingent's civil-military operations team.[33]

The resultant effect on Australian artillery of the 'Defence of Australia' policy setting, and its attendant support to global peacekeeping during this period was profound. The emphasis placed on operational employment of conventional artillery firepower waned, as Australian foreign policy trended from a post-Cold War outlook towards concentrating on low-level threats at home, and overt support to these 'blue beret' United Nations commitments.

A member of 107th Field Battery with unexploded ordnance and ammunition for transport to a dump for explosive disposal, Baidoa, Somalia, 29 March 1993 (Courtesy AWM P01735.518)

Changing Strategic Stance: 1997–1999

Australia's overseas peacekeeping missions in the 1990s were generally successful, and were popularly supported domestically. This support may have contributed to the shift in strategic guidance that resulted from a change of national government in 1996, and was reflected in the document Australia's Strategic Policy 1997 (ASP 97). ASP 97 cited the nation's wider security interests in avoiding de-stabilising competition between regional major powers, maintaining a benign security environment in South-East Asia, and preventing the positioning of foreign military forces.[34] It foresaw greater engagement in the Asia-Pacific, and identified a role for the ADF in defending regional interests and supporting global interests, as well as continental defence.[35]

This change occurred midway through the RTA process. In releasing the RTA Plan in 1997, the Minister for Defence stated that the land force should be capable of conducting offshore operations alone or as part of a coalition, reflecting the new government's greater policy emphasis on collective action with traditional allies.[36] As this was not the basis on which the RTA plan had been developed, a second phase of trials was proposed to cover defence of regional interests after the initial restructuring trials were completed.[37] Initially, however, the ADF remained underprepared for regional involvement, as the ASP 97 settings were not sufficient to drive any comprehensive change in its force posture, nor trigger significant reinvestment in force structure.[38]

Focus on continental defence of Australia from the mid-1980s onwards was reflected in the ADF's reliance on other nations to provide the enabling support and command elements for the majority of its peacekeeping missions. The consequence was that by 1999, the ADF had little practical experience in large scale force generation, or in the planning and command requirements for force projection and protection beyond Australia's maritime area of interest. With the limited exception of the Gulf War, Australia's recent tactical experience in warlike operations was equally minimal. Whether Defence's heavily reorganised and commercialised support infrastructure would prove adequate for future operations was also untested.[39]

In the eyes of some commentators, restructuring for the defence of Australia against low-level threats in times of limited defence expenditure had resulted in a 'hollow force' of modest scale and depth, with little current doctrine for, or experience in, strategic planning and rapid expansion, and with limited capacity for sustainment, expansion or interoperability with allies in conventional operations.[40]

As the end of the decade approached, 8th/12th Medium Regiment and the 1st Brigade finalised relocation to Darwin as part of the 'Army Presence in the North'.[41] Australian artillery was at its lowest capability ebb since between the world wars. In terms of technology, force structure and scale, the RAA was not ready to respond to a significant conflict against a state adversary, and was reliant on the ten-year strategic warning time that Defence planners anticipated at the time to be able to do so. Although its field artillery was technically proficient, it was in practice limited to the close-support role using conventional ammunition. Its air defence and locating capabilities were also limited. Some re-equipment proposals were in train, and it remained to be seen how the change in strategic policy might play out for Gunners. However, for some time senior commanders and defence planners had seen little use for the arm in low-level operations, envisaging deploying guns in widely dispersed positions, if at all, and exploiting the artillery's command, liaison and observation elements in the civil-military cooperation roles intrinsic to low-level operations such as evacuation scenarios.

CHAPTER 14

Intervention and Expansion: 1999–2006

Protection of the wider strategic interests foreshadowed in the strategic policy shift of 1997 became reality for the Australian Defence Force (ADF) between 1999 and 2006, initially in providing security in East Timor and then in combat and mentoring operations in Iraq and Afghanistan as part of the 'War on Terror'. With the reductions in the ADF in the previous decade, these commitments, along with concurrent peacekeeping, border security and homeland tasking, stretched the Army.

Artillery elements participated in all Australia's deployments, providing civil–military liaison, joint offensive support coordination, surveillance and target acquisition, and point air defence. For the Army, these more demanding operations, along with the strategic guidance from 2000 onwards that increasingly contemplated a broader range of contingencies, resulted in a 'Hardened and Networked Army' plan in 2005.

This plan allowed the gunners to program re-equipment. It consolidated the earlier force structure decision to position two-battery field regiments in support of manoeuvre brigades, maintain an air defence regiment, and deliver on the promise of an expanded surveillance and target acquisition capability. However, while the Army and the RAA maintained doctrine for employment in higher-level operations, in practice artillery employment was focussed on support at brigade- or joint task force-level and below. Australia's use of artillery resources remained similar to the previous two decades, involving secondary roles or deployment of only command, liaison and observation groups. No guns were deployed, and the Australian artillery's relative decline in comparison to coalition partners continued.

East Timor Operations: 1999

In August 1999, violence by pro-Indonesian militias following a United Nations (UN)-supervised referendum in favour of independence for East Timor led to the deployment of an Australian-led stabilisation force. The International Force-East Timor (Interfet) was tasked to restore peace and security, and to facilitate humanitarian assistance until such time as a UN peacekeeping force could be deployed.

The Army deployed over 5500 personnel to Interfet, initially drawn from the 3rd Brigade. In the low-threat, low-lethality environment, the gun batteries supporting each Australian battalion group deployed their command, liaison and observation elements, along with other Gunners performing infantry and other non-artillery roles. Guns from the battery accompanying the first rotation were pre-positioned in Darwin in case they were required.[1] While the threat was uncertain, commanders at all levels retained options for the deployment of field artillery to provide close support from fire-bases similar to those used previously in Malaysia and Vietnam, if required.

INTERFET proved a relative success for the Gunners in reprising their secondary all-arms role, while refining new skills in civil-military affairs, and reaffirming traditional artillery command, liaison and observation functions. Nevertheless, INTERFET proved a major force projection and sustainment challenge for the ADF overall. Australia had not provided full logistic support for a deployed force since World War II, and the reductions in defence spending over the previous decade had diminished the ADF's deployable logistic support force.[2] The widely dispersed force elements were especially reliant on communications equipment and vehicles, and the deployed Gunners experienced challenging shortfalls, requiring regiments remaining in Australia to cross-level equipment to address deficiencies.

Following INTERFET, Australia later contributed around 2000 personnel to the UN Transitional Administration in East Timor (UNTAET) Mission and to other UN agencies during Timor-Leste's protracted move towards independence. In this period, artillery command and observation parties continued to perform civil-military roles alongside humanitarian and development agencies. Gunners also took the opportunity to field test new surveillance technologies including ground surveillance radars and the hand-launched Codarra CX-1 'Avatar' Uncrewed Aerial Vehicle (UAV), which was used for tactical reconnaissance.[3]

Gunners of 131st Locating Battery, Surveillance Section (call-sign Cracker) with some of their surveillance equipment, Operation Tanager, August 2001 (Courtesy Defence Image Gallery V0111802.jpg)

Evolving Defence Policy

The 2000 Defence White Paper (DWP 2000) identified three priority tasks for the ADF: the defence of Australia – including attacking hostile forces 'as far from our shores as possible'; contributing to security in Australia's immediate neighbourhood; and supporting the nation's wider interests by contributing to international coalitions. DWP 2000 stated that while land-force planning had been dominated by a focus on lower-level contingencies on Australian territory for much of the last two decades, 'the focus now will be broadened to meet a wider range of possible contingencies, both on Australian territories and beyond'.[4]

DWP 2000 foreshadowed an increase in defence expenditure over the forthcoming decade. The Army was to be based around three regular and four reserve brigades; the logistic support force was to be improved; and a range of new equipment acquired, stemming from the RTA trials and the ADF's East Timor experience. The role of the reserves in supporting and sustaining the regular Army was confirmed, and call-out regulations short of a declaration of war were implemented accordingly.[5]

DWP 2000 announced a suite of artillery projects to meet three objectives. The first was to address the looming life-of-type of certain equipment, and included purchasing a missile system to supplement RBS-70 and replace Rapier. The second was to improve surveillance and target acquisition capabilities, and incorporated projects for the acquisition of tactical UAVs, upgrades to the AN/TPQ 36 weapon-locating radar, ground surveillance radars, and a thermal imaging surveillance system.

The third objective sought to enhance the employability of field artillery across the spectrum of conflict settings. With the RAA's field guns reaching their end of life-of-type in 2010, the intention was to introduce lighter-weight towed and self-propelled weapons to improve mobility. The self-propelled howitzers were to complement the concurrent mechanisation of Army's manoeuvre brigades and increase survivability in higher-intensity conflict. The prospect of self-propelled artillery some 50 years after the abortive Yeramba project foreshadowed a welcome step-change in Australian artillery capability.

The replacement guns were to be capable of firing both conventional and precision guided ammunition. They would have inbuilt fixation, orientation and gun-data computation capability; and would use 'sensor-to-shooter' links between the observer/target-designator and the offensive-support coordinator through a digital fire control system featuring enhanced firing data computation software. Supporting projects looked to a new family of conventional 155-millimetre ammunition, and an artillery orienting system as a complement to the Global Positioning System.[6] Collectively, this recapitalisation was to be the most extensive since before the Vietnam War, and, if realised, provided for a limited but highly capable and potent artillery force.

Shortly after release of DWP 2000, on 17 May 2001, the Chief of Army formally reinstated auxiliary roles for Heads of Corps across the Army. An Artillery Head of Regiment was duly appointed to be the Chief of Army's 'principal adviser on regimental matters connected with the Royal Australian Artillery'.

The force elements of Land Command Artillery at this point are shown at Appendix 1, Table 19. Headquarters Land Command Artillery articulated the four capabilities the RAA then provided to the ADF: joint offensive support coordination and targeting; indirect firepower; surveillance and target acquisition; and ground-based air defence.[7] The separation of offensive support coordination from the provision of indirect fire support was a novel development, reflecting the progression of the RAA towards a 'joint fires' methodology.

The War on Terror

The attacks by al Qaeda terrorists in New York on 11 September 2001 precipitated what was known as a global 'War on Terror'. This took the form of a succession of interventions by the USA and its coalition partners in support of multilateral security objectives and the global rules-based order. For forces more designed for 'force-on-force' conflict like the RAA's field and air defence artillery, the prospect of a largely counter-terrorist/counter-insurgency 'war' presented limited scope for employment.

The first of these interventions took place in Afghanistan in October 2001, aimed at preventing that country remaining a terrorist base, defeating al Qaeda, and ending the Taliban Government's rule. Australia's contribution, designated Operation Slipper, entailed a Special Forces Task Group, RAN warships, and RAAF aircraft. Involvement by Australian land forces continued until the end of 2002, with 16th Air Defence Regiment on two occasions providing troops of RBS-70 for point protection of RAN support ships in the Persian Gulf.[8] While no other RAA units participated, the Air Mobility Group periodically assigned individual artillery Ground Liaison Officers to Air Force transport elements in the Middle East, the beginning of an enduring commitment that would last until 2012.[9]

16th Air Defence Regiment RBS-70 detachment at 'weapons hold' on HMAS *Kanimbla*, 12 March 2003. A Coalition Sea King passes overhead (Courtesy Defence Image Gallery JPAU12MAR03WG07A.jpg)

Artillery Technology: Naval and Air-Ground Fire Support

Since the earliest campaigns of the 20th century, Australian Gunners have acted as the coordinators between the air, sea and land domains in providing fire support for the land forces. At Gallipoli, Australian artillery officers provided aerial observation, while others worked with Royal Navy warships, coordinating shore bombardment. Later, over the battlefields of the Western Front, artillery observers converted to aircrew in the fledgling No. 3 Squadron Australian Flying Corps, while other Gunners served as observers in artillery spotter aircraft, such as the venerable R.E.8.

Naval and air-ground cooperation soon developed as three functions, consolidated during World War II and carried through to today:

Liaison facilitated the understanding of tactics and procedures, allowed the exchange of ideas, and the establishment of mutual trust and confidence. It is embodied by artillery Naval Gunfire Support Liaison Officers aboard vessels, and usually reciprocated by Naval Fire Support Officers embedded in artillery headquarters ashore. The 1st Naval Bombardment Group that supported the landing of the 9th Division at Lae was a World War II example of such cooperation. Correspondingly, Artillery Air Liaison Officers were installed in Air Force squadrons and Air Operation Centres. Similarly, Brigade and Divisional Air Liaison Officers have provided the reciprocal Air Force presence in artillery Fire Support Coordination Centres and, in later theatres, Tactical Artillery Command Posts, and their successor Joint Offensive Support Coordination Centres and Joint Fires and Effects Coordination Centres.

HMAS Anzac providing Naval Gun Fire Support to 3 (UK) Commando Brigade and other Coalition forces on Al Faw Peninsula, Iraq, 22 March 2003 (Courtesy Defence Image Group NIUW8094997_20030322_333)

Effective communications linkages have and always will remain crucial to joint fire support coordination. The extended range, lethality and diverse communications platforms of naval and air fire support has always required fire support coordinators to master HF, VHF and UHF radio systems alike. More recently, standardised digital communications linkages such as the Link series of battlespace communication systems has been integrated into joint fires coordination measures.

Fire control is delivered through observers trained in the use of naval, air and land fire support, using a precise and unambiguous language developed to call for and control joint fires. Artillery doctrine has continually cultivated a lexicon of joint fire control in concert with naval and air partners, to ensure accurate understanding and computations across diverse combat systems.

The 21st century has since witnessed the advent of Strike cells, where joint fires coordination is fused and applied to a degree only dreamed of a century beforehand. Yet, the fundamentals of joint fires coordination remain, entrusted principally to artillery coordinators acting on behalf of the manoeuvre commander.[11]

A second intervention began in March 2003 when a US-led coalition, including Australia, invaded Iraq, maintaining that the country had failed to abide by UN Security Council resolutions concerning the surrender of weapons of mass destruction. For Australia, this was Operation Falconer. The US and Britain provided the principal combat forces, with Australia's contribution being similar to that for Operation Slipper. Australian artillery involvement again consisted of elements of 16th Air Defence Regiment providing point air defence, this time aboard the amphibious vessel HMAS *Kanimbla*.[10]

Stabilising the New Iraqi Government: 2005–2006

Australian ground combat forces were withdrawn in 2003 after the fall of the regime of Saddam Hussein, with the exception of a Security Detachment that provided protection to the Australian Embassy in Iraq and escort to Australian personnel under Operation Catalyst until 2008, and extended under Operation Kruger until mid-2011.

In April 2005, the Army's commitment to Operation Catalyst was broadened, with the deployment of two land-based task groups, as well as a substantial commitment of additional embedded staff positions. The first was the Al-Muthanna Task Group (AMTG), within which armoured/infantry battle groups served on rotation to provide a stable and secure environment for the humanitarian tasks of the Japanese Reconstruction and Support Group in Al-Muthanna Province. The second task group was the Australian Army Training Team-Iraq (AATT-I), which, along with embedded staff officers in coalition and Iraqi units, assisted in training the new Iraqi Army.[12] RAA officers and NCOs featured prominently in both contingents as instructors, and as plans and operations headquarters staff.

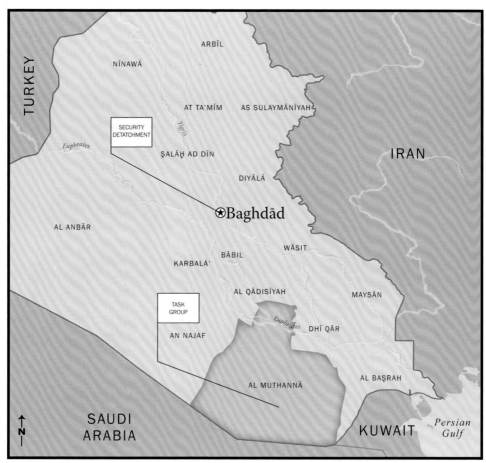

Map 14.01: Operation Catalyst Area Of Operations, Iraq, 2005. The map depicts the Area of Operations for the Al Muthanna Task Group 1 (AMTG-1) and Security Detachment (SECDET), February-October 2005. These groups were deployed as part of Australia's military contribution toward the reconstruction of Iraq. Each successive AMTG and ensuing Overwatch Battle Group (OBG) was supported by an integral Artillery Joint Offensive Support Coordination Centre and associated surveillance and target acquisition assets.

Elements from 101st Medium Battery joined the initial AMTG rotation, which was based on the 2nd Cavalry Regiment. Threats from insurgent indirect fire and improvised explosive devices were low, although potentially highly lethal. The battery command group formed a Joint Offensive Support Operations Centre (JOSCC) to provide the AMTG's offensive support targeting and liaison functions. Its observation group provided the Joint Offensive Support Teams (JOSTs) supporting the task group's combat teams. Australian guns were not deployed, with Coalition air assets providing fire support if required. AMTG 1 also included an AN-TPQ 36 weapon locating radar to warn the contingent of mortar or rocket attacks.[13]

In November 2005, 103rd Medium Battery provided the JOSCC and JOSTs for the 5/7RAR-based AMTG 2. It also commanded an assigned weapon-locating radar and a 'Skylark' UAV detachment from 131st Surveillance and Target Acquisition Battery drawing on the success of tactical reconnaissance UAVs in Timor.[14] The latter provided intelligence, surveillance and reconnaissance (ISR) support, reprising the Australian artillery's links with aerial observation and target location in previous conflicts dating back to World War I.

Bombardier Andrew Hamilton, 8/12th Medium Regiment provides protection to the Japanese Iraq Reconstruction Support Group (Courtesy Defence Image Gallery 20051005adf8182062_030.jpg)

Increased Army Commitments: 2000–2005

The commitments to Afghanistan and Iraq and a new peacekeeping mission in 2003 to the Solomon Islands (Operation Anode) added significantly to existing demands on the Army stemming from deployments to East Timor and simultaneous peacekeeping in Bougainville. By 2001 the Army was providing 80 per cent of all ADF personnel deployed on operations.[15] Meanwhile, the Brisbane-based 7th Task Force, which had earlier transformed into the 7th Brigade, began steadily increasing the ARA proportions across its major combat units, including 1st Field Regiment.[16]

Along with routine training and support to homeland events, these commitments dramatically raised unit operating tempos from the low levels of the 1990s, and exposed difficulties in meeting concurrent tasks.[17] Gunner units, both regular and reserve, regularly performed out-of-role tasks. In 2000, personnel from the 2nd/10th Medium, 7th and 23rd Field Regiments and 105th Battery assisted with security at the Sydney Olympics.

Between 2000 and 2004, the 4th Field and 8th/12th Medium Regiments, along with 131st Locating Battery, contributed detachments to peacekeeping in the Solomon Islands. 8th/12th Medium Regiment sent a contingent to the rifle company at Butterworth, Malaysia, in 2003 to fulfil Five-Power Defence Arrangements obligations. Between 2002 and 2004 every regular regiment and 131st Locating Battery provided Transit Security Elements for several months' duration to assist the Navy with border security operations off Australia's north coast, a task to which the reserve Gunner units also contributed supplementary personnel.[18]

Throughout the period, the RAA's regiments and independent batteries sought to retain their gunnery skills despite the operational and out-of-role commitments. Annual training cycles for reserve units focussed primarily on individual and battery-level training, while the regular units commonly went beyond this to conduct regimental-level exercises and participate each year in all-arms exercises and a major joint firepower exercise. 16th Air Defence Regiment elements joined periodic Five-Power Defence Arrangements exercises in Malaysia, and contingents from both the regular and reserve field regiments deployed to occasional sub-unit exchanges to New Zealand, and others to Hawaii.[19]

A battery civil military affairs team briefing COMD Sector West, East Timor 2002 (Courtesy private collection)

The Hardened and Networked Army: 2005–2006

It was clear from the growing operational tempo of the early 2000s that the Army's permanent force was inadequate to meet government commitments. In 2005, the Chief of Army noted that the diversity of recent deployments reflected both a change in world politics and an increasing complexity in the conduct of military operations across a broad spectrum of conflict. Consequently, the Army needed to be flexible, adaptable and agile, and proficient at conducting joint, coalition and multi-agency operations. It had to develop well-protected forces to fulfil all potential operational demands, based on infantry, armour, artillery, aviation and engineers working together in an increasingly lethal, volatile and complex threat environment. The Chief of Army also reaffirmed the earlier RISTA trial's recommendation to expand the RAA's surveillance and target acquisition capability into a dedicated regiment.[20]

The resulting Hardened and Networked Army (HNA) program was announced in December 2005, and endorsed by the government in March 2006 for implementation over the succeeding decade. The Army's full-time strength was to be increased by 1485, and a High-Readiness Reserve created to assist in supplementing regular manpower.[21] However, no additional personnel were allocated to artillery units.

As the Rapier surface-to-air missile system had been withdrawn from service earlier in the year, the HNA program envisaged a mobile air defence capability based on 16th Air Defence Regiment equipped with RBS-70 missiles. This modest investment in ground-based air defence was based on a prevailing counter-terrorist/counter-insurgency threat, and provided a limited foundation for the regiment's timely expansion in scale and systems capability to contend with a medium-threat peer adversary.

The regular field artillery was to sustain capabilities to support combined arms operations in the following conflict settings: medium-intensity conflict, with 8th/12th Medium Regiment (155-millimetre howitzers) supporting the mechanised 1st Brigade; light scale deployments supporting the 3rd Brigade with 4th Field Regiment (105-millimetre guns); and motorised deployments supporting the 7th Brigade with 1st Field Regiment, re-equipped with 155-millimetre M198 howitzers – whose longer range was better suited to the improved mobility of the formation.

In response, the RAA proposed that each regular regiment would have two six-gun batteries, with those in 8th/12th Regiment projected to become self-propelled. Two of the regular regiments would each produce a brigade-level JOSCC, and each battery would field a battle group-level JOSCC, and three JOSTs. In the reserve, the three remaining gun regiments and three independent batteries were to support the six reserve infantry brigades, whose task was to provide a capability for protective operations, peacekeeping and border security.

In addition to supporting the reserve brigades, the HNA program envisaged that reserve artillery units together would generate 150 high readiness soldiers to supplement the regular regiments. Those augmenting the gun regiments would be trained in offensive support coordination and targeting duties. However, the intention within the HNA program to standardise on 155-millimetre artillery presented practical problems for the reserve in terms of increasing training and maintenance times required, and contingency planning began to consider alternatives, including the employment of mortars.

Formation of 20th STA Regiment

Just prior to the HNA endorsement, but integrated into its implementation, and following the decision that the RAA would be responsible for deploying formation-level UAVs, on 1 January 2006 the Army announced the raising of the 20th Surveillance and Target Acquisition (STA) Regiment. Created from 131st STA Battery and a UAV trial unit, the regiment comprised the 131st Battery equipped with the AN/TPQ 36 Radar and other surveillance devices, and the 132nd Battery operating medium 'ScanEagle' and small 'Skylark' UAVs.[22]

The operational employment of the artillery's UAVs helped address the Army's concurrency pressures arising from a wide range of commitments by reducing the need for infantry and armoured elements to gather intelligence and conduct surveillance. For a fraction of the manpower resources previously required, the capability provided reliable situational awareness for tactical commanders that considerably enhanced force protection and command and control of their manoeuvring troops. The new capability also saw the Gunners called upon to support special operations, as Army's only tactical UAV operator.

Reflections: 1999–2006

The HNA Plan acknowledged that the first half-decade of the 21st century had stretched the standing Army to a degree unprecedented since World War II. Multiple operational and non-operational deployments at a high operating tempo contrasted sharply with the previous quarter-century, placing great stress on the ADF's ability to conduct concurrent operations, and revealed defence investment had previously been insufficient for Australia's renewed interventionist policy.

The RAA had played its part in meeting the commitments of the new century. Operational focus had remained on action at below brigade level, and little if any thought was given to more substantial conflict. The regular artillery capability remained small, while the reserve capacity continued to decline. Nevertheless, Gunner training kept alive the skills and procedures required for accurate close support, and the regular regiments continued to practice the provision of joint and coalition fires. On operations, the opportunity to deploy guns had not arisen, but the capability provided by artillery surveillance and target acquisition had grown in value. So, too, had the value of artillery JOSCCs and JOSTs in targeting and joint and coalition fire support coordination, due to the demonstrated need to integrate Australian joint fires elements within larger coalition forces.

The period saw the beginnings of the first sustained efforts to modernise the artillery for some time. Projects to improve the artillery's capability had been set in train, though their fruition would take time. The Army's efforts to modernise through the HNA represented the most extensive since prior to the Vietnam War, and bore promise of at least providing the foundations of a capable expansion base for the field artillery. The formation of the STA regiment incorporated under HNA was a positive step for the locating Gunners, as was the recognition that external engagements and a greater range of threats still required the fire support provided by artillery in formation and battle group level operations.

Artillery Technology: Aerial Surveillance and Terminal Control

The use of airborne observation to provide artillery intelligence and, ultimately, control of artillery and joint fires has accompanied the employment of Australian artillery since the Gallipoli landings in 1915. The Royal Navy swiftly instigated aerial surveillance using Gunner officers to assist in locating targets for its naval surface bombardment support to the Anzacs.

Meanwhile, Royal Flying Corps (RFC) aviators over France were experimenting with improving means to communicate with artillery batteries while airborne, using weighted handwritten messages, aerial photographs, lamps and finally Morse-code wireless radio to direct fire. The Australian Flying Corps (AFC) soon joined their RFC comrades, flying R.E.8 reconnaissance aircraft, and by November 1917, No. 3 Squadron AFC was flying in direct support of the new Australian Corps. Many aviators transferred from or remained Australian Field Artillery (AFA) personnel, and maintained extremely close relationships with the AFA batteries they supported. New systems of fire control emerged, including the 'clock code' system for corrections, and shared ortho-photographic maps gridded with easily readable alphanumeric coordinates – foundations for terminal control systems still in use a century later.

Lieutenants Stanley Brearley, pilot, and Robert Taylor, observer, of No. 3 Squadron AFC, starting out for a night bombardment operation, Northern France, 22 October 1917. (Courtesy AWM, E01178).

During World War II, RAA officers flew as artillery observers with RAAF pilots, usually in Auster light aircraft, operating in both Mediterranean and Pacific theatres. During the Korean War, RAA observer pilots were seconded to the British Air OP Flight in the Commonwealth Division, coordinating both artillery and close air support.

Vietnam saw increasing use of RAAF pilots as Forward Air Controllers (FACs) to complement RAA airborne observers with Army Aviation flights, reflecting the increasing technical and specialist training that 'fast air' support coordination and terminal control of munitions onto target demanded.

Throughout the eighties and nineties, most FACs were RAAF officers, although many RAA forward observers qualified as Air Contact Officers (ACOs), providing land force tactical insight, and augmenting artillery support and coordination.

The demands of multiple operations in the Middle East post-INTERFET saw the resurgence of Army observers – both RAA and Special Forces – as FACs, rapidly evolving into the Joint Terminal Attack Controller (JTAC) role. As JTACs, Gunner observers are again qualified to perform terminal control for effectively all natures of joint fire support, employing laser rangefinders and target designators, and integrated communications suites.

Meanwhile, the introduction of UAVs into the RAA inventory during the Reconnaissance, Intelligence Surveillance & Target Acquisition Trials saw the Gunners reclaim their own aerial surveillance and terminal control platforms. The uncrewed assets operated today by 20th and 9th Regiments perpetuate a rich legacy stretching over a century. [23]

CHAPTER 15

Iraq, Afghanistan and the 'Adaptive Army': 2006–2014

Between 2006 and 2014, the ADF's resurgence into East Timor and Afghanistan – along with continuing engagement in Iraq, peacekeeping obligations, and international and domestic commitments – placed sustained pressure on the Army and confirmed the need for continuing expansion. While operations by 2005–2006 were far more joint in nature than previously, Army's contribution still comprised two-thirds of all defence personnel deployed.[1]

The RAA participated in all the operational deployments of the period, playing a key role in targeting, joint fires coordination and countering indirect fire attacks. It also provided mentoring and training components. No Australian guns were deployed, but RAA gun detachments served for a period with the Royal Artillery (RA) in Afghanistan, marking the first time Australian field Gunners had fired on operations since Vietnam.

The period between 2006 and 2014 also saw the beginning of the transition towards a 21st century combat-capable artillery force, driven in large part by demonstration in Iraq and Afghanistan that locating and field artillery undeniably had a valid role. By 2014, the RAA's 20th STA Regiment was regularly deploying and operating its UAVs, and a newly formed Air-Land Regiment comprising air defence, counter-rocket artillery and mortar, and air-ground operations batteries was also deploying and employing force elements in their primary roles. The RAA's regular field regiments would all be equipped with a lightweight 155-millimetre howitzer and a digital fire control system, while its reserve batteries were in the process of converting to mortars, following the Army's decision to withdraw its 105-millimetre guns from service, which ironically coincided with RAA gun detachments deploying with RA batteries firing those very guns. Further restructuring under the Army's Plan Beersheba was also in prospect.

An Enhanced Land Force: 2006–2007

In August 2006, contemplating continued strategic volatility and increasing operational tempo, and notwithstanding the increase in strength already promised under the HNA initiative, the Government announced a further increase in the size of the Army. The Enhanced Land Force (ELF) would deliver approximately 2700 additional personnel, including two further infantry battalions in the short term. Combined with the previous HNA announcements, this foreshadowed an Army of 31,000 by 2016.[2] The increase in numbers was timely, as by May 2007, almost 7 per cent of the permanent defence force would be deployed overseas in Iraq, the Solomon Islands, Timor-Leste and Afghanistan.[3]

Despite this growth in numbers, headquarters rationalisation in 2006 saw the disestablishment of Headquarters Land Command Artillery, and the consequent loss of its centralised technical control of the RAA regiments. Command of the 16th Air Defence Regiment transferred to the Deployable Joint Force Headquarters, and the School of Artillery became the centre of artillery technical excellence.[4] Advice on artillery matters to the Chief of Army would now be provided through the senior artillery officer appointed as Head of Regiment as an auxiliary duty.

The rapid implementation of the ELF initiative generated a dramatic influx of recruits for the newly raised battalions. Accordingly, the Chief of Army directed the RAA to provide officers and NCOs as supplementary instructors at the 1st Recruit Training Battalion at Kapooka, allowing their infantry comrades to support raising the battalions. Despite the consequent draw on their junior leaders, the regiments managed to maintain their technical capabilities, and meet their operational and out-of-role commitments.[5]

In 2007, service conditions also began to change relating to the employment of women in the Defence Force. In advance of formal policy changes in 2011 allowing women to serve in combat roles, two female artillery officers graduated from Royal Military College into the RAA in late 2007, with a female soldier joining Gunner ranks at the same time.[6] The Head of Regiment had previously identified employment opportunities for women in the artillery meteorological and survey trades.[7] Meanwhile, some reserve artillery units had regularly accepted female soldiers in the decade prior, fulfilling roles as drivers, signallers and headquarters personnel.

As the regular Army steadily expanded, the reserve again stepped in to assist in meeting the Army's commitments. In the period between 2006 and 2014, hundreds of reserve personnel, including many Gunners, undertook Continuous Full-Time Service, filling vacancies in regular units or in support of operations, international commitments, or homeland tasks such as transit security and bushfire relief. By June 2008, reserve members on full-time service constituted 15 per cent of Army personnel deployed on operations.[8] This, together with the transfer of reserve members to the regular Army in the same period, made recruitment, maintenance of technical training standards and retention in the reserve increasingly difficult.[9]

Regional Commitments: 2006–2013

The regional commitments the ADF faced at this time comprised a mixture of long-standing activities, and new demands. As the call for manoeuvre force elements continued to mount across Australia's concurrent deployments throughout the Indo-Pacific and Middle East, it became inevitable that RAA units would be called on in response. The Gunners had deployed elements to these areas for some years, but to reduce the pressure on infantry and armoured sub-units, in early 2006, the Chief of Army formally authorised the commitment of field artillery and air defence batteries to fulfil rifle company tasks. These included operational deployments in East Timor and the Solomon Islands, and rotation of contingents re-roled as rifle companies into Butterworth in Malaysia, as part of Australia's long-standing Five-Power Defence Arrangements commitment.[10]

Commitment to the Solomon Islands arose when, in April 2006, riots in Guadalcanal necessitated an infantry company group to be deployed to provide security, as a part of Operation Anode. The 101st Medium Battery deployed in May, and was followed by 103rd Medium Battery four months later. The batteries conducted joint training and security patrols with the Australian Federal Police and the Solomon Islands Police Force, as well as independent remote island patrols and assistance to local authorities with security, medical support and transport. Other batteries with similar tasks followed, until the commitment ended in 2013.[11]

Bombardier Michael Cross, Golf Company (16th Air Defence Regiment, leads a group of Australian and New Zealand soldiers to a forward operating base in Dili, East Timor, 3 February 2009 (Courtesy Defence Image Gallery 20090203adf8262658_329.jpg)

Following civil unrest in mid-2006, the Timor-Leste Government sought increased assistance, and the Australian-led International Stabilisation Force (ISF) deployed in response, marking the beginning of a commitment that would remain in place until April 2013. Together Australia and New Zealand, as part of Operation Astute, provided an ANZAC Timor-Leste Battle Group, as well as continuing the Australian individual personnel contributions to other ongoing UN peacekeeping operations. Between 2006 and 2009 're-roled' RAA batteries served in the first, second, fifth and sixth rotations of the Timor-Leste Battle Group, undertaking functions ranging from infantry duties through to operations staff, interagency liaison and communications within the ISF. Sixty RAA personnel also deployed as individual headquarters staff in the third battle group rotation.[12]

Iraq Operations: 2006–2008

In Iraq by 2006, the original Al-Muthanna Task Group (AMTG) mission had transitioned to an operational overwatch role in support of fledgling Iraqi Government security control of the provinces of Al-Muthanna and later, Dhi Qar. Accordingly, the Australian task group was renamed as the Overwatch Battle Group (West) (OBG (W)). AMTG 3 became OBG (W) 1, and was followed by three more rotations.

During the AMTG 3/OBG(W) 1 rotation, the task group's various artillery surveillance and target acquisition assets were employed cooperatively to provide the functional components of a counter-rocket, artillery and mortar (C-RAM) capability in response to random and indiscriminate indirect fire from highly mobile firers. The improvised arrangement incorporated locating radars to detect incoming rounds and feed the information directly into the JOSCC's operating picture. The JOSCC then manually cued the base's force protection measures, and initiated responses using UAVs and other reconnaissance assets.[13]

During the last Australian battle group deployment in 2008, a British AS90 self-propelled howitzer was temporarily incorporated in the OBG(W) 4 Battle Group to provide a C-RAM response capability, which was demonstrated on several occasions. By this time it had become the norm to provide multi-disciplinary artillery batteries comprising field, locating, air defence and offensive support coordination elements, capable of coordinating coalition fires and effects in support of Australian forces.[14]

The artillery contribution to each overwatch battle-group typically comprised a Joint Offensive Support Coordination Centre (JOSCC), a surveillance and target acquisition component with an AN/TPQ36 radar and an Uncrewed Aerial Vehicle (UAV) troop, an Air Liaison Officer/Joint Terminal Attack Controller (JTAC – formerly a Forward Air Controller) element, and two Joint Offensive Support Teams (JOST), one for each combat team.[15]

Artillery Commanders: Colonel David Edwards, CSC

In 2005, Major David Edwards, then commanding 108th Field Battery, was deployed to Iraq as the battery commander of Overwatch Battle Group West, where he faced the challenge of commanding not only Gunners, but a diverse range of combat support elements.

Edwards came to this position after ten years' service, beginning in 4th Field Regiment, and including deployment to East Timor as a forward observer,

Chief of Army Lieutenant General Peter Leahy (left) reviews the terrain as Major David Edwards (right) delivers a ground brief from the top of the Ziggurat at Ur. Iraq, 31 Jul 2006 (courtesy Defence Image Gallery 20060731adf8243116.032

instructional postings at the School of Artillery and Duntroon, and secondment to a British battle group in Bosnia.

In Iraq, Edwards led an ad-hoc sub-unit comprising personnel from approximately 25 units, 18 corps and the Royal Australian Air Force. It was a complex challenge, met by 'those well-worn leadership tenets of looking after your people, understanding what they are doing and their difficulties, and making sure administration is not a distraction. Getting people together to identify as a team and making sure they knew they were valued and part of the broader battle group was one of the most important things I had to do.'

From an artillery viewpoint, Edwards considered it vital that all Gunners had a sound general artillery knowledge. This enabled the planning and execution of support in such a manner as to meet the expectations and earn the trust and confidence of the supported arm while adapting to the complex problems of the operational environment. Those problems included new and unusual terrain, incredible heat, limited communications bandwidth, and an enemy determined to remain below detection thresholds. He found the quality of the artillery members of the battle group to be excellent, a testament to their pre-deployment training.

Edwards observed two distinct lessons from his deployment in command. The first was 'maintaining a strong foundation of artillery knowledge within our training system is essential, even as we expand to more technical or specialised capabilities into the future'. The second was to 'train with your personnel, challenge them, and then give them trust and space when you deploy'.

Colonel Edwards later served in Afghanistan, and as a senior officer contributed with distinction in training, planning, and professional military education appointments.

British AS90 155-millimetre self-propelled howitzer of the 26th Regt, Royal Artillery, Iraq, 2003 (Courtesy UK MoD)

As an example of a battle group's tasks, during OBG (W) 3, the 5RAR Battle Group deployed combat teams to Al Muthanna and Nasiriya, where they undertook security and training tasks with the Iraqi Army and Police. The 103rd Battery's JOSCC deployed with the battle group headquarters, and the battery provided a JOST to each combat team, as well as individual gunners as signallers and drivers for the Bushmaster protected mobility vehicles.[16]

Gunners from the Surveillance and Target Acquisition detachment with OBG (W) 4 prepare to launch a Skylark small UAV, Camp Terendak, Tallil, Iraq, 5 April 2008 (Courtesy Defence Image Gallery 20080405adf8246638_098.jpg)

Afghanistan – Reconstruction and Mentoring: 2005–2010

Map 15.01: Operation Slipper: Map depicting Australian Area of Operations within Uruzgan Province, Southern Afghanistan, 2010.

Following the ADF commitments earlier in 2001–2, an Australian Special Forces Task Group returned to Afghanistan in September 2005, in response to the growing Taliban insurgency. While it was deployed, Australia was encouraged to make a further contribution to North Atlantic Treaty Organisation's (NATO's) ongoing International Security Assistance Force (ISAF) operations established in 2003. Accordingly, in September 2006, an Australian Reconstruction Task Force, based on a combat engineer regiment, was deployed to Uruzgan Province to undertake civil aid projects as part of a Dutch-led Provincial Reconstruction Team within ISAF's Task Force Uruzgan (TF-U). Another Special Operations Task Group deployed to Uruzgan in April 2007, and a Rotary Wing Group arrived at Kandahar in February 2008.[17] These forces deployed into an environment of moderate threat from mortar and rocket fire, but an escalating threat from ground fire and improvised explosive devices.

Although Australia did not deploy organic artillery fire assets, Gunner elements provided JOSCCs and JOSTs as part of each task force rotation as the mission transitioned from reconstruction to mentoring. Their task was to provide artillery and joint fires advice and coordination, which was imperative to Australian targeting and essential for gaining access to coalition fires and effects. JOSTs comprised artillery Joint Fires Observers (formerly Forward Observers), along with artillery, special operations and air force Joint Terminal Attack Controllers (JTACs). [18] They coordinated joint fires and effects for both defensive and patrol operations.[19] For most Australian rotations, the RTF JOSCC was at Kamp Holland in the TF-U Joint Operations Room, located with the Dutch – and later, US – Fire Support Coordination Centres. This co-location made for effective cross-coalition sharing of information, fire support coordination and battle-tracking.[20]

Joint Fires Observer Bombardier Thomas Grieve confirms his position during a five-hour contact, which occurred during Operation Zamarai Lor in southern Afghanistan, 27 May 2009. (Courtesy Defence Image Gallery 20090527adf8185016_0098.jpg)

Australian special operations and conventional forces in Uruzgan province and beyond relied on ISAF and US artillery, mortar, attack aviation and close air support throughout the campaign. At Tarin Kot, close fire support was provided mostly by a Dutch PzH2000 155-millimetre self-propelled artillery element, and at times by US mortar teams.[21] Collectively, the JOSCC and the JOSTs' ability to interoperate with US and ISAF forces proved essential, and the JTACs who were accredited to call in and control US and ISAF close air support were particularly valuable. The operational experience afforded to the participating Australian Gunners was invaluable, providing a rare insight into modern, peer joint force coordination. It also revealed comparative deficits in RAA field artillery capability, and offered practical avenues for resolution.

At this time, the overall growth in the ADF's UAS capability at all tiers of operation was becoming indispensable in providing timely and responsive surveillance and intelligence to deployed units. Over Uruzgan, RAA-controlled drones operated alongside RAAF 'Heron' UAVs and coalition manned and unmanned air assets, providing multiple layers of surveillance and reconnaissance support. A network of Australian and ISAF coordination centres analysed the information gained, and generated intelligence to inform the tactical manoeuvre of both conventional and special forces. The result proved the worth of 20th STA Regiment's formation as a dedicated surveillance and target acquisition unit.[22]

The second Australian RTF deployed in May 2007, supported by 'Scan Eagle' UAVs operated by 20th STA Regiment's Gunners, converting later to the 'Shadow 200' UAS.[23] The STA assets divided their support between the Australian Special Operations Task Group and the conventional troops in Uruzgan Province, and sustained their employment throughout all the remaining Australian rotations in Uruzgan province until 2014.[24]

The AAI Shadow 200 tactical unmanned aerial system is recovered post-mission at Multi National Base Tarin Kot, 18 September 2013 (Courtesy Defence Image Gallery 20130918adf8514423_001.jpg)

Concurrent Re-Equipment: 2006–2008

When communicating his vision for the HNA Plan earlier in 2005, the Chief of Army had challenged the RAA not only to support Army's manoeuvre forces with reliable and intimate fire, but to enable combat teams to gain access to joint fires from other arms and services, enabled by a widespread communications network connecting each 'sensor' to the optimal 'shooter'.[25] In response, the RAA set out to develop its capability to coordinate all forms of offensive support, to grow its surveillance and target acquisition capability, and to update its air defence capability both on operations overseas, and in organisational developments in Australia.

Several significant re-equipment projects came to fruition between 2006 and 2008, in large part the culmination of materiel processes that had been in train since the 2000 Defence White Paper. One saw the upgrade of RBS-70's build standard, and the provision of associated surveillance and target acquisition radars along with an immersive 'dome' trainer. Others resulted in the upgrade of the AN/TPQ 36 weapon-locating radar, and the introduction into service of a new artillery orienting system, ground surveillance radars and thermal imaging systems.[26] Planning also continued for the replacement of its L118/L119 guns and M198 howitzers with modern 155-millimetre field howitzers, along with new precision and conventional ammunition.

The decision to transition solely to 155-millimetre calibre adversely affected the reserve artillery. Under the HNA plan, the reserve Gunners had responsibility for producing high-readiness JOSTs and battalion JOSCCs. However, the greater time required to train the larger 155-millimetre detachments and the fewer guns that batteries could field diminished the reserve batteries' ability to conduct the firing practices necessary to produce suitably qualified, 'high-readiness' personnel. Accordingly, trials commenced in 2nd/10th Field Regiment to determine if it would be viable to re-equip reserve batteries with 81-millimetre mortars.[27]

During the commitments to Iraq and Afghanistan, some Gunners were involved in developing tactics and technologies to support the operations and, more broadly, ADF counter-insurgency and counter-terrorism operations. Perhaps the most prominent example was the Counter Improvised Explosive Device Task Force, raised in March 2006 and headed by Brigadier Phil Winter, who was then the RAA Head of Regiment. Adapting artillery and weapons intelligence techniques along with explosive ordnance and joint fires expertise, the task force developed means of defeating improvised devices on the battlefield, as well as strategies to defeat and disrupt insurgent supply networks.[28]

In 2008, with a new Defence White Paper looming, and in light of operational experience over the previous decade, the RAA began studies into future artillery roles. One rapidly evolving aspect was that the tactical effects available to support the manoeuvre commander had broadened beyond the lethal methods of traditional fire support, to include non-lethal effects such as the use of cyber, electronic or psychological warfare.[29] Reflecting this development, from February 2008, RAA terminology changed once more. JOSCCs became Joint Fires and Effects Coordination Cells (JFECC), and JOSTs were renamed as Joint Fires Teams (JFT).[30]

Afghanistan – Alongside British Gunners: 2008–2011

Separate to the Australian operations in Uruzgan, following a proposal by the Australian Army in 2007, between 2008 and 2011 a series of Australian field artillery troops were embedded into Royal Artillery (RA) batteries serving elsewhere in the Regional

Command-South area of operations. These batteries formed part of the British Army's Operation Herrick in neighbouring Helmand Province, where the ground and indirect threat was markedly higher.[31] The three regular Australian gun regiments each contributed two troops, drawn in rotation, to what was the first operational deployment of gun-line personnel in their primary role since the Vietnam War. Each contingent underwent pre-mission training in Britain before being deployed to Afghanistan. The deployments provided the opportunity for those involved to develop, practice and retain the artillery tactics, techniques and procedures employed in the Afghanistan theatre.[32]

In the first of the deployments, a troop of 15 Gunners from 101st and 103rd Batteries, 8th/12th Medium Regiment travelled to Britain for work-up exercises and training with the 105-millimetre L118 Light Gun.[33] Embedded with I Parachute Battery (Bull's Troop), 7th Parachute Regiment, Royal Horse Artillery (RHA), the troop then deployed to Forward Operating Base (FOB) Armadillo in March 2008, as part of the direct support battery to the UK's Battlegroup Centre. Here, the battery's fire was augmented by support from attack helicopters and aircraft.[34]

In this first rotation, illumination was the only indirect fire support initially required, but this changed once the traditional fighting season commenced in June, after which time suppression, danger close and counter-battery missions became commonplace. The troop fired 2911 rounds during 153 fire missions in support of British, Danish and American troops, and participated in a combined airmobile insertion at Kajaki, which led to the successful destruction of four insurgent mortar teams, the mission cued by a Danish weapon-locating radar. Later in the tour, the battery's fire support to an Irish Operational Mentoring Liaison Team and a company of the Afghan National Army (ANA) involved firing as close as 60 metres from unprotected troops, and the engagement of Final Protective Fire targets on multiple occasions.[35]

Each successive rotation of Australian Gunners confronted different experiences as the British mission evolved. During the fourth national rotation with Operation Herrick, Gunners from 8th/12th Medium Regiment served with forward elements of B Battery 1st Regiment, RHA in September 2009, occupying FOB Armadillo (later renamed FOB Budwan), located in the Upper Gereshk Valley. The British-Australian battery supported the 11th British rotation of forces into Helmand Province, providing indirect fire support to the Danish Operational Mentoring Liaison Teams of Task Force-Helmand. The composite battery fired constantly in support of numerous planned operations, as well as contacts across the 'Green Zone'.

The battery gained a significant reputation for accurate, aggressive, and responsive fires, utilising both its guns and smaller direct fire support weapon systems. The Gunners fired HE, smoke and illumination missions, expending 1027 rounds during their six-month tour. This Rotation XI of Operation Herrick witnessed some of the worst losses of British and Danish forces within Helmand Province since ISAF operations commenced. In mid-March 2010, the troop handed over to fellow Gunners from 4th Regiment, RAA.[37]

Quo Fas Et Gloria Ducunt: Sergeant Simon Hastings

Sergeant Simon Hastings deployed as part of 4th Field Regiment's first contribution with the Royal Artillery (RA) in Helmand, known as 'Wallaby Troop'. Embedded with the British 8 (Alma) Battery, 29 Commando Regiment RA, the Australians initially trained in Britain prior to deploying. Some members, including Hastings were located at FOB Edinburgh.

In January of 2009, after a difficult reconnaissance during which two British Gunners were wounded, the composite battery established a direct-fire single gun position at the nearby Roshan Tower, a small clearing atop a feature commanding the Musa Qaleh district. Under cover of darkness, the Gunners and an accompanying platoon from the Royal Gurkha Rifles manhandled a 1.8-ton 105-millimetre British Light gun (equivalent to the Australian Hamel gun) to the top of the steep-sided feature, where it was concealed when not in action. Hastings was the first commander of its mixed Australian/British detachment, and he and other Australian Gunners rotated through this isolated location for up to a month at a time.

In its direct fire role, the gun provided devastatingly accurate fire out to 3000 metres, dominating the valley below. Freed from the constraints of seeking airspace clearance to fire, Hastings accrued a significant record of targets suppressed or destroyed.

The Taliban sporadically attacked the tiny FOB with machine gun fire, but, despite their best efforts, the Gunners continued to deal effectively with targets that had previously withstood coalition attack by mortars, 105-millimetre HE, Apache Hellfire missiles and aerial bombs. The moniker 'Dragon Gun' was coined by the Taliban who were on its receiving end, and its fearsome reputation passed into local folklore – at least for a time.[36]

18 Jan 2012. Sergeant Simon Hastings briefing Afghan National Army Gunners (Courtesy Defence Image Gallery 20060731adf8243116_032).

Gunner Jake Hyland, 107th Battery, 4th Regiment, maintains security during piquet duty at Forward Operating Base Budwan, Helmand Province Afghanistan, July 2010 (Courtesy Defence Image Gallery 20100705adf8266070_0024.jpg)

The overall combat tempo and intensity experienced by each of the Herrick rotations in Helmand were considerable. The Gunners' artillery fire – both indirectly supporting Coalition manoeuvre forces, and directly in local defence of the troop's own position – regularly required significant augmentation by joint fires from helicopter attack aviation and close air support. In an illustrative example, later in October 2010, the British-Australian-Danish forward operating base at FOB Budwan was attacked by Taliban insurgents with rocket-propelled grenades and small arms. Assisted by fire support from a hastily assigned helicopter gunship, the Gunners defended their position by using the 105-millimetre Light Gun in a direct fire role, along with small arms and an armoured vehicle's turret chain-gun.[38]

Over three years, the Herrick operational deployments provided a next generation of Australian Gunners with mission-critical tactical experience.[39] The quality of the embedded Australians was acknowledged by their peers, and indicated that that the RAA could have provided competent, effective and accurate indirect fire support to deployed Australian task groups. The fact that the RAA had not been tasked to do so in either Iraq or Afghanistan was perhaps a combination of the perceived threat levels, the presence of other nations' artillery, abundant availability of air support in an environment of air superiority, logistic considerations, and restrictions on the size and composition of the Australian contingents. That few, if any, senior Australian commanders serving at that time had ever previously relied on live artillery support may also have been a contributing factor.

Gunners of Tiger troop, 1st Regiment RAA, in front of the 105-millimetre light gun at their remote patrol base in Helmand Province, Afghanistan, 12 March 2011 (Courtesy Defence Image Gallery 20100705adf8266070_0024.jpg)

Modernisation

Australian Operations in Iraq had recently ceased, and those in Afghanistan were still in train, when the government issued the 2009 Defence White Paper. This document reaffirmed the priority tasks for the Defence Force set out in 2000, and confirmed the ADF's conventional land forces would continue to be based around three combat brigades.

The paper also stated that by 2030, the ADF would need to be more potent in certain conventional warfare areas. One of those areas of direct interest to the RAA was strike capability, through the acquisition of long-range land-attack missiles. This would be a deep battle capability that had been hinted at previously, but not pursued. A long range strike capability in the RAA would align it more closely with its British and American peers, and counter a similar capacity in competitor artillery forces.

The White Paper also announced the government's intention to replace the RBS-70 air-defence system, and to proceed with the replacement field gun. These acquisitions were the focus of the RAA's flagship Land 19 (air defence artillery) and Land 17 (field artillery) projects respectively.[40]

That same year, the American M777A2 155-millimetre howitzer was selected to fill the lightweight field gun role, and the Advanced Field Artillery Tactical Data System (AFATDS) was chosen as the new digital command and control system. AFATDS marked the Gunners' first true step into the digital age, and assisted in meeting the challenge issued by the Chief of Army four years previously to provide not only reliable and intimate fire, but enable combat teams to reach back to joint fires enabled by a widespread and disaggregated sensor-shooter network.[41] With AFATDS, the RAA became digitally interoperable with the Army's overall battle management system, and those of Australia's allies, a capability hitherto not fully attained. The M777 and accompanying tactical data system were fielded in 2011, with the L119 phasing out as part of the replacement.

The advent of these new capabilities took the Gunners a step closer to American equipment and doctrine, and reflected a growing emphasis on interoperability in coalition warfare. To complement the data system, a Digital Terminal Control System – a combination of rangefinders, designators and communication components allowing JFTs and JTACs to request and coordinate offensive support missions – was planned for introduction in 2012.[42]

Changes also occurred at an organisational level. Following the earlier establishment of an ADF Joint Operations Command, the paper announced the replacement of Army's Land and Training Commands with Forces Command, which thereafter commanded all artillery units, except those on operations and those being prepared for deployment under the 1st Division. A small cell was established in Forces Command to advise on artillery matters, somewhat redressing the demise of Headquarters Land Command Artillery, three years beforehand.[43]

For a period as well, the artillery experimented with a reorganisation that reflected the growth in importance of fires and effects coordination. Under the change, the regular gun regiments transformed to a single gun battery of 12 guns and three 'observer' batteries. The descriptor 'field' or 'medium' was removed from their titles. Each observer battery was structured to provide a JFECC to support a battle group, and three JFTs to support its combat teams.[44] The restructure proved short-lived, but for a short time batteries providing such support in Afghanistan were considered to be 'observer' batteries.[45]

Afghanistan Mentoring: 2010–2014

In Afghanistan, the role of the Australian task force changed to increase focus on mentoring the Afghan National Army (ANA) battalions – known as Kandaks – in Uruzgan Province, just prior to the Dutch-led TF-U transitioning to the US-led Combined Team Uruzgan (CTU). The mentoring role had been introduced earlier in October 2008 with the Mentoring and Reconstruction Task Force-1 (MRTF-1), and involved considerably more patrolling across the province. The more active profile triggered an increased need for joint fires coordination from the Australian Gunners accompanying those mentoring operations.

The first Australian Mentoring Task Force (MTF-1) based on 6RAR provided mentoring and liaison teams as a sole mission role. Further mentoring task force battle groups followed. As a typical example of Coalition artillery task sharing of that period, from late 2009 until late 2010, the Tarin Kot base accommodated a tri-nation group of Gunners comprising the Australian JFECC and ScanEagle UAS group, Singaporean weapon locating radars, and

Dutch 155-millimetre self-propelled howitzers.[46] This multinational grouping represented a considerable accomplishment in coalition interoperability and integration of joint fires coordination.

Bombardier Glen Swain and Gunner Ashley Kerr (L) of a Joint Fire Team with MTF-1 cross fields near Sinha, Mirabad Valley, Uruzgan, 25 March 2010 (Courtesy Defence Image Gallery 20100325adf8246638_388.jpg)

The indirect fire threat in the area of operations was an enduring concern. When Singapore withdrew its weapon-locating radar, the risk to Australian forces was elevated as the ADF had no organic locating assets deployed at that time. Australia then rapidly acquired the SAAB 'Giraffe' Agile Multi-Beam radars and TPQ/38 Lightweight Counter-Mortar Radars to provide a C-RAM system to protect the base at Tarin Kot. The Giraffe radars were manned by re-roled Gunners of 110th Air Defence Battery, as the equipment had combined air defence and weapon locating capabilities, and 20th STA Regiment had no spare capacity. The combined JFECC integrated the data provided by the two sources, cueing force protection and search responses, foreshadowing impending capabilities for the RAA in the near future. The 'sense and warn' system successfully detected incoming indirect fire on all occasions, thereby reducing the potential for personnel casualties. It was a highly successful example of a rapidly acquired technology that was intrinsically capable of integration into the coalition fires network, and fielded directly upon acquisition.[47]

In 2010, while 103rd Battery's JFECC and JFTs were deployed with the 5RAR-led Mentoring Task Force (MTF-2), the battery was caught up in the RAA's organisational change to 'gun' and 'observer' batteries'. The 103rd Battery's deployed JFECC and JFTs became 115th Battery. Adding to the disruption, the battery's observer elements

Artillery Commanders: Colonel Simon Hunter

As a Major commanding 103rd Medium Battery, Simon Hunter deployed with Mentoring Task Force (MTF) 2 in Afghanistan in 2010–11. The challenges he faced were typical of those experienced by Gunners during counter-insurgency–style operations, when artillery command and observation elements only were deployed, and where manning restrictions were in place.

Hunter was well placed to take on his role in Afghanistan, having completed a range of regimental appointments that included deployment to East Timor as a Civil-Military Cooperation Team Leader, and a period as a forward observer in an Overwatch Battle Group in Iraq.

The principal challenge Hunter encountered in Afghanistan flowed from the national manning cap imposed on the MTF. The resulting pressure was exacerbated by the MTF commander's decision to split the deployed force into smaller groups with the ambition of providing maximum coverage throughout Uruzgan Province.

Hunter's battery contingent had to adapt and manage the resultant risk as best as possible, even though it meant that observation groups and fire support coordination assets were employed in an unconventional fashion, the artillery 'independent check' was not always achievable, and there was insufficient depth in teams, leading to low sustainability and fatigue. The risks were offset to some degree by modern artillery equipment, and procedures that served to reduce human error and the requirement for the independent check. MTF 2's manoeuvre elements also had equipment that assisted them conducting an all-arms call for fire.

Hunter's experiences showed how care should be taken to deploy in a manner that maintains the integrity of observer teams and fire support coordination cells, permitting safe handling of targeting information and firing data, and ensuring teams remain able to sustain high tempo operations.

Following Afghanistan, Colonel Hunter went on to command 1 Regiment RAA, and serve on the operations staff of joint headquarters.

30 November 2010: Major Simon Hunter, Multinational Base Tarin Kot.

were equipped early with the new Digital Terminal Control System prior to its general introduction into service.[48]

The Giraffe Counter Rocket Artillery and Mortar (C-RAM) radar above Multi National Base Tarin Kot (Courtesy Defence Image Gallery 20110422adf8214577_001.jpg)

Taking their reorganisation in stride, the Gunners in Uruzgan adapted successfully. During its tour, 115th Battery coordinated the fire of over 300 rounds of M777 155-millimetre, over 200 rounds of Afghan artillery D-30 122-millimetre and over 200 rounds of Australian 81-millimetre mortars. Bombardier David Robertson earned the Medal for Gallantry for his actions during a fighting patrol, and the battery also suffered several casualties, including a member of a JFT who was severely wounded.[49]

Afghanistan – Other Gunner Commitments: 2010–2013

Alongside the Uruzgan-based reconstruction and mentoring task forces, many individual Gunners were embedded in various ISAF headquarters and bases in the wider mentoring mission, within the Afghan National Army Officer Academy, and elsewhere. The RAA also deployed several joint fires and effects training teams, including personnel within ISAF combat-support mentoring and liaison teams, whose mission was to train individual Afghan National Army field artillery batteries to combat readiness.[51]

Quo Fas Et Gloria Ducunt: Bombardier David Robertson, MG

Bombardier David Robertson deployed to Afghanistan in October 2010 as part of Mentoring Task Force 2. Deploying from Patrol Base Qareb, he accompanied a mixed patrol of 5RAR and Afghan National Army soldiers to the village of Moruch, to interact with locals and search for caches. However, as the patrol approached the village, SIGINT reports warned of insurgents observing them and preparing to attack.

Not long after the patrol's arrival, Australian snipers in overwatch engaged a number of insurgents who could be seen carrying PKM machine-guns in the next village. This triggered insurgent small-arms fire from the high ground overlooking the patrol.

Robertson with his signaller and a small infantry team pushed out to a nearby low feature that was exposed to the insurgent fire from higher ground, with little cover available. Undaunted, Robertson called in a mortar fire mission, and after one correction and three rounds fire for effect, the elevated insurgent position was silenced. He then turned his attention to the other insurgent machine-gun, opening at three rounds fire for effect, using airburst proximity high explosive rounds. Both insurgent locations were neutralised within 20 minutes.

When the infantry commander ordered the patrol forward to a second village, Bombardier Robertson called in another fire mission to suppress Taliban machine gunners on the nearby high ground while the patrol searched the village for insurgents and weapons. This suppression continued until sundown when the patrol moved back to its patrol base.

Although Bombardier Robertson said he feared for his safety during the patrol, he was more concerned about his mates. 'When the time came, everyone else was relying on me to do my job and I really didn't want to let anyone down.'[50]

Combat Support Mentors and Training Teams

In the first half of 2010, a small ISAF artillery training team deployed to Uruzgan Province with MTF-1 to train the gun battery of the combat support Kandak of the 4th Brigade ANA, which was equipped with three Russian-designed 120-millimetre D-30 howitzers. This required the Australians to first learn how to operate the 'Russian gun', in the process acquiring dial sights from the international arms market. At times, the lesson development preceded instruction by only a couple of steps, with delivery through interpreters a constant challenge. However, the experience of the instructors and their knowledge of gun design won through – although the D-30 dial sight's Soviet bloc 6000-mil (instead of NATO standard 6400-mil) circle subdivision caused some initial head-scratching. In late July, the fledgling Afghan battery undertook its first live fire exercise, a direct fire shoot on Tarin Kot's anti-armour range.[52]

Warrant Officer Class Two David Nutini from the First Mentoring Task Force mentors an Afghan National Army gunner with the alignment of a gun at Multi National Base Tarin Kot, 26 April 2010 (Defence Image Gallery 20100426adf8246638_232.jpg)

Artillery Training Team-Kabul, Afghanistan

From April 2010, the RAA also provided the ISAF Artillery Training Team – Kabul (ATT-K). Gunners from 8th/12th Medium Regiment provided the first team, charged with the establishment of an Afghan School of Artillery, while other Gunners were embedded in the Afghan National Army Officer Academy and elsewhere. In 2011, the ATT-K transitioned into the Artillery Training Advisory Team (ATAT), and was staffed by rotational deployments, until it was withdrawn in April 2013. During its existence, the Training Team delivered up to 20 courses per year, and ultimately became part of the ANA School of Artillery, which in 2012 graduated approximately 1100 soldiers, non-commissioned officers and officers.[53]

ISAF mentoring and training commitments under Operation Slipper continued until 31 December 2014, at which point the Australian commitment concluded. By that time, more than 26,000 ADF personnel had served in Afghanistan and the wider Middle East region.

Plan Beersheba

While the Australian military commitment to Afghanistan was still in progress, the ADF turned to considering its future force structure. For the Army, the result was 'Plan Beersheba', promulgated in 2011, and confirmed in the 2013 Defence White Paper. Under this plan, between 2014 and 2017 the Army's three regular combat brigades were to be restructured into standardised multi-role formations, each based around an armoured/cavalry unit, and two infantry battalions with enhanced mobility. Plan Beersheba also employed the Army's recently established operational generation model, in which in any given year, one brigade would be 'ready', another 'readying', and the third brigade in 'reset'. Two reserve brigades were paired with each of the regular brigades, and expected to produce a battalion-sized force if mobilised during the 'ready' period.[54]

The M777 howitzer and accompanying tactical data system were fielded in 2011, but plans to acquire 155-millimetre self-propelled guns were cancelled in 2012 by the Chief of Army to meet cost saving measures required under the government's strategic reform program.[55] Instead, each of the regular combat brigades was to be supported by an artillery regiment of three batteries of four M777 howitzers. Each battery provided a battle group-level JFECC and three combat team-level JFTs. A separate amphibious battalion was identified, along with a battery to provide its support.

The 16th Air Defence Regiment was re-titled as 16th Air-Land Regiment (ALR) in January 2012, and restructured to consist of an air-defence battery, a counter-rocket and mortar battery, and an air-ground operations battery, the latter responsible for coordination and allocation of air assets, and including a JTAC troop. The restructure afforded improved coordination across the various natures of air-land coordination provided by the Gunners, and essential to the modern multi-dimensional battlespace. Organisationally, 16th ALR and 20th STA Regiment would become components of a separate 6th Combat Support Brigade.

The Beersheba plan saw the demise of the remaining regimental headquarters in the reserve, whose artillery was shrunk to a Joint Fires Cell in Headquarters 2nd Division, and six light batteries. With 105-millimetre guns withdrawn from service, these batteries were equipped with 81-millimetre mortars. Each battery became part of an infantry battalion, although their members remained RAA, and wore artillery cap badges and lanyards. Their task was to provide integral fire support for the battle group from their parent brigades that would reinforce the associated 'ready' regular formation. Each battery was expected to provide a tactical-level JFECC and two JFTs.[56] This presented a real challenge for the reserve artillery Gunners, in terms of retaining links to the wider RAA for individual and collective training, as well as in terms of remaining part of the Gunner fraternity and ethos.[57] It also widened the training gap to be bridged for reserve Gunners to provide effective individual reinforcements to regular units.

Plan Beersheba, like the HNA Plan before it, consolidated the place of the regular artillery in support of brigade operations while consigning the reserve artillery to a lesser role as mortar companies of infantry battalions. In doing so, it continued the Army's contemporary focus for artillery on close support to tactical manoeuvre, and overlooked fires support for operational manoeuvre and the deep battle. How this structure would deliver against strategic policy references in white papers to greater capability in conventional operations and the potential employment of long-range missiles was not clearly articulated.

Reflections: 2006–2014

The period between the advent of the HNA plan and the cessation of Operation Slipper in the Middle East was one of continual high tempo for the ADF. In contrast to the strategic expectations of the continental defence era, national commitments had demanded a reconfigured, responsive ADF with higher readiness levels, better force protection, enhanced force projection capability and greater flexibility in role and employment. In short, the ADF had had to become 'harder to hit, and harder-hitting'. It had encountered adversaries that were determined, hard to detect and even harder to discriminate from their societal environment, demanding a rapid evolution of tactics, techniques and procedures.

The period stretched the standing ADF, the Army and its artillery across concurrent operations to a degree unprecedented since World War II, and it was noteworthy that – with the exception of the commitment to Korea in 1950 (and arguably to Soudan in 1885) – the response was provided solely by full-time service personnel, without resort to call-out, mobilisation, or reliance on a national service scheme. Nevertheless, the ADF met the Australian Government's commitments, aided by voluntary reserve reinforcements, urgent investment programs that delivered qualitative and quantitative expansion, and rapid adaptation to the exigencies of the lethal, asymmetric style of conflict typified in Iraq and Afghanistan.

Artillery units and personnel played their part in all the regional and peacekeeping deployments of the period. Although their contribution was perhaps not as central as in earlier conventional warfare against peer adversaries, for many Gunners this tempo entailed multiple tours of duty. In the operational theatres of Iraq and Afghanistan, Australian forces regularly needed to call on joint fires support, and in the course of its provision the artillery principles involved in lethal-fires engagements were expanded to provide methodologies for the employment of non-lethal effects such as information operations, electronic warfare or psychological operations.

A combination of factors led to circumstances where – apart from Korea – Australian land manoeuvre forces deployed overseas for the first time in a 'shooting war' since 1885 without their own Gunner comrades providing close indirect fire support. Even though no Australian gun batteries were deployed, the gun troops that served with British batteries demonstrated that Australian field artillery support could have been a viable option. By contrast, artillery surveillance and target acquisition devices were deployed extensively across all theatres and played a vital part in intelligence gathering and targeting. Similarly, Australian artillery command, liaison and observation teams and individuals in coalition headquarters performed key roles in providing advice on fire support, gathering the data to employ it, and putting it into effect.

CHAPTER 16
The Artillery after 2014

The Army's support to operational deployments, including peacekeeping, international commitments and homeland support tasks, continued after 2014, although at a lesser intensity than before. The Army used the opportunity of ebbing concurrency pressures to reflect on recent experience, reorganise, respond to evolving strategic guidance, and bring new materiel into service. The RAA Head of Regiment characterised the end of major involvement in the Middle East as a 'strategic pause to allow the Regiment to home in on effectively harnessing advancements in all its capabilities and new organisations'.[1]

By 2021, the RAA's regular gun and surveillance and target acquisition regiments fielded modern equipment, and were structured to provide accurate and responsive fire support to brigades and battle groups in mid- to low-level conflict, and to coordinate joint and coalition fires. However, they were few in number, and reserve Gunners provided but a single regiment armed with mortars. Evolving defence guidance and related equipment announcements pointed to the acquisition of greater capability to undertake more conventional high-level conflict settings, but such advancements had yet to come to fruition.

In the same period, the RAA's anti-aircraft artillery defence continued its evolution into a more comprehensive ground-based air and missile defence system, capable of being incorporated into complex integrated air and missile defences. By 2021, projects to re-introduce standoff ground-based air and missile defence in the ADF had been announced to complement the RAA's extant very low-level air defence capability. Meanwhile, the use of drones in the contemporary Russia-Ukraine and Armenia-Azerbaijan conflicts had become prevalent, and the prospect of future Australian military operations where a multi-layered enemy air threat existed, provided a compelling motive for the need for counter-drone systems to complement other air and missile defence systems.

Implementing Plan Beersheba

The RAA began the period after the end of Operation Slipper with the ongoing implementation of Plan Beersheba. This posed few challenges for the regular field regiments, as the new structure largely resembled existing practice, albeit involving the relocation of some batteries, and the re-raising of others.[2] The same was largely true for the 20th Surveillance and Target Acquisition Regiment and the restructured 16th Air-

Land Regiment, although in 2016 the latter reorganised internally so that both its weapon batteries had a radar troop and a weapons troop.[3]

For the reserve Gunners, the Beersheba reorganisation was considerably more problematic. The incorporation of batteries into infantry battalions led to a significant dislocation in training, capability and camaraderie with the regular artillery units. Nevertheless, by 2017, combined reserve batteries were fielding mortar fire units, Joint Fires and Effects Coordination Centres (JFECC) and Joint Fires Teams (JFT), reinforcing the annual cyclic 'ready formation' exercises for the regular brigades.[4]

A gun detachment from 4th Regiment, Royal Australian Artillery, prepares to reload an M777A2 lightweight howitzer during the combined-arms live-fire training activity near Townsville, Queensland, 14 March 2016 (Courtesy Defence Image Gallery 20160314adf8252964_01.jpg)

Then, in 2018, the integration of reserve Gunners into infantry battalions was reversed, and the RAA reserve batteries were instead grouped into the re-raised 9th Regiment RAA, equipped with 81-millimetre mortars and small observation drones. The restructured Regiment was tasked to field a composite battery in direct support of the reserve battle group reinforcing the 'ready' combat brigade, provide individual round-outs for regular fire coordination centres, and manage reserve artillery training.[5]

Afghanistan – Operation Highroad: 2015–2021

Overseas, from January 2015, ADF operations in Afghanistan under the NATO Resolute Support mission transitioned to a 'train, advise and assist' mission with Afghan Army, Air

Artillery Tactics: Firepower and Manoeuvre

The provision of fire support to Iraqi forces during Operation Okra illustrated once more that the choreography between opposing manoeuvre forces and the artillery firepower that supports them is akin to a sophisticated and continually evolving ballet. Dramatic changes in opposing forces' mobility and tempo, and their firepower's terminal effects, alter the interplay between each element.

Historically, flexible and responsive positioning of artillery's firepower for target effect in accordance with tactical plans is the prime determinant of how and where artillery batteries themselves are manoeuvred.

Until the early 20th century, infantry and cavalry formations tactically manoeuvred, while artillery gunners provided direct fire support from nearby. Artillery fire and its effects were directly observed and controlled from the gun-lines. Commanders directed the priorities for artillery support of manoeuvring infantry and cavalry. While artillery ranges were short, they were usually sufficient to keep the guns out of the close battle and remain effective.

While range and effectiveness of infantry weapons increased over time, assaults and close combat around tactical objectives ultimately remained essential in establishing battlefield dominance. Terrain and the nature of operations determined the speed of infantry movement. Increasing artillery ranges saw a transition from dedicated direct fire, to providing an umbrella of indirect artillery fire coverage.

Firing indirectly, the location of gun positions remained linked to infantry manoeuvre, but less strongly. Skilful positioning of artillery gun positions now provided numerous fire support options to engage multiple dispersed targets. Indirect fire multiplied the power and potential of artillery fire. Manoeuvre of fire from guns in concert with infantry manoeuvre now became more responsive, and therefore increasingly effective. The ability to switch flexibly between targets across much larger areas meant artillery fire became increasingly available as battles unfolded, and increasingly influential as a battlefield determinant.

From World War I onwards, commanders carefully selected the most versatile supporting artillery gun *areas* in their plans as key considerations. Gun areas now permitted allocation of a variety of gun positions, such as primary, secondary, alternate, step-up, and pistol gun, creating scope for artillery's own manoeuvre tactics, to allow batteries to deliver continuous, responsive and accurate fire in support of the manoeuvre commander. Such tactics also enabled gun position protection from hostile artillery, air and ground attack.

and National Police forces, known as Operation Highroad. Approximately 300 Australian personnel, Gunners amongst them, deployed at any one time, primarily undertaking mentoring and advisory roles, but also providing force protection and logistic support. This commitment ceased in 2021.[6]

Defeating Da'esh in Iraq – Operation Okra: 2014–2024

In August 2014, at the invitation of the Iraqi government, an international American-led intervention commenced to defeat the self-styled Islamic State in Iraq and Syria (ISIS), otherwise known as 'Da'esh'. [7] Fourteen nations, including Australia, participated in what was known internationally as Operation Inherent Resolve. The militants posed a significant threat in terms of scale, intensity and lethality, and by 2015 had brutally conquered large swathes of Iraqi and Syrian territory.

Operation Okra, Australia's contribution to Inherent Resolve comprised an Air Task Group aircraft, a Special Operations Task Group in an 'advise and assist' role with the Iraqi Security Forces (ISF), and a training Task Group at Taji base. All were supporting the coalition's mission to build ISF capability. Australian defence personnel, including many Gunners, also served in individual plans and operations positions in coalition headquarters and bases. Artillery Ground Liaison Officers assigned by the Air Mobility Group deployed periodically with the Air Task Group supporting close air support, air interdiction and strike operations in Iraq and Syria until 2018.[8]

Coalition ground and air forces provided vital tactical information, joint fires and enabling support to the ISF, and facilitated the targeting of ISIS fighters through coalition JTACs and joint fires observer mentors with the Iraqi artillery. These coalition advisers coordinated strikes in close support and in depth, using both precision-guided and conventional munitions from coalition guns, rockets and mortars. Some fires were delivered at long range, some using artillery raids. Advisers also aided Iraqi Army artillery in providing close support to ISF manoeuvre forces. Coalition Strike Cells coordinated all coalition joint fires on behalf of the Iraqi armed forces, while the Iraqis began to develop their own fledgling theatre-level joint fires coordination capability. Australian Gunners were embedded as part of targeting and joint fires and effects coordination staffs within coalition component and combined joint task force headquarters at all echelons, from unit to corps level.[9]

By December 2017, after significant clearance operations around Mosul, Sinjar and the Euphrates River Valley, Iraqi and supporting coalition forces had recaptured all of Iraq. ISIS was declared defeated in Syria on 23 March 2019, though remnant resistance remained. The Taji training Task Group concluded in June 2020, by which stage well over 4000 Australian personnel had deployed as part of Operation Okra, and Australian aircraft had flown over 2700 strike sorties. By September 2021, approximately 110 ADF personnel remained deployed in support of the ongoing Operation Okra.[11]

Artillery Tactics: Artillery Gun Raids

The concept of the artillery raid is both simple and lethal. Artillery raids are conducted in a similar approach to the more familiar 'direct action' raids employed throughout military history, and made famous through the commando operations during World War II.

In an artillery raid a fire unit is deployed rapidly and discreetly to a firing position – potentially via a temporary hide location prior – from where the system's lethality and range and can be applied to achieve an unanticipated and damaging effect, before the unit withdraws equally swiftly to a secure or concealed location.

Artillery raids are designed to generate tactical and even operational shock, with consequent psychological demoralisation. They exploit field artillery's characteristics of range, precision, accuracy and reliability, and the surprise of employing predicted fire.

The artillery raid can be used simply to provide destruction of key point targets, or harassment and interdiction of deep targets. In the close support role, artillery raids can be employed to provide a diversion to draw enemy attention from friendly manoeuvre elsewhere in the battlespace, or to provide close fire support to tactical action.

During World War I at Pozieres, Lieutenant Sam Thurnhill of the Australian Field Artillery conducted a limited, carefully planned single gun raid to support Australian infantry advances near Mouquet Farm. In Vietnam, US Field Artillery conducted raids with composite 105-millimetre/155-millimetre fire units, deployed by air from and to fire support bases, accompanied by an infantry local protection element, in order to range targets otherwise out of reach.

In more recent battles in 2022 and 2023, Ukrainian field and rocket artillery have conducted numerous raids employing High Mobility Artillery Rocket System, and towed or self-propelled artillery units in the war against Russia.[10]

Evolving Strategic Guidance

At the height of these overseas operations, and while the Army was reorganising at home, the government released the 2016 Defence White Paper. Continuing the themes of its predecessors, it identified Australia's defence objectives as deterring or defeating any attack on Australia, supporting the security of maritime South-East Asia, and providing contributions to international responses to threats to the rules-based global order. The Commonwealth reiterated its commitment to a regionally superior defence force, and repeated intentions to acquire a long-range rocket system for the land force by the mid-2020s. It also signalled the introduction of armed medium-altitude unmanned aircraft, the replacement of RBS-70, and, later, the acquisition of a medium-range, ground-based air defence system.[12]

The prospect of operating in a more hostile environment gave rise in Australian defence planning to projects providing self-propelled guns, ammunition, long-range rocket artillery and an enhanced ground-based air and missile defence.[13] In 2019, the Commonwealth announced the Raytheon/Kongsberg National Advanced Surface-to-Air Missile System (NASAMS) as the successor to RBS 70. The following year, the Commonwealth began the process to acquire self-propelled 'protected mobile fires' howitzers to re-equip several gun regiments, and a new family of 155-millimetre precision-guided and conventional ammunition.[14]

The National Advanced Surface to Air Missile System (NASAMS) Canister Launcher firing an AMRAAM missile. The Australian Army NASAMS will provide a Beyond Visual Range Ground Based Air Defence capability against airborne threats such as aircraft, unmanned aerial vehicles and cruise missiles through Project LAND 19 Phase 7B (Courtesy Defence Image Gallery rtn_222610.jpg)

With continuing international tension in South-East Asia and the South China Sea, Australia's Defence Strategic Update 2020 reprised the prospect of operating in a more hostile environment, and in a littoral setting.[15] The update implied potential artillery employment in coalition operations against capable opponents across a spectrum of conflict in an environment of high political interest, demanding a capability for long-range precision surface fires, and 'multi-domain' fires encompassing all physical domains (land, sea, air and space) as well as exploiting the cyber domain and electro-magnetic spectrum. For the Gunners, this translated as a continued and expanded requirement for joint fires and effects planning, coordination and advice.

Bombardier Samuel Jessep (left) and Lance Bombardier David Cater, embedded with Army's amphibious battalion, operate a scouting drone during a ship to shore swim serial as part of Exercise Sea Explorer, Cowley Beach, Queensland, 4 June 2021 (Courtesy Defence Image Gallery 20210604adf8609651_0541.jpg)

Global Context: Delivering Target Effects in the 21st Century

The conflicts of the early 21st century occurred primarily in settings where modern capable coalition forces faced determined irregular adversaries with no air capability. However, by 2019, it had become clear that the same circumstances would not be guaranteed in future.

Across the world's armed forces, the array of available joint fires systems now included surface-to-surface missiles and rockets, traditional 'tube' artillery, mortars, naval gunfire, attack aviation, and close air support and air interdiction from both crewed and uncrewed aircraft. After the collapse of the Intermediate-Range Nuclear Forces Treaty in 2019, a growing echelon of major power and developed nation militaries increasingly pursued developments in long-range precision surface strike, including ballistic and hypersonic missiles. These were closely matched by a revitalisation of ground-based air and missile defence.

Elements of artillery surveillance and target acquisition systems – ground sensors, surveillance radars and acoustic sensors – had been used in earlier conflicts by Australia and its coalition partners not only for targeting, but to create counter-rocket, artillery and mortar (C-RAM) capabilities. In response to random and indiscriminate indirect fire from highly mobile, low-detectability platforms in several contemporary conflicts, C-RAM systems were regularly improved to provide better warning, along with better targeting of associated surveillance devices, and more-responsive counter-bombardment. Coalition forces had exploited these and other dramatic improvements in information-gathering and analysis, and their air and electronic warfare superiority to attain uncontested, highly effective targeting of irregular adversaries.

Similar acceleration occurred with 'multi-domain' fires encompassing the cyber and electro-magnetic domains that could support disruptive electronic frequency attack, cyber-attack, information operations and psychological operations. These developments reaffirmed the enduring importance of joint fires and effects planning, coordination and advice. The RAA's prudent, ongoing interoperability arrangements with its allies and coalition members now offered the promise of unprecedented access to joint fires systems beyond Australia's national resources.

However, while 'detection' was often possible, 'discrimination' – the separation of the target from the non-combatant surrounding – had remained difficult, and lethal engagement of irregular adversaries had rightly remained governed by internationally codified rules of engagement. Moreover, more contemporary conflict elsewhere between more evenly matched conventional forces, such as in Ukraine from 2014 and Armenia-Azerbaijan in 2021, demonstrated that target development and prosecution was less simple when the air and electro-magnetic spectrums were strongly contested.

Meanwhile, artillery command, liaison and observation groups, also known as 'tactical' or 'tac' groups, still provided manoeuvre arm commanders with access to and advice on fire support and the use of non-lethal effects. Observation had been dramatically enhanced by UAVs, providing the artillery with pervasive and persistent air observation, feeding data directly to coordination centres and strike cells. 'Trusted' communications networks[16] comprising strong electronic protection of voice and data integrity through standards, protocols and hardware devices, permitted a return to centralised decision-making and allocation of fire support assets, albeit always conscious that communications remained potentially susceptible to contestation, disruption and interdiction.

Theatre-level precision for location and orientation via satellite geo-location had also become prevalent, but the growing threat of electro-magnetic signal interference reinforced the need for independent geo-location and orientation systems. Artillery meteorological data remained essential, and though provided automatically, remained challenging to disseminate in a timely fashion.

By 2022, the ongoing Russia-Ukraine conflict had demonstrated beyond doubt that surface artillery's capacity to provide intimate fire support had been dramatically enhanced by precision-guided munitions, and still offered a persistent fire support capability when aerial platforms were grounded or unable to acquire a target. Parallel advances across modern artillery forces in ballistics technology, and the consistent application of survey, meteorological, calibration and ordnance corrections saw continued improvement in the predicted-fire accuracy of conventional and rocket artillery into the 2020s.

Effective employment of all of these 'high end war-fighting' resources against peer adversaries now brought the depth battle to the forefront once more, alongside long-established concepts for shaping the 'close' battlespace. Australia's recent commitments to counter-insurgency conflicts, opposing asymmetric adversaries with no air capability had resulted in such concepts being largely overlooked since the end of World War II.

High Mobility Artillery Rocket Systems (HiMARS) of the United States Army and United States Marine Corps launch rockets during a firepower demonstration held at Shoalwater Bay Training Area in Queensland, during Talisman Sabre, 18 July 2021 (Courtesy Defence Image Gallery 20210718adf8443968_515.jpg)

Australia's Artillery in 2021

One hundred and fifty years after Australia's first continuous permanent artillery force was established, and after two decades of continuous expeditionary operations, the ADF had become considerably more proficient in preparing, mounting, projecting and sustaining sizeable forces on both military and peacekeeping operations. Its joint planning capacity and experience had increased considerably, and the ADF was now far more versatile and experienced across a wider range of missions – short of major, state-on-state warfighting.

The RAA had also undergone dramatic re-equipment, expansion and modernisation in the preceding decade, the Head of Regiment noting in 2019:

> The Royal Regiment today is unrecognisable from the Royal Regiment of ten years ago.
>
> The Hamel Gun, M198, Q-36 Radar, P-Star Radar and ScanEagle have made way for the M777A2, the Giraffe AMB radar, the LCMR, the Shadow UAS and the full networking and digitisation of the kill chain with AFATDS and DTCS.
>
> Binoculars have made way for Vector 21 binocular laser rangefinders and SOPHIEs (long-range hand-held thermal imager and target locators), whilst Copperhead has made way for the M982 Excalibur and M1156 Precision Guidance Kit.[17]

The structure of the RAA in 2021 is shown at Appendix 1, Table 20. Its principal elements comprised three regular gun regiments, a reserve mortar regiment, a surveillance and target acquisition regiment, and a regiment equipped with air-defence missile systems and extended-range radars.

Gunners from 9th Regiment RAA firing the F2 81-millimetre mortar during Exercise Chong Ju, at Puckapunyal Training Area, Victoria, 8 May 2019 (Courtesy Defence Image Gallery 20190508ara8517500_148.jpg)

Australian artillery tactics, techniques and procedures retained all standard artillery mission types – blinding, obscuration, illumination, suppression, destruction, neutralisation and even direct fire missions, and were still practised consistently. Deliberate and quick fire planning remained integral parts of the RAA skillset.

The RAA also continued to provide joint fires and effects staff and advice to the wider Army and ADF through the JFECC within Headquarters 1st Division/Deployable Joint Force Headquarters, the Supported Arms Coordination Centre within Headquarters Amphibious Task Group, and the Directorate of Army Air Support within the RAAF Headquarters Air Command. These staffs were supported by various embedded artillery entities – such as the JTAC Troop and Ground Liaison staff – as well as JFTs in the Army's amphibious battalion. Additionally, the Gunners contributed staff at higher joint headquarters, such as the Effects Cell within Headquarters Joint Operations Command. By 2021, the School of Artillery continued to conduct artillery and joint fires and effects training for all artillery trades, as well as individual training for infantry mortars.

By 2021, the RAA had also emerged at the forefront of the Army's modernisation program. Arrayed before the gunners were a number of projects arriving in future decades that would embody the Artillery Modernisation Plan produced at this time.[18] The Artillery Modernisation Plan was put in place to substantially upgrade the RAA's current weapons systems, platforms and support force elements, to attain parity with, or generate overmatch of potential enemy threats, and to provide ongoing upgrades to those systems to ensure their ongoing potency and relevance. Each capability area identified in the Artillery Modernisation Plan aligned to the 2020 Force Structure Plan,[19] and supported the strategic defence objectives identified in the 2020 Defence Strategic Update released the same year.[20]

Gunners from 109th Battery Alpha detachment, 4th Regiment, fire their M777 howitzer during a demonstration at Shoalwater Bay Training Area in Queensland during Exercise Talisman Sabre, 18 July 2021 (Courtesy Defence Image Gallery 20210718adf8638673_0176.jpg)

While acknowledging gaps in protected mobility artillery, air and missile defence and long-range fires capability existed in 2021, the Artillery Modernisation Plan vision foresaw that by 2040, the Regiment would either comprise – or be able to access – improved surveillance, reconnaissance and target acquisition, command, control and communications systems, with accompanying launch platforms and weapons delivery assets, across all the known domains. Together, these initiatives aimed to deliver combat systems for short-range ground-based air and missile defence; self-propelled artillery; long-range rocket artillery; surveillance, reconnaissance and targeting developments; digital terminal control systems to engage targets; and next-generation artillery ammunition.

Additionally, the value of artillery to modern coastal defences had again become apparent, with the prospect of mobile, long-range surface-to-surface rocket systems and land-based mobile strike missile platforms offering an 'anti-access, area-denial' capability in Australia's littoral maritime environment. The capability would comprise an Australian Army-operated deployable land-based anti-ship system.[21]

Progressively, the RAA became considered as the logical protagonists to fight Australia's future depth battles, with the prospect of a future artillery fires formation providing a potentially effective organisation and structure. The RAA's joint fires system was primed to become truly ubiquitous, and fulfil its stated vision of 'mastering multiple domains, delivering one effect'.

AS9 Huntsman and AS10 Ammunition Resupply Vehicle (Courtesy of Hanwha Defense Australia.)[22]

Beyond 2021

With the growth in regional military capabilities during the early 2020s, Australia's strategic guidance turned to the prospect of higher intensity conflict, and of the importance of field artillery, air and missile defence and long-range fires in settings where allied air superiority could not be assumed. Increasingly, Australia's planners and policymakers acknowledged artillery's role in providing not only sustained close support, but support to both 'shape the battlefield' in depth, and defend against a range of air, drone and missile threats – all illustrated by the major conflict then unfolding in Ukraine.

These considerations reinforced RAA plans for acquisition of long-range missiles, self-propelled howitzers, modern conventional and precision ammunition, improved UAS and advanced air defence capabilities. Together with new digitised artillery command and control systems, these developments returned the RAA to a more central position within Australia's land forces, and indeed the ADF's joint force capabilities as a whole.

In the 2023 Defence Strategic Review, the Commonwealth unequivocally expressed its policy on future artillery capability, confirming that the projects for acquiring long-range fires including High Mobility Artillery Rocket System (HiMARS) and land-based maritime strike would be accelerated and expanded immediately. At the same time, the second regiment of Army's self-propelled howitzers would be immediately cancelled, reflecting the Commonwealth's revised prioritisation in rebalancing between Army's manoeuvre and long-range strike capabilities.[23] The Review also identified an 'enhanced integrated targeting capability' and 'enhanced all-domain, integrated air and missile defence capability' capable of operating in the littoral regions surrounding Australia as critical.[24] Later that year, the

Commonwealth formally announced the raising of a new 10th Brigade as a 'fires brigade' that would field Australia's future long-range strike capabilities. Both the long-range strike and new NASAMS integrated air and missile defence capabilities would be based in Adelaide.[25]

The Artillery Modernisation Plan had earlier articulated how self-propelled artillery would allow increased protection and range with the ability to maintain a mechanised force's battle tempo, while new improvements to ammunition would allow in-service and future artillery systems to deliver firepower with improved accuracy. The long-range fires program would provide Australia an increased ability to shape the battlespace by defeating threats at ranges out to 300 kilometres and in time, beyond. Similarly, the RAA's projected Digital Terminal Control System would enhance the speed of engagement – as well as access to a larger number – of weapon platforms to engage targets. Planned new UAS assets would also provide better sensors to improve targeting, allow better situational awareness for commanders, and enhance artillery intelligence, surveillance and reconnaissance capabilities.[26]

CHAPTER 17

Conclusion – Change and Constancy

Artillery has been a constant presence in Australia's military history. From colonial times onwards, coastal gun batteries formed Australia's first line of defence, their procedures becoming increasingly complex as the range of naval guns increased. Because the forts had to be kept at higher levels of readiness, garrison Gunners, as they were known, constituted the majority of the permanent forces. Such pre-eminence extended into World War II, but afterwards air power and the development of long-range missiles rendered fixed coastal defences obsolete. Paradoxically, the circle appears to be turning once more, with the range and accuracy of modern missiles now offering the prospect of mobile land-based maritime strike.

Field artillery evolved alongside the coastal defences, the units in peacetime being provided predominately by the citizen force. A separate field artillery was raised as part of the expeditionary divisions of the AIF in World War I, and these Gunners, within the larger artillery of the British Expeditionary Force, developed expertise in massing fires and accurately engaging targets with predicted indirect fire. Australian artillery commanders planned and controlled fire support at divisional and corps level, incorporating heavy artillery groups and exploiting artillery intelligence to coordinate the location and engagement of depth targets, particularly hostile batteries.

Between the wars, citizen force and then militia field artillery units absorbed the expertise gained in World War I, and with the lessons from that war in mind, the first Australian anti-aircraft artillery units were formed in the 1920s, and the first anti-tank units in 1940. The latter played an important role in the Middle East and the Pacific in World War II before the armoured threat dissipated during the jungle fighting of the war's latter years. In the same conflict, anti-aircraft artillery protected Australia's cities, fixed defences and ground forces, for which purpose they were incrementally equipped with moving-target aiming devices, radar and searchlights. After the war, technological evolution led to countering armour becoming an all-arms responsibility, and the Army sharing the responsibility for air defence with the Air Force. Currently, anti-aircraft artillery's missiles and associated radars defend manoeuvre units and critical points.

Early in World War II, the field Gunners of the 2nd AIF effectively employed divisional artillery capabilities in the Middle East, building on the practices developed in World War I. As Japanese forces advanced into Australia's region, militia artillery units were mobilised, leading to the greatest artillery force Australia had ever fielded. However, when the threat abated after the Japanese reversals in the battles of the Coral Sea, Milne Bay and the Kokoda Track, not all were required, and the size of the militia force was progressively scaled back. On the ground, a revised approach in artillery employment was required from 1942 onwards as the terrain and tropical vegetation on the islands in the archipelagos of the South-West Pacific limited the size of the infantry formations, and the supporting AIF and militia artillery.

The Gunners adapted successfully, maintaining wherever possible the survey and meteorological foundations for accurate fire, and, during larger operations, establishing artillery intelligence capabilities to locate and engage enemy guns. They developed particular techniques for adjustment and observation of fire in close country, and strengthened affiliations between forward observers and infantry companies, and likewise between battery commanders and battalion headquarters. In these littoral campaigns, coordination of fire expanded beyond the artillery to include air and naval gunfire support.

During the Korean War, individual Australian Gunners experienced a brief reprise of artillery employment in conventional operations, before Australia engaged in the counter-insurgency campaigns of the Forward Defence policy of the 1950s and 1960s. In support of operations in Malaysia, Borneo and Vietnam, rapid and accurate fire support, at battery and, sometimes, regimental level, remained indispensable. It was provided by permanent Gunners, supplemented, in the case of Vietnam, by national servicemen. The limited regional conflicts of this period signalled a reduced need for a follow-on or expansion force, and, accordingly, the citizen force artillery was reduced in size.

Until this point, Australia's field artillery firepower had been used primarily to protect the manoeuvre arms, reflecting General Monash's observation that:

> The true role of infantry was not to expend itself upon heroic physical effort, not to wither away under merciless machine gun fire, not to impale itself on hostile bayonets, nor tear itself to pieces in hostile entanglements … but on the contrary, to advance under the maximum possible protection.[1]

In the Defence of Australia period that followed the Vietnam War, the strategic setting envisaged that only low-level threats would be encountered. The perceived requirement for artillery protection waned. Combined with constrained defence spending, this resulted in the RAA's force structure, being reduced, with the citizen force Gunners becoming a reserve for the permanent force rather than continuing as a limited expansion base. The artillery played a part in the domestic deployments and regional and international peace support operations of the 1990s and 2000s, but employment in this fashion did not drive substantive artillery modernisation, beyond the key step of the Gunners assuming responsibility for coordination of all forms of joint fires and effects.

When Australian forces deployed on operations in the Middle East during the early 21st century, the requirement for accurate and persistent fire support arose once more. Australian guns would have been quite capable of meeting the requirement, but they were not used, the ADF opting instead to rely on coalition artillery and air support. However, Australia did deploy artillery command, liaison, and observation elements, which played a vital role in providing fire support advice and in coordinating the support of joint and coalition assets, a process which advanced beyond lethal-fires engagements to include such effects as information and psychological operations, and electronic warfare. The contribution of artillery surveillance and target acquisition elements also grew in importance, while other Gunners successfully performed training and mentoring roles.

By the time those operations drew to a close, the RAA comprised a small but technically competent force centred on three regular gun regiments and six reserve gun batteries, a surveillance and target acquisition regiment, and an air-land regiment. Australian Government strategic guidance, reflecting developments in the Pacific and South-East Asia, increasingly identified a need to modernise this artillery, to upgrade its air defence capability, and to introduce a capacity for long-range strike to counter that of potential adversaries and complement that of allies. Projects to put this guidance into effect were put in train. Combined with a focus on artillery command and control and targeting capabilities, these aimed to return artillery to a more central position should future conflict occur, and to underpin operational and strategic advantage in Australia's envisaged threat environment.

An Australian Army battery from the 1st Regiment, Royal Australian Artillery, fires its M777 howitzer during Exercise Southern Jackaroo at Shoalwater Bay, 24 May 2019. Courtesy Defence Image Gallery 20190524adf8567820_053.jpg)

Throughout the 150 years of evolving employment and character of Australian artillery since 1871, some enduring observations are evident. Most importantly, the contribution Gunners provide is responsive to the particular strategic circumstances, national resources, technological developments and nature of the conflict. The unique character of each conflict and corresponding national strategic commitment will continue to drive artillery's configuration, employment and constraints.

That said, artillery will continue to have a role as the principal provider of defensive and offensive firepower in both the close and depth battle, and through the provision of joint fires and effects advice, surveillance and target acquisition, and airspace, targeting and strike coordination. In turning that role into effect - whether in deterring attacks on Australia, at Gallipoli, on the Western Front, in jungle warfare, or in coalition fire support coordination in recent times - successful artillery commanders at all levels have had to possess adaptability, innovation and flexibility.

The continuing relevance of the principles of employment of the artillery has equally remained evident. Successive campaigns have seen the need for combined arms and joint cooperation, concentration of artillery's power, economy of effort through the massing and switching of fires and effects, and effective logistic sustainment. These principles will undoubtedly remain relevant in future operations that are likely to see dispersed artillery employment at scale, across extended lines of operation for prolonged periods and involving demanding rates of fire.

In employing these principles over successive campaigns, the command and control of artillery has necessarily evolved differently to the other manoeuvre arms such as infantry and armour. Artillery's ability to acquire and engage targets over a wide area without physical manoeuvre has meant that the command of its units, and the control of their fire or effort have needed to be approached separately. This contrasting approach has made the provision of sound artillery advice vital to the manoeuvre arms commander, and equally called for artillery commanders to play a central and ongoing role in joint fires and airspace coordination.

This history has shown that, at its core, artillery has been a technical arm requiring detailed training to master its intricacies. Regardless of moment in history, Australia's Gunners have grappled with the 'gunnery problem', the constant challenge to acquire targets, determine the requisite effect, and conduct an effective engagement. Modern technologies such as digital 'Sensor-to-Shooter' linkages and GPS have made this easier in some regards, but recent experience emphasises that future solutions will still need to engage at ranges beyond which an adversary can respond. They will need to encompass the cyber, information and electro-magnetic domains as well as the physical, and to discriminate as well as detect in each. In addition, effective future artillery air defence systems will need to operate and engage in multiple ways and at speeds that defeat all types of adversary aerial munitions and delivery systems, including the rapidly evolving array of uncrewed systems. The future application of artillery will continue to demand considerable scientific application and technical mastery.

Even so, an enduring quality of Australian artillery has been an inherent culture that has sought to strike a balance between the science of gunnery and the art of its employment. That culture is founded upon a cooperative human spirit that has been exemplified in Gunners of all ranks and branches, devoted to both their tactical and technical roles, working together as part of a team. That team ethos is perhaps what remains most distinctive of Gunners, and what they will continue to value most.

Australia's Gunner community has remained a reflection of its longstanding battery, regimental, and branch heritages. Throughout 150 years of diverse operations and shifting strategic policy, Gunners have been able to orchestrate these disparate aspects into a concerted application of fires and effects in each theatre, deservedly earning the battle honour, *Ubique*. Australia's artillery employment has ebbed and flowed, but its intrinsic nature has endured. True to their motto, the Gunners have advanced and will continue to advance:

Where right and glory lead

Acknowledgements

Action! Action! Action! could have taken many shapes. The concept was for a short history with a friendly format complementary to the Australian Army History Unit's (AAHU) *Campaign Series*, including only 'essential' parts of the Gunners' long history. With only 200-odd pages, deciding what would, and would not be included was an unenviable judgement. Nick Floyd's insight to build the book around a backbone of the employment of artillery over the 150 years until 2021 became the key.

Nick Floyd and Paul Stevens agreed to be joint authors, sharing the research and writing, generously giving their time and expertise freely. Long-term members of the Regimental History Committee; David Brook, Kevin Browning, Keith Glyde, and Bob Lowry researched, drafted sections, and provided insight and counsel on many parts of the history. They were critical to achieving accuracy, synonymous with Gunner culture. Jason Cooke, Peter Dean, James Eling, Mark Mankowski and William Westerman provided select expert contributions. Nevertheless, the project is responsible for any error. Matt Hodda (as Deputy Head of Regiment), former Head of Regiment Phil Winter, and Dr Rhys Crawley helped steer the content, considering the balance of treatment of subjects, the appropriateness for the audience, and accuracy. Their observations increased the project's confidence in the content and its presentation. Strategic advice was obtained from the AAHU. Its Senior Historian, Mr Paul McAlonan along with Ms Miesje de Vogel, and especially Dr Garth Pratten generously provided counsel and comment on the direction and specifics of the book's early drafts. The outcome is all the better for their involvement.

Without funding however, the book would not have seen the light of day. The RAAHC covered the costs associated with publication, in keeping with its purpose to preserve and promote the history and heritage of Australian Artillery. The commemorative value of the book was recognised with a grant from the Department of Veterans Affairs. The Australian War Memorial (AWM)'s Director, Matt Anderson, also provided generous support in accessing the numerous AWM photographs used to illustrate the book. In its decisions, the not-for-profit, volunteer RAAHC has not planned for a profit, although it is hoped there will be some return from ongoing book sales.

Special assistance in various forms was also provided by former Gunners Wade Cooper, Darryl Kelly and Brett Sprague, by Regimental Master Gunner Anthony Hortle, and by Susan Touch. Denny Neave with his Big Sky Publishing team provided a professional partnership. Space has prevented including ranks of the Army members acknowledged.

John Cox
History Director, RAA Historical Company

APPENDICES
Appendix 1: Artillery Organisation Tables 1-20

Table 1: Australian Artillery 1903[1]

New South Wales	Victoria	Queensland
FIELD FORCE		
Brigade Staff	Brigade Staff	Brigade Staff
A Instr Cadre RAAR	C Instr Cadre RAAR	No 1 Qld Bty AFA
No 1, 3 & 4 NSW Bty AFA	No 1, 2 & 3 Vic Bty AFA	No 2 Qld Bty AFA
GARRISON FORCE		
Garrison Artillery Staff District Establishment	Garrison Artillery Staff District Establishment	District Establishment
District Reserve: No 2 NSW Bty AFA	District Reserve: No 5 & 6 Vic Bty AFA	District Reserve: B Instr Cadre RAAR
Sydney Fortress: No 2, 3 & 4 Coy RAAR No 4 NSW Coy AGA	Port Phillip Fortress: No 5, 6, & 7 Coy RAAR No 1 to 8 Vic Coy AGA	Fort Lytton Garrison: No 8 Coy RAAR (-) No 1 Qld Coy AGA
Botany Garrison: No 1 Coy RAAR No 4 NSW Coy AGA		Townsville Garrison: Det No 8 Coy RAAR No 2 Qld Coy AGA
Wollongong Garrison: No 4 NSW Coy AGA		Thursday Is Garrison: No 9 Coy RAAR No 3 Qld Coy RAA
Newcastle Garrison: No 1 Coy RAAR (-) No 3 NSW Coy AGA		

Table 1: Australian Artillery 1903[1]

South Australia	Western Australia	Tasmania
FIELD FORCE		
No 1 SA Bty AFA	No 1 WA Bty AFA	No 1 Tas Bty AFA
GARRISON FORCE		
District Establishment	District Establishment	District Establishment
District Reserve:	District Reserve: No 2 WA Bty AFA	Southern Reserve: Sect No 2 Tas Bty AFA
Adelaide Garrison: Det No 10 Coy RAAR No 1 SA Coy AGA	Albany Garrison: Det No 10 Coy RAAR No 1 WA Coy AGA	Northern Reserve: Sect No 2 Tas Bty AFA
		Hobart Garrison: Det No 10 Coy RAAR No 1 Tas Coy AGA

Table 2: Divisional Artillery July 1916[2]

1st Australian Division	2nd Australian Division	3rd Australian Division(1)	4th Australian Division	5th Australian Division
HQ 1st Divisional Artillery	HQ 2nd Divisional Artillery	HQ 3rd Divisional Artillery	HQ 4th Divisional Artillery	HQ 5th Divisional Artillery
1st AFA Bde: 1st, 2nd, 3rd Btys 101st How Bty	4th AFA Bde: 10th, 11th, 12th Btys 104th How Bty	7th AFA Bde: 25th 26th 27th Btys 107th How Bty	10th AFA Bde: 37th, 38th, 39th Btys 110 How Bty	13th AFA Bde: 49th, 50th 51st Btys 113th How Bty
2nd AFA Bde: 4th, 5th, 6th Btys 102nd How Bty	5th AFA Bde: 13th 14th, 15th Btys 105th How Bty	8th AFA Bde: 19th 30th, 31st Btys 108th How Bty	11th AFA Bde: 41st, 42nd, 43rd Btys 111th How Bty	14th AFA Bde: 53rd, 54th, 55th Btys 114th How Bty
3rd AFA Bde: 7th, 8th, 9th Btys 103rd How Bty	6th AFA Bde: 16th, 17th, 18th Btys 106th How Bty	9th AFA Bde: 33rd, 34th, 35th Btys 109th How Bty	12th AFA Bde: 45th, 46th, 47th Btys (119th How Bty)	15th AFA Bde: 57th, 58th, 59th Btys (120th How Bty)
21st AFA Bde; 22nd, 23rd, 24th Btys (116th How Bty)	22nd AFA Bde: 19th 20th, 21st Btys (117th How Bty)	23rd AFA Bde: 28th, 32nd, 36th Btys 118th How Bty	24th AFA Bde: 40th, 44th 48th Btys 112th How Bty	25th AFA Bde: 52nd, 56th, 60th Btys 115th How Bty
V1A Heavy Mortar Battery	V2A Heavy Mortar Battery	V3A Heavy Mortar Battery	V4A Heavy Mortar Battery	V5A Heavy Mortar Battery
X1A, Y1A, Z1A MTM Btys	X2A, Y2A, Z2A MTM Btys	X3A, Y3A, Z3A MTM Btys	X4A, Y4A, Z4A MTM Btys	X5A, Y5A, Z5A, MTM Btys
1st Div Ammn Column	2nd Div Ammn Column	3rd Div Ammn Column	4th Div Ammn Column	5th Div Ammn Column

Notes:
The organisation of the 3rd Division's artillery along these lines was not completed until September 1916.
The howitzer batteries shown in brackets were yet to be raised.

Table 3: Australian Field Artillery Early 1917 Onwards[3]

1st Australian Division	2nd Australian Division	3rd Australian Division	4th Australian Division	5th Australian Division	'Army' Brigades AFA
HQ 1st Divisional Artillery	HQ 2nd Divisional Artillery	HQ 3rd Divisional Artillery	HQ 4th Divisional Artillery	HQ 5th Divisional Artillery	
1st AFA Bde: 1st, 2nd, 3rd Btys 101st How Bty	4th AFA Bde: 10th, 11th, 12th Btys 104th How Bty	7th AFA Bde: 25th 26th 27th Btys 107th How Bty	10th AFA Bde: 37th, 38th, 39th Btys 110th How Bty	13th AFA Bde; 49th, 50th, 51st Btys 113th How Bty	3rd Army Bde AFA: 7th, 8th, 9th Btys 103rd How Bty Bde Ammn Column
2nd AFA Bde: 4th, 5th, 6th Btys 102nd How Bty	5th AFA Bde: 13th, 14th, 15th Btys 105th How Bty	8th AFA Bde: 29th, 30th, 31st Btys 108th How Bty	11th AFA Bde: 41st, 42nd, 43rd Btys 111th How Bty	14th AFA Bde 53rd, 54th, 55th Btys 114th How Bty	6th Army Bde AFA: 16th, 17th, 18th Btys 106th How Bty Bde Ammn Column
					12th Army Bde AFA: 45th, 46th, 47th Btys 112th How Bty Bde Ammn Column
V1A Heavy Mortar Bty	V2A Heavy Mortar Bty	V3A Heavy Mortar Bty	V4A Heavy Mortar Bty	V5A Heavy Mortar Bty	
X1A, Y1A, Z1A MTM Bty	X2A, Y2A, Z2A MTM Bty	X3A, Y3A, Z3A MTM Bty	X4A, Y4A, Z4A MTM Bty	X5A, Y5A, Z5A MTM Bty	
1st Div Ammn Column	2nd Div Ammn Column	3rd Div Ammn Column	4th Div Ammn Column	5th Div Ammn Column	

Notes:
All batteries raised from four to six guns by absorbing equipment from disestablished batteries.
In addition to the field artillery, Australia provided the 36th Heavy Artillery Group, artillery training units, and periodic schools

Table 4: Australian Artillery 1924[4]

Table 4A: Field Force

AHQ Melbourne	1st Cav Div (NSW/QLD)	2nd Cav Div (VIC/SA)	1st Inf Div (NSW /QLD)	2nd Inf Div (NSW)
Chief of Artillery			Artillery Commander	Artillery Commander
Artillery School of Instruction	XXI. Bde AFA Paddington	XXII. Bde AFA Richmond	I Bde AFA Newcastle	IX. Bde AFA Paddington
			V. Bde AFA Brisbane	XIV. Bde AFA Marrickville
			VII. Bde AFA Nth Sydney	XVIII Bde AFA Goulburn

Table 4B: District Base

1st Military District (QLD)	2nd Military District (NSW)	3rd Military District (VIC)
Brisbane: 8th Bty RAGA 22nd Bty AGA	Middle Head: 1st Coast Artillery Bde 2nd Bty RAGA 14th Bty AGA	Queenscliff: 2nd Coast Artillery Bde 4th Bty RAGA
Townsville: 21st Bty AGA	Paddington: 1st Bty RAFA 15th, 16th Bty AGA	Geelong: 18th Bty AGA 19th Bty AGA
	South Head: 1st Bty RAGA	Nepean: 5th Bty RAGA
Thursday Island; 9th Bty RAGA	Newcastle: 3rd Bty RAGA 13th Bty AGA	

Table 4: Australian Artillery 1924[4]

Table 4A: Field Force

3rd Inf Div (VIC)	4th Inf Div (VIC/SA)	11th Brigade (QLD)	12th Brigade (TAS)	13th Bde (WA)
Artillery Commander	Artillery Commander			
II. Bde AFA St Kilda	X. Bde AFA Albert Park	XI. Bde AFA Brisbane	VI. Bde AFA Hobart	III. Bde AFA Perth
IV. Bde AFA St Kilda	XV. Bde AFA Albert Park			
VIII. Bde AFA Carlton	XIII. Bde AFA Adelaide			

Table 4B: District Base

4th Military District (SA)	5th Military District (WA)	6th Military District (TAS)
Fort Largs: 10th Bty RAGA 20th Bty AGA	Fremantle: 6th Bty RAGA 23rd Bty AGA	Hobart: 7th Bty RAGA 17th Bty AGA
	Albany: Det 6th Bty RAGA 24th Bty AGA	

Table 5: Armaments of Defence Ports 1940[5]

Table 5A: Coast Armaments of Defended Ports 1940

Northern Command	Eastern Command	Southern Command	Western Command	7th Military District
HQ Brisbane Fortress:	HQ Sydney Fortress:	HQ Port Phillip Fortress:	HQ Fremantle Fortress:	HQ Darwin Fortress:
Cowan Bty 2x6-in Mk XI	Banks Bty 2x9.2-in Mk X	Queenscliff Bty 3x6-in Mk VII	Oliver's Bty 2x9.2-in Mk X	East Bty 2x6-in Mk XI
Bribie Bty 2x6-in Mk XI	Signal Bty 2x6-in Mk XI	Nepean Bty 2x6-in Mk VII	Bickley Bty 2x6-in Mk XI	Emery Bty 2x6-in Mk XI
Lytton Bty 1x4.7-in	Hornby Bty 2x6-in Mk VII	Pearce Bty 2x6-in Mk VII	Swanbourne Bty 2x6-in Mk VII	4xDE Lights
4xDE Lights	Middle Head 2x6-in Mk VII	Franklin Bty 1x4.7-in	Arthurs Bty 2x6-in Mk VII	
	1x12pr	12xDE Lights	7xDE Lights	
	North Bty 2x9.2-in Mk X			
	West Bty 2x4.7-in			
	Kembla Bty 2x6-in Mk XI			
	12xDE Lights			
Townsville: 2x4.7-in				
2xDE Lights				
Thursday Island:	HQ Newcastle Fortress:	HQ Hobart Fortress:	HQ Albany Fortress:	
Goods Bty 2x6-in Mk XI	Scratchley Bty 2x6-in Mk XI	Direction Bty 2x6-in Mk VII	Princess Royal Bty 2x6-in QFC	
Milman Bty 1x4.7-in	Wallace Bty 2x9.2in Mk X	Pierson Bty 1x4-in	2xDE Lights	
5xDE Lights	5xDE Lights	3xDE Lights		
Port Moresby Fortress:		HQ Port Adelaide Fortress;		
Paga Bty 2x6-in Mk XI		Largs Bty 2x6-in Mk VII		
2xDE Lights		2xDE Lights		

Table 5B: Anti-Aircraft Armaments of Defended Areas 1940

Northern Command	Eastern Command	Southern Command	Western Command	7th Military District
	Sydney: 1st AA Bty 4x3.7-in 8x3-in 20cwt 32 AA Lights	Melbourne: 4th AA Bty 4x3.7-in 8x3-in 20cwt	Fremantle: 5th AA Bty 2x3-in 20cwt 13 AA Lights	Darwin: 2nd AA Bty 4x3.7-in 6x3-in 20cwt 21 AA Lights
	Newcastle: 3rd AA Bty 4x3.7-in 6x3-in 20cwt 24 AA Lights			

Table 6: Militia Artillery June 1940[6]

Northern Command (QLD)	Eastern Command (NSW)	Southern Command (VIC/SA/TAS)	Western Command (WA)	7th Military District (NT)
Artillery Commander	Brigadier RAA	Brigadier RAA	Artillery Commander	Artillery Commander
Commander Coast Defences/8th Heavy Bty 121 Heavy Bty 122 Heavy Bty	Commander Coast Defences/CO 1st Heavy Bde 5th Heavy Bde 1st AA Bde	Commander Coast Defences/CO 2nd Heavy Bde 6th Heavy Bde 4th AA Bty	Commander Coast Defences/CO 3rd Heavy Bde 7th Heavy Bde	
Port Moresby Defences 126 Heavy Bty	1st Cavalry Division: 21st Field Bde	2nd Cavalry Division: 22nd Field Bde	3rd Field Bde	Darwin Field Bty
5th Field Bde	1st Infantry Division: Artillery Commander 1st, 7th Field Bdes	3rd Infantry Division: Artillery Commander 2nd, 4th, 8th Field Bdes		
11th Field Bde	2nd Infantry Division: Artillery Commander 9th, 14th, 18th Field Bdes 1st Medium Bde	4th Infantry Division: Artillery Commander 10th, 15th Field Bdes 2nd Medium Bde		
	2 Arty Survey Company	3 Arty Survey Company		
		4th Military District: 13th Field Bde 48 Field Bty, 22nd Field Bde 120 heavy Bty		
		6th Military District: 6th Field Bde 117 Heavy Bty		

Table 7: 2nd AIF Artillery - Middle East Mid-1941[7]

HQ 1st Aust Corps	6th Australian Division	7th Australian Division	9th Australian Division
CCRA: Brig-Gen CA Clowes	Divisional Artillery Commander/ Commander Royal Artillery (CRA): Brig-Gen EF Herring	Divisional Artillery Commander/ Commander Royal Artillery (CRA): Brig-Gen EJ Milford	Divisional Artillery Commander/ Commander Royal Artillery (CRA): Brig-Gen AH Ramsay
Corps Troops Field Artillery: 2/9th Army Field Regt 2/11th Army Field Regt 2/13th Army Field Regt 2/1st Survey Regt	2/1st Field Regt 2/2nd Field Regt 2/3rd Field Regt	2/4th Field Regt 2/5th Field Regt 2/6th Field Regt	2/7th Field Regt 2/8th Field Regt 2/12th Field Regt
	1st Anti-Tank Regiment	2nd Anti-Tank Regiment	3rd Anti-Tank Regiment
Corps Troops AA Artillery: HQ 1st AA Bde 1st AA Regt 2nd HAA Regt 3rd LAA Regt			

Note:
This organisation was based on 1938 British establishments.

Table 8: Field Force Artillery: July 1942[8]

First Army	Second Army
Toowoomba	Melbourne
Brigadier Royal Artillery (BRA)	BRA
	2nd Mdm Regt, 2nd Svy Regt
I Aust Corps. (Toowoomba)	2nd Aust Motor Div:
CCRA	22nd Fd Regt, 48 Fd Bty,
2/9th, 2/11th Army Fd Regts, 2/1st Mdm Regt, 2/1st Svy Regt	105th A-Tk Regt
3rd Aust Inf Div:	
2nd, 4th, 8th Fd Regts	*32nd US Div*
106th A-Tk Regt	*41st US Div*
7th Aust Inf Div:	
2/4th, 2/5th, 2/6th Fd Regts	12th Aust Inf Bde Gp:
2/2nd A-Tk Regt	6th Fd Regt, 110th A-Tk Regt
II Aust Corps (Sydney)	
CCRA	
1stMdm Regt, 12th Army Fd Regt;	
Z Tp,18 Fd Bty; 1st Svy Regt	
1st Aust Div:	
9th, 19th Fd Regts, 111th A-Tk Regt	
2nd Aust Div:	
7th, 18th Fd Regts, 104th A-Tk Regt	
10th Aust Div:	
1st, 20th Fd Regts, 103rd A-Tk Regt	
5th Aust Div:	
2/3rd, 5th, 17th Fd Regts, 101st A-Tk Regt	
1st Aust Motor Div:	
21st Fd Regt, 102nd A-Tk Regt	

Table 8: Field Force Artillery: July 1942[8]

III Aust Corps	NT Force	Reserve
Perth	Darwin	
Corps Commander Royal Artillery (CCRA)	BRA	
4th Aust Div: 3rd, 10th 15th Fd Regts, 109th A-Tk Regt	2/14th, 11th Fd Regts; Y Tp, 18Fd Bty. M & 14th A-Tk Btys	1st Aust Armd Div: 16th Fd Regt, 108th A-Tk Regt

	NG Force	Overseas
	Pt Moresby	6th Aust Div (Ceylon) 2/1st, 2/2nd Fd Regts,
	CRA	1st A-Tk Regt
	13th, 14th Fd Regts	9th Aust Div (M-East) 2/7th, 2/8th, 2/12th Fd Regts, 3rd A-Tk Regt, 4th LAA Regt

Table 9: Fixed Defences Artillery July 1942[9]

	Qld LofC Area	NSW LofC Area	VIC LofC Area	SA LofC Area	WA LofC Area	TAS LofC Area	NT	New Guinea
Heavy Artillery								
HQ Fixed Defences	Brisbane Townsville Thursday Is	Sydney Newcastle Kembla Jervis Bay	Port Phillip	Adelaide	Fremantle Albany	Hobart	Darwin	Port Moresby
Anti-Aircraft Artillery								
HQ AA Defences	South Queensland 2/2nd HAA Regt (-) 113th LAA Regt 6th, 38th AA Btys North Queensland 223rd, 224th LAA Btys	Sydney AA Gp: 110th LAA Regt 111th LAA Regt 1st, 7th, 9th, 15th 19th, 20th, 25th AA Btys; 221st LAA Bty Newcastle AA Gp: 3rd, Sec 7th, 18th AA Bty 222nd LAA Bty Kembla AA Gp: 8th AA Bty	Melbourne AA Gp: 112th LAA Regt 4th, 10th, 11th, 28th, 30th, 31st AA Btys	12th, 26th AA Btys	2/3rd LAA Regt (-) 116th LAA Regt 5th, 29th AA Btys	13th AA Bty	Darwin AA Gp: 2/1st LAA Regt (-) 2nd, 14th, 22nd AA Btys	AA Bde NG Force: HAA Regt LAA Regt Milne Bay: sec 23rd AA Bty; 2/6th HAA Bty; 2/9th LAA Bty

Table 10: Operational Formations July 1943[10]

LHQ Melbourne	HQ First Army Toowoomba	HQ Second Army Sydney	HQ III Aust Corps Perth	HQ NG Force Port Moresby	HQ NT Force Darwin	LHQ Reserve
MGRA Maj-Gen Whitelaw	BRA Brig-Gen Barker	BRA Brig-Gen St Clair	CCRA Brig-Gen Klein	CCRA Brig-Gen Sewell	BRA Brig-Gen O'Brien	
BRA Brig-Gen Chalmers	Brigadier AA and Coast Artillery: Brig-Gen Neylan					
	II Aust Corps: CCRA Brig-Gen Ramsay	1st Div: CRA Brig-Gen Friend	1st Armd Div: CRA Brig-Gen Kitto	3rd Div: CRA Colonel Jackson (US Army)		4th Div: CRA Brig-Gen de Low
	6th Aust Div: CRA Brig –Gen Cremor		2nd Div: CRA Brig-Gen Doyle=	5th Div: CRA Brig-Gen Moriarty		
	7th Aust Div: CRA Brig-Gen Eastick			11th Div: CRA Brig-Gen Daly		
	9th Aust Div: CRA Brig-Gen Goodwin					
	3rd Armd Div					

Table 11: Anti-Aircraft Units in New Guinea October–November 1943[11]

Location	Type	Commander	Equipment
Port Moresby	AA Defence Command	COL J Wrean (USA)	30 static 3.7-in guns; 29 mobile 40mm Bofors
Milne Bay	AA Defence Command	LTCOL J Mc Conkey	13 static, seven mobile 3.7-in guns
Oro Bay	2/2nd Composite AA Regt	LTCOL K Dalton	Eight 3.7-in guns; twelve 40mm Bofors at Buna
Wau	LAA Bty		Six 40mm Bofors at Wau; six 40mm Bofors at Bulolo
Merauke	52nd Composite AA Regt	LTCOL J England	Eight static 3.7-in guns; twelve 40mm Bofors
Morobe	HAA Bty; 162 LAA Bty		Eight static 3.7-in guns; six 40mm Bofors
Nassau Bay	LAA Bty		Twelve 40mm Bofors
Lae	2/3rd Composite AA Regt		Eight mobile 3.7-in guns; twelve 40mm Bofors
Finschhafen	2/1st Composite AA Regt	LTCOL A Hitchman	Eight static 3.7-in guns; twelve 40mm Bofors
Sattelberg	2/4th LAA Regt	MAJ J Pagan	Thirty-six 40mm Bofors

Table 12: Artillery December 1944[12]

First	Army (Lae)	I Aust Corps (Atherton)	Second Army (Sydney)	NT Force
BRA 2/11th Fd Regt (Nadzab) 'U' heavy Battery (Bougainville) HQ II Aust Corps 2nd Mountain Bty 3rd Division: 2nd, 4th Fd Regts 3rd Svy Bty Torokina Base Area: 554 LAA Bty (static) Outer Islands: 32nd HAA Bty (static) (New Britain) 5th Division: 2/14th Fd Regt 5th Svy Bty Jacquinot Bay Base Area: 472 HAA Tp (static)	(Aitape-Wewak) 6th Aust Division: 2/1st, 2/2nd, 2/3rd Fd Regts 2/1st Tk-A Regt 2/6th Svy Bty Port Moresby Base Area: Moresby Coast Arty 801 AA/CA Bty Lae Base Area: 31 HAA Bty **First Army Rear Details** 11th Division: 2/1st Mdm, 13th Fd Regt 1st Mountain Bty 4th Svy Bty 2/3rd Force Spt Bty Merauke Force: 52nd Composite AA Regt Brisbane, Townsville, Torres Strait Coast Arty	CCRA Corps Troops: 2/9th Fd Regt 2nd Mdm Regt 2/1st Composite AA Regt 53rd Composite AA Regt 2/4th LAA Regt 1st Base Sub-Area; 2/2nd Composite AA Regt 2/3rd Composite AA Regt 7th Aust Division: 2/4th, 2/5th, 2/6th Fd Regts 2/2nd Tk-A Regt 2/7th Svy Bty 9th Aust Division: 2/7th, 2/8th, 2/12th Fd Regts 2/3rd Tk-A Regt 8th Svy Bty	BRA 16th Fd Regt 51st Composite AA Regt 112th LAA Regt Sydney, Newcastle, Kembla Fortresses 2nd AA Group **Western Command (Perth)** Fremantle Fortress 8th AA Group	1st Fd Regt 2nd Svy Bty AA Defence Command: 54th Composite AA Regt 55th Composite AA Regt **LHQ Melbourne** LHQ Schools Of Arty (Fd/AA/CA/AASL) 1st Aust Naval Bombardment Group

Table 13: Field Force Artillery 1947[13]

Army HQ	1st Infantry Bde / ARA / Three Inf Bn / One Armd Regt	2nd Division / CMF / One Inf Bde (Qld) / Two Inf Bde(NSW)	3rd Division / CMF / Two Inf Bde (Vic) / One Inf Bde (SA)	1st Armd Bde Gp / CMF / Two Armd Bde / Four Armd Regt	13th Inf Bde Gp / CMF / Two Inf Bn	Corps Troops / CMF
Directorate of Artillery						
School of Artillery	1st Fd Regt Georges Hts, NSW	HQ RAA Sydney, NSW	HQ RAA Melbourne, Vic			2nd Mdm Regt St Kilda, Vic
		5th Fd Regt Marrickville, NSW	2nd Fd Regt Melbourne, Vic	22nd Fd Regt Brighton, Vic	3rd Fd Regt Karakatta, WA	
	4th Tk-A Bty Puckapunyal, Vic	7th Fd Regt Willoughby, NSW	10th Fd Regt Melbourne, Vic			1st HAA Regt Haberfield, NSW
	5th LAA Bty Sth Head, NSW	11th Fd Regt Kelvin Grove, Qld	13th Fd Regt Keswick, SA			3rd Comp AA Regt Bulimba. Qld
		3rd Tk-A Regt Belmore, NSW	6th Tk-A Regt Tasmania			Combined Ops Bombardment Regt Sth Head, NSW
		1st LAA Regt Mosman, NSW	2nd LAA Regt Melbourne/ Geelong Vic			1st Corps Obsn Regt (Raising deferred)
		2nd Div Loc Bty Sth Head, NSW (Raising deferred)	3rd Div Loc Bty Richmond, Vic (Raising Deferred)			HQ 1st Air OP Sqn (Raising deferred)
		'A' Air Op Flt Sydney, NSW (Raising deferred)	'B' Air OP Flt Melbourne, Vic (Raising deferred)			'C' Air Op Flt (Raising deferred)

Table 14: Fixed Defences 1947[14]

Eastern Command (NSW)	Western Command (WA)	4th Military District (SA)	6th Military District (Tas)	8th Military District (NT)
HQ 1st Fixed Def Bde ARA South Head	HQ 3rd Fixed Def Bde ARA Fremantle	4th MD CA Cadre Fort Largs	6th MD CA Cadre Fort Direction	
1st CA Bty ARA South Head	6th CA Bty ARA Fremantle/Rottnest			8th CA Bty CMF Dudley Point
2nd CA Bty ARA South Head	11th CA Bty ARA Fremantle/Rottnest			9th CA Bty ARA Dudley Point (Part raised)
5th CA Regt CMF (Raising deferred)	7th CA Regt CMF (Raising deferred)			
1st Static AA Regt CMF (Raising deferred)	5th Static AA Regt CMF (Raising deferred)			

Table 15: Artillery Organisation 1953[15]

Army HQ	Northern Command (Qld)	Eastern Command (NSW)	Southern Command (VIC)	Central Command (SA)	Western Comd (WA)	Tasmania Command	NT Comd
Directorate of Artillery		1st Fd Regt					
School of Artillery		2nd Division: 5th Fd Regt 7th Fd Regt 21st Fd Regt 3rd Lt Regt 1st Amphibious Observation Regt 1st Movement Light Bty(1) 31st Div Loc Bty	3rd Division: 2nd Fd Regt 10th Fd Regt 22nd Fd Regt (SP)	13th Fd Regt		6th Fd Regt	
	HQ 5 AGRA: 11th Fd Regt 30th Mdm Regt 12th Lt Regt 3rd LAA/SL Regt 22nd Mobile Coast Artillery Bty	HQ 1 AGRA: 1st HAA Regt 23rd HAA Regt 1st LAA Regt 18th LAA Regt	HQ 2 AGRA: 2nd Mdm Regt 31st Mdm Regt 15th Lt Regt HQ 4 AGRA: 2nd HAA Regt 36th HAA Regt 40th HAA Regt 2nd LAA Regt 38th LAA/SL Regt 3rd AA Control & Reporting Tp 30th AA Fire Comd Bty		3rd Fd Regt 25th Coast AA Bty		26th Mdm Coast Bty
		25th Coast Regt					

Australian Regular Army elements shown in blue

Notes:

1. A Movement Light Battery was a searchlight sub-unit whose task was to provide battlefield illumination

Table 16: Pentropic Artillery Organisation 1960-63[16]

1st Division	3rd Division
HQ RAA (Sydney)	HQ RAA (Melbourne)
1st Fd Regt (Sydney)	2nd Fd Regt (Melbourne)
4th Fd Regt (Brisbane)	3rd Fd Regt (Perth)
5th Fd Regt (Brisbane)	11th Fd Regt (Brisbane)
7th Fd Regt (Sydney)	13th Fd Regt (Adelaide)
23rd Fd Regt (Sydney)	15th Fd Regt (Melbourne)
131st Div Loc Bty (Sydney)	132 Div Loc Bty (Melbourne)

Combat Support Group

10th Mdm Regt (Geelong)

18th LAA Regt (Sydney)

130th Corps Loc Regt (Melbourne)

Combat Support Group

112th Fd Bty

Australian Regular Army elements shown in blue

Table 17: Artillery Structure 1976[17]

Table 17A: Field Force Command

HQ Field Force (FF) Command	1st Division	1st FF Gp	2nd Div FF Gp	3rd Div FF Gp	4th FF Gp	5th FF Gp	6th FF Gp
Commander FF Arty	Commander Divisional Artillery		Colonel, Artillery	Colonel, Artillery			
	Holsworthy (1st TF) 8th/12th Mdm Regt 131st Div Loc Bty	Brisbane 5/11th Fd Regt	Willoughby/ Newcastle 7th Fd Regt 113rd LAA Bty	Melbourne 2nd/15th Fd Regt	Keswick 48th Fd Bty	Karrakatta 7th Fd Bty	Launceston 16th Fd Bty
	Townsville (3rd TF) 4th Fd Regt		Belmore 18th/23rd Fd Regt	Geelong 10th Mdm Regt			
	Enoggera (6th TF) 1st Fd Regt		Manly 133rd Div Loc Bty	Brighton 132nd Div Loc Bty			
	Div Troops 16th AD Regt						

Australian Regular Army elements shown in blue

Table 17B: Training Command

School Of Artillery (North Head).
Seven Training Groups

Table 18: Land Command Artillery June 1991[18]

ARA

Ready Deployment Force (3rd Bde) (Townsville)	1st Brigade (Holsworthy) (1)	Force Troops (Adelaide)
4th Fd Regt	8th/12th Mdm Regt	16th AD Regt (2)
131st Div Loc Bty (Enoggera)		

Notes:
It was planned that 1st Brigade would move to Darwin in the coming decade.
16th AD Regt included a RRES component

RRES

Ready Reserve (7th) Task Force
(Brisbane)

1st Fd Regt

ARES

4th Bde (Vic)	5th Bde (NSW)	7th Bde (Qld)	8th Bde (NSW)	9th Bde (Tas/SA)	11th Bde (Qld)	13th Bde (WA)
2nd/10th Mdm Regt	23rd Fd Regt	5th Fd Regt	7th Fd Regt	6th/13th Fd Regt	11th Fd Regt	3rd Fd Regt

Table 19: Land Command Artillery 2000[19]

ARA

3rd Bde (Townsville)	1st Brigade (Darwin)	Force Troops (Adelaide)
4th Fd Regt	8th/12th Mdm Regt	16th AD Regt
107th Fd Bty	A Fd Bty	110 AD Bty (Rapier)
108th Fd Bty	101st Mdm Bty	111 AD Bty (RBS-70)
	103rd Mdm Bty	

ARA/ARES

7th TF
(Brisbane)

1st Fd Regt
102nd Fd Bty (RTA Trials)
13th Fd Bty
41st Fd Bty
104th Fd Bty
105th Fd Bty

131st Div Loc Bty

ARES

4th Bde (Vic)	5th Bde (NSW)	8th Bde (NSW)	9th Bde (Tas/SA)	11th Bde (Qld)	13th Bde (WA)
2nd/10th Mdm Regt	23rd Fd Regt	7th Fd Regt	48th Fd Bty	16th Fd Bty	7th Fd Bty
38th Mdm Bty	10th Fd Bty	28th Fd Bty			
22nd Fd Bty	11th Fd Bty	113th Fd Bty			

Table 20: Forces Command Artillery 2021[20]

1st Brigade	3rd Brigade	7th Brigade	6th Combat Support Brigade	16th Aviation Brigade	17th Sustainment Brigade
8/12th Regiment RAA	4th Regiment RAA	1st Regiment RAA	16th Regiment RAA		
101st Bty	106th Bty	A Bty	110th Air Land Bty		
102nd Bty	107th Bty	104th Bty	111th Air Land Bty		
103rd Bty	109th Bty	105th Bty	1st Air-Ground Ops Bty		
			20th Regiment RAA		
			131st STA Bty		
			132nd UAV Bty		

2nd DIVISION

4th and 9th Brigades	11th and 13th Brigades	5th Brigade
	9th Regiment RAA	
2nd/10th Lt Bty	15th/11th Lt Bty	7th Lt Bty
6th/13th Lt Bty	3rd Lt Bty	23rd Lt Bty

Australian Regular Army elements shown in blue

Appendix 2: Glossary of Artillery and Military Terms

TERM	MEANING
Advanced Field Artillery Tactical Data System (AFATDS)	Digital fire support command and control system employed by US Army, Marine Corps and Australian Army units to provide automated support for planning, coordinating, controlling and executing fires and effects.
Al-Muthanna Task Group (AMTG) later, Overwatch Battle Group (West) (OBG(W))	Australian Army unit-level combat task group deployed to Al Muthanna province in Southern Iraq under Multi-National Force-Iraq, providing security initially to the Japanese Iraq Reconstruction and Support Group and other forces, to contribute to the security and rehabilitation of Iraq. The AMTG (2005–6) transitioned to the OBG (W) (2006–2008) in July 2006.
Army	A group of corps.
Army Brigades Field Artillery	Field artillery brigades at the disposal of an Army Commander.
Army Group Royal Artillery (AGRA)	A group of artillery units at the disposal of an Army Commander.
Artillery Board	A square board with a gridded cover to which is affixed a range arm pivoted at the battery location and a bearing arc. Used the determine bearing and range to a target.
Artillery Intelligence	The collation of material relating to hostile batteries and artillery systems.
Artillery Training Team – Kabul (ATT-K): later Artillery Training Advisory Team (ATAT)	Australian Army-led artillery training team composed primarily of RAA personnel, and was responsible for wider artillery training within the Afghan National Army's Training Command 2010–2013.
At Priority Call	A control term denoting priority of effort to a nominated entity.
Australian Army Training Team-Iraq (AATT-I)	Australian Army contribution to the reconstruction and rehabilitation of Iraq under Multi-National Force-Iraq, responsible for training and supporting the Iraqi Army, mostly in the Al Muthanna province 2004-2008.
Australian Field Artillery (AFA)	The title of the militia and Australian Imperial Force field artillery from 1903 to 1936.
Australian Garrison Artillery (AGA)	The title of the militia garrison artillery from 1903 to 1936.
Australian Imperial Force (AIF)	The title of the Australian expeditionary forces in World War I (AIF) and World War II (2nd AIF).
Australian Regular Army (ARA)	The title of the permanent military forces post-1947.
Battlespace domains	Physical and virtual divisions of the modern battlespace, including the physical: land, air, space, sea (and sub-sea); and virtual: (electromagnetic and information/cyber).
Bearing Picket (BP)	A survey control point in the form of a picket at the gun position bearing the surveyed map coordinates and bearing to a reference point.
Brigadier General Heavy Artillery (BGHA)	The senior Heavy Artillery officer at Corps HQ in World War I.
Brigadier General Royal Artillery (BGRA)	The artillery adviser appointment employed at Corps HQ from 1914 to mid-1916.

TERM	MEANING
British Expeditionary Force (BEF)	The British military forces employed on the Western Front in World War I.
Centre of Arc (CoA)	Term for the bearing from the gun position to the centre of the target zone on which guns were aligned, in use from the mid-1950s onwards. See also Zero Line.
Civil-Military Cooperation (CIMIC) (related to Civil-Military Operations and Civil Affairs)	Cooperative efforts among military and civil authority agencies, including host nation governments and agencies, and Non-Government Organisations, for facilitating understanding of military intent sand actions in the community.
Commander Royal Artillery (CRA)	The Commander of the Divisional Artillery.
Concentration	Fire applied to a single target location.
Concurrency pressure	Stress imposed on military forces arising from multiple contemporary commitments, leading to shortfall in capacity and increased burnout of forces, due to the extended scale and tempo of operations.
Continuous Full-Time Service (CFTS)	Form of Australian Army Service where Reserve personnel are employed under Regular Army conditions of service for a contracted period.
Corps	A group of Divisions.
Corps Commander Royal Artillery (CCRA)	The title of the artillery commander at Corps HQ in World War II.
Corps Troops	Troops commanded by a Corps outside of the Divisional structures.
Counter-Battery/ Bombardment (CB)	Engagement of the enemy's guns and mortars.
Counter-Rockets, Artillery and Mortar (C-RAM) System	Early warning, cueing and response system that detects incoming indirect fire, and initiates warning alarms to targeted personnel, as well as initiating responses, such as the launch of reconnaissance and surveillance systems to search the point of origin, and in some cases retaliatory indirect fire at the calculated point of origin.
Counter-Improvised Explosive Device Task Force (CIEDTF)	Joint ADF task force created to develop counter-measures against the production, provision and employment of improvised explosive devices by global terrorist and non-conventional forces.
Creeping Barrage	A barrage with a number of lines covering the area from the enemy front to the objective and beyond, in which the fire is lifted from line to line at intervals determined by the attacker's planned rate of advance.
Defensive Fire (DF)	Fire planned and recorded to provide rapid and effective defensive engagement.
Depression Range Finder	A coast artillery fire control instrument measuring range and bearing to a target from an elevated position.
Digital Terminal Control System (DTCS)	Targeting system utilised by Joint Terminal Attack Controllers (JTACs) and Joint Forward Observers (JFOs) to request and coordinate offensive support missions delivered by land, sea or air platforms.
Direct Fire	Fire where the target is visible from the gun or weapon system.
Disappearing Gun	A gun on a hydro-pneumatic mounting where the force of recoil lowers the gun into a pit for loading in defilade, at the same time storing the energy for it to be raised to the firing position.
Division	A group of brigades or land force formations.
Empty Battlefield/Empty Battlespace	Describes the perception that a soldier is virtually alone on the battlefield; describes the changed appearance of the battlefield when soldiers begin dispersing and seeking cover in response to increasing lethality of weapon systems.

TERM	MEANING
Enhanced Land Force (ELF)	Australian Government growth initiative and commitment to the Australian Army, announced in August 2006.
Field Artillery Brigade (FAB)	A group of field artillery batteries (see also Field Regiment).
Field Regiment (Fd Regt)	A group of field artillery batteries.
Fixation	The map location of a (fixed) point.
Formation	The collective name for a group of Army units. See also Brigade.
Forward Operating Base (FOB)	A secure forward operational-level military position, commonly a military base that is employed to support tactical objectives and strategic goals.
General Officer Commanding Royal Artillery (GOCRA)	The artillery commander at Corps HQ from mid-1916 to 1918.
Green Zone	Term used to describe vegetated and often irrigated land flanking natural and artificial watercourses across Afghanistan. Contrasts to the 'Dasht' (desert plain), describing the more open flat or undulating arid terrain beyond the watered land.
Gunnery Problem, The	The persistent and fundamental challenge for artillery to acquire adversary targets, determine the requisite effect, and engage those targets effectively. Key functional elements include the target, the observer (target acquisition), the computation mechanism, the decision mechanism, and the delivery system.
Hardened and Networked Army (HNA)	Australian Government growth initiative and commitment to the Australian Army, launched in December 2005.
Heavy Artillery Group (HAG)	A unit containing heavy artillery batteries.
High Trust Communications	Communications networks considered highly reliable in persistence and reach, and having negligible potential to be hacked or intercepted.
Impromptu Fire	Fire that is not programmed.
In Direct Support (DS)	A control term denoting provision of observation, communication and liaison to a designated unit, along with immediate response to calls for fire
In Support	A control term denoting the provision of fire to a designated unit if not employed on a higher priority task.
Indirect Fire	Fire in which the target is not visible from the gun.
Infantry Division	A group of infantry brigades, with an integral allocation of artillery and other arms and services, so as to be able to operate independently.
Integration	The arrangement of military forces and their actions to create a force that operates by engaging as a whole.
Intelligence Preparation of the Battlespace (IPB) also Intelligence Preparation of the Operating Environment (IPOE)	The prior acquisition of all natures of intelligence necessary to inform the effective planning and execution of military operations.
International Stabilisation Assistance Force (ISAF)	Multinational military mission led by NATO in Afghanistan 2001–2014, initially to facilitate the formation of the Afghan Transitional Administration, then expanded to provide and maintain security beyond the capital across the country.
International Stabilisation Force (ISF)	Australian-led intervention force deployed under Operation Astute 2006–2013, on request from the Timor-Leste government in August 2006, in response to loss of internal security and law and order.
Interoperability	The ability of military equipment or groups to operate in conjunction with each other.
Joint Fires	Fire Support originating from, and coordinated across, all Defence Services.

TERM	MEANING
Joint Offensive Support Coordination Centre (JOSCC) later, Joint Fires and Effects Coordination Centre (JFECC)	Artillery-led coordination centre established at manoeuvre unit-level or higher, designed to coordinate all forms of joint fires and effects, including non-lethal effects.
Joint Offensive Support Team (JOST) later, Joint Fires Team (JFT)	Artillery forward observer party, capable of coordinating joint forms of offensive support.
Joint Terminal Attack Controller (JTAC)	Military term replacing 'Forward Air Controller' to reflect the appointment's enhanced ability to terminally control all forms of joint fires, in particular the terminal guidance of air- or artillery-delivered precision guided munitions.
Jungle Division	The Divisional structure for fighting in New Guinea adopted by Australia in 1942.
Land 17, Project	An Australian Defence land capability acquisition project. Land 17's purpose was to enhance the Australian Army's indirect fire system through the replacement of the L119 field and M198 medium howitzers, and the introduction of enhanced battle management and targeting systems and precision/near precision munitions.
Limber	A wheeled trailer carrying ammunition and gun stores positioned between the horse team/towing vehicle and the gun.
Locating Artillery	Artillery entities providing survey, meteorology, target location and artillery intelligence to assist the field artillery.
Major-General Royal Artillery (MGRA)	The senior artillery officer at an Army Headquarters.
Mentoring & Reconstruction Task Force (MRTF)	Two rotations of Australian Army contribution to the Dutch-led Task Force-Uruzgan, with the mission of providing reconstruction support and assistance to local Afghan government and community, and provision of mentoring support to Afghan National Army Kandaks (battalions) 2008–2010.
Mentoring Task Force (MTF)	Five rotations of Australian Army contribution to the US-led Combined Team-Uruzgan (CTU), with the mission of providing mentoring support to Afghan National Army Kandaks (battalions) 2010–2012. The final MTF-5 was replaced by two successive rotations of Advisory Task Force (ATF) 2012–2014.
Militia	Paid, part-time soldiers.
Neutralisation	The prevention of an enemy from using his weapons or carrying out his intentions effectively. See also Suppression.
Non-Lethal Effects (NLE)	Battlespace effects generated to impede, obstruct or neutralise adversaries, such as information operations, electronic warfare and cyber operations.
Non-Lethal Targeting	The application of the same principles of approach used in targeting for lethal force – that is, precision acquisition of the target, identification, discrimination, application of Rules of Engagement, collateral damage assessment, mechanism for engagement effects assessment, and options for re-attack as required and recording – to the employment of non-lethal force.
Operation Anode	The Australian operational commitment to stabilisation operations in the Solomon Islands, 2003–2017.
Operation Catalyst	The Australian operational commitment to stabilisation operations in Iraq 2003–2009.
Operation Falconer	The Australian operational contribution to the direct combat operations by United States and other coalition forces against Saddam Hussein's Iraqi military forces 2003.
Operation Okra	The Australian contribution to the international effort to combat the Islamic State in Iraq and the Levant (Da'esh) terrorist threat in Iraq and Syria from 2014.

TERM	MEANING
Operation Slipper	The Australian operational commitment to stabilisation operations in Afghanistan 2001–2014.
Operational Mentoring Liaison Team (OMLT)	ISAF military teams partnering with elements of Afghan National Security Forces, to provide training and mentoring to Afghan forces, liaison with ISAF forces, and coordination of planning operations and provision of enabling support.
Orientation	Alignment of the guns in relation to grid (map) North.
Pentropic Division	A divisional structure based on five battle groups adopted for a short period in the 1960s.
Point Defence (missile launcher)	Air defence systems deployed in individual or small array, thus able to defend one geographic point only.
Position Finder	A coast artillery fire control instrument measuring range and distance to a target.
Preliminary Bombardment/ Preparatory Fire	Bombardment/fire prior to an assault or offensive operation
Programmed Fire	Fire that is laid out in a program, typically to support an attack or to defend a position. Also called a fire plan.
Provincial Reconstruction Team (PRT)	Intervention team concept originally devised by the United States government, consisting of military officers, diplomats, and reconstruction subject matter experts, working to support reconstruction efforts in unstable states. Their purpose was to empower local governments to govern their constituents more effectively.
Quick Firing (QF)	A type of ordnance where a brass cartridge case contains the propellant and prevents the rearward escape of propellant gases.
Ranging	The adjustment of fall of shot onto a target.
Ready Reserve (RRES)	Form of Army Reserve Service that commenced with one year of permanent service, followed by a higher requirement of Reserve commitment from 50 to 100 days per year.
Reconstruction Task Force (RTF)	Four rotations of Australian Army contributions to the Dutch-led Task Force-Uruzgan, with the mission of providing reconstruction support and assistance to local Afghan government and community, and provision of engineer training to Afghan National Army 2006–2008.
Regional Force Surveillance Units (RFSU)	Specialised infantry units of the Australian Army Reserve responsible for patrolling northern Australia.
Registration	The determination of firing data for the purpose of future engagement either by ranging or by prediction (silent registration).
Revolution in Military Affairs (RMA)	A momentous change in the conduct of military operations that fundamentally alters the nature and conduct of warfare.
Royal Australian Artillery (RAA)	The title granted to the permanent artillery forces of Queensland, New South Wales and Victoria in 1899, remaining in force until 1902. The title granted to the permanent artillery in 1927, and the part-time artillery in 1936.
Royal Australian Artillery Regiment	The title of the permanent artillery from 1902 to 1911.
Royal Australian Field Artillery (RAFA)	The title of the permanent field artillery from 1911 to 1927.
Royal Australian Garrison Artillery (RAGA)	The title of the permanent Garrison artillery from 1911 to 1927.
Royal Regiment of Australian Artillery	The title of the Royal Australian Artillery from 1962 onwards.

TERM	MEANING
Security Detachment (SecDet)	Australian armoured and infantry elements committee to Iraq, 2003–2011, to protect the Australian Embassy and diplomats, and to provide escort security for Australian staff and VIPs.
Sensor-to-Shooter network	Describes the nodes and linkages required to connect one or more acquisition sensors, through analysis, decision and execution decision mechanisms, to response assets that may be lethal or non-lethal in nature.
Siege Brigade	A heavy artillery group/brigade formed by RAGA (and RGA) personnel for service in World War I.
Standing Barrage	A single line of barrage fire, normally placed on a line of enemy defences.
Standoff	Characteristic of engagement whereby the adversary can be engaged successfully at sufficient range or under such conditions where the adversary is unable to respond with retaliatory fire.
Strike Cell	Coordination and execution centre for US or Coalition joint fires and effects, and fusion of intelligence surveillance, target acquisition and reconnaissance information, established at divisional or higher levels of command.
Superimposition	The firing during programmed shooting of two batteries on the same target, so that one might be removed to engage an un-planned target without diminishing the required programmed effect.
Support or Suppression (SOS) Lines	A line of close defensive fire on which guns were laid when not involved in other tasks.
Suppression	See Neutralisation.
Task Force	A task-organised formation of combat and supporting units within a Pentropic, Tropical Warfare or contemporary division.
Theatre (of Operations)	Geographically defined area within which a series of related and grouped military operations and/or campaigns are undertaken.
Threat to Force	Military threat defined through its potential to inflict physical or moral damage to personnel and organisations deployed.
Threat to Mission	Military threat defined through its potential to impede or prevent the successful outcome of a mission.
Tropical Warfare Division	The Divisional structure adopted in the mid-1960s.
Under Command	A command term meaning the artillery unit and its fire is at the disposal of the entity to which it is so allotted.
Uncrewed Aerial System (UAS)	Describes the entire capability system of military unmanned flight operations, including airframes, ground control station, command and control nodes, observation and advice elements), whereas the term UAV describes the airframes specifically.
Uncrewed Aerial Vehicle (UAV)	Aircraft controlled from a terrestrial control station, commonly known as a drone, equipped with on-board sensors and in some instances weapon munitions. UAVs such as the Shadow also termed Tactical UAVs (TUAV).
Zero Line	The name of the bearing from the gun position to the centre of the target zone on which guns were aligned until the mid-1950s. See also Centre of Arc.

Appendix 3: Significant Dates in Colonial Australian Artillery History

This appendix summarises the significant changes in the organisation and deployment of Australian artillery formed contingents, batteries and organisations. For operational deployments of formed artillery contingents, the first rotation only is denoted.

Date	Federal	New South Wales	Victoria	Queensland	Tasmania	South Australia	Western Australia
1854		21 August: first volunteer artillery corps raised in New South Wales.[21]				14 September: first volunteer artillery corps raised in South Australia.[22]	
1856			1 January: first volunteer artillery corps formed in Victoria by redesignation and reorganisation of an existing volunteer infantry corps.[23]				
1858			2 October: Her Majesty Queen Victoria grants the accolade 'Royal' to the Victoria Volunteer Artillery Regiment.[24]				
1859					10 December: first Volunteer Artillery corps raised in Tasmania.[25]		
1862				30 August: first volunteer artillery unit raised in Queensland.[26]	8 March: School of Artillery established in Argyle Street, Hobart, Tasmania, fitted out partially as a battery and partially as a lecture room.[27]		
1870	25 August: The 1st Battery, 1st Brigade of the Royal Artillery, and the 2nd Battalion, 18th (Royal Irish) Regiment of Foot, the last British garrison, depart the Australian colonies.[28]		20 October: The Victorian Government announces the establishment of the Victorian 'Artillery Corps'.[29]				

Date	Federal	New South Wales	Victoria	Queensland	Tasmania	South Australia	Western Australia
1871		1 August: New South Wales Artillery raised as a component of the NSW Permanent Force.[30]	1 January: first permanent artillery unit, the Victorian Artillery Corps, raised.[31]				
1873							23 January: The Union Troop of Western Australian Mounted Volunteers, which had undergone training with field guns since early 1871, were renamed the "Western Australian Troop of Volunteer Horse Artillery", the first formed artillery corps in WA.[32]
1880			31 December: the Victorian Artillery is effectively disbanded.[33]				
1882			31 July: Establishment of a Battery of Garrison Artillery, totalling 125 all ranks.[34]			25 July: South Australian Artillery raised as a permanent battery.[35]	
1885	27 February: a field battery, part of the *Soudan Expedition Contingent*, formed from the New South Wales Artillery and the New South Wales Volunteer Artillery for service in the Soudan.[36]	8 September: School of Gunnery established as a permanent training establishment of the NSW Military Forces.[37]		24 February: permanent artillery unit raised in Queensland.[38]			
1886					10 September: Tasmanian Permanent Artillery raised.[39]		
1891			9 October: precedence of 'Right of the Line' over the Victorian Cavalry granted to the Victorian Horse Artillery when on parade with its guns.[40]				
1892			Victorian Garrison Artillery redesignated as the Victorian Permanent Artillery.[41]				

Date	Federal	New South Wales	Victoria	Queensland	Tasmania	South Australia	Western Australia
1893							28 February: Western Australian Artillery formed as a permanent corps, originally from personnel recruited and trained in South Australia.[42]
1899	14 July: A despatch of this date from the Secretary of State for the Colonies to the Governors of Queensland, New South Wales, and Victoria, notifies that the designation of Queensland, etc., Regiment of Royal Australian Artillery, was conferred on the Permanent Artillery of Queensland, New South Wales and Victoria by Her Majesty Queen Victoria.	The effective dates on which these three colonies acted to change the designation of their Regiments are: Queensland – Chief Secretary's Office letter dated 23 August 1899.[43] New South Wales – Premier's Office letter dated 01 September 1899 with an effective date of 24 August 1899.[44] Victoria – Premier's Office letter dated 13 September 1899.[45]					
1899		30 December: A Battery, NSW Regiment RAA, embarked for service in the Anglo-Boer War.		1 November: the Machine Gun Section, Queensland Regiment RAA, embarked for service in the Anglo-Boer War with the First Queensland Contingent.			

245

Appendix 4: Significant Dates in Commonwealth Australian Artillery History

Date	Event
1902	1 July: The three state Regiments of Royal Australian Artillery and the permanent artillery of the remaining three states amalgamate as the Royal Australian Artillery.[46]
1903	1 July: The volunteer and partially paid artillery of the six states reorganized as the Australian Field Artillery and the Australian Garrison Artillery.[47]
1904	1 March: The Royal Australian Artillery Regiment (if mounted), and the Batteries of Australian Field Artillery (if allotted to units of the Light Horse) on ceremonial parade with their guns, to take the right, and march at the head of the Light Horse Regiments.[48]
1904	14 November: The King's Banner was presented to the Royal Australian Artillery in recognition of its services during the Second Anglo-Boer War 1899-1902 at a Royal Review in Melbourne commemorating the birthday of His Majesty King Edward VII.[49]
1908	23 January: Field Marshal The Right Honourable Earl Frederick Sleigh Roberts VC KG KP GCB OM GCSI GCIE KStJ VD PC was appointed Colonel-in-Chief of the Australian Artillery (Field and Garrison).[50]
1910	1 December: Two field artillery batteries were created from the Royal Australian Artillery Regiment as the Australian Field Artillery (Permanent).[51]
1911	10 March: Approval granted by His Majesty King George V for The Royal Australian Artillery and the Permanent Batteries of Field Artillery to be redesignated respectively as The Royal Australian Garrison Artillery and The Royal Australian Field Artillery.[52]
1914	3 August: Elements of the Citizen Military Forces responsible for manning the fixed defences, including the Australian Garrison Artillery, were called out for active service.[53]
1914	5 August: Gunners at Port Phillip heads fire the first Australian shot of the war across the bows of the German steamer *Pfalz* as she attempts to leave the bay.[54]
1914	18 August: The artillery of the Australian Imperial Force is recruited from volunteers who had attested for service outside Australia for the duration of World War I and any period thereafter as proclaimed necessary by the Governor-General.[55] This force eventually included five complete divisional artilleries and components of a corps artillery. The Australian Imperial Force ceased to exist on 31 March 1921.
1915	21 May: An Australian Siege Artillery Brigade (Heavy) consisting of a HQ and two Siege Batteries is raised from members of the Royal Australian Garrison Artillery who volunteered for service abroad with the Australian Imperial Force. The initial contingent included some volunteers from the Royal Australian Field Artillery, and the brigade was reinforced during the war with volunteers drawn equally from the permanent Royal Australian Garrison Artillery and the Australian Garrison Artillery of the Citizen Military Forces. It departed to Lydd, Kent, in July 1915 for training and equipping with guns.[56]

Date	Event
1919	31 May: Army Order 58/1919 notifies the granting of an alliance between The Royal Regiment of Artillery of the British Army and the Artillery of the Commonwealth of Australia by His Majesty King George V.[57]
1925	1 July: The first medium artillery brigades and artillery survey companies were raised as part of the Australian Garrison Artillery.[58]
1926	1 August: The first anti-aircraft battery was raised as part of the Australian Garrison Artillery.[59]
1927	1 July: The Royal Australian Field Artillery and The Royal Australian Garrison Artillery amalgamated as the Royal Australian Artillery.[60]
1930	19 June: The permanent and part-time elements of the Australian Artillery adopted a hat badge incorporating a field gun with a scroll bearing the battle honour UBIQUE (Everywhere) and a Tudor Crown above, and scrolls below the gun bearing the motto CONSENSU STABILES (Strong in Agreement) and the word AUSTRALIA.[61]
1935	31 March: The alliance of the 110th Field Battery (Howitzer) RAA(M) with the 100th Field Battery RA was approved.[62]
1935	18 November: His Majesty King George V conferred the title Royal on the Militia units of the Australian Field Artillery and Australian Garrison Artillery. These titles were abolished and the two branches were amalgamated as the Royal Australian Artillery (Militia). At the same time the Royal Australian Artillery adopted the title Royal Australian Artillery Regiment.[63]
1939	2 September: The Citizen Military Forces are called up for War Service. The heavy artillery immediately began manning the coast defences. All units commenced extended camps of continuous training and began to assimilate conscripted Universal Service Personnel.[64]
1939	13 October: The artillery of the Second Australian Imperial Force is recruited for war service from volunteers who had attested for service outside the Commonwealth of Australia for the duration of the Second World War and any period thereafter as proclaimed necessary by the Governor-General.[65] This force eventually included four complete divisional artilleries, a corps artillery, and certain miscellaneous units. The Australian Imperial Force ceased to exist on 30 June 1947.
1940	27 January: The anti-tank branch of the RAA is established.[66]
1941	24 February: Coast defences directed to be continuously manned.[67]
1941	31 August: Citizen Military Force artillery unit cadres comprising all officers, warrant officers, NCO not below the rank of corporal, and specialists are called up for full-time duty for the duration of the war to facilitate the mobilisation of units.[68]
1941	25 November: The Victoria Cross was awarded to Lieutenant Arthur Roden Cutler, 2/5th Aust Field Regiment, for the "…most conspicuous and sustained gallantry during the Syrian Campaign and for outstanding bravery during the bitter fighting at Merdjayoun" during June and July 1941.[69]
1943	26 March: The nomenclature 'anti-tank' was altered to 'tank-attack'.[70]
1943	3 December: The nomenclature 'Fixed Defences Heavy Artillery' was altered to 'Coast Artillery'.[71]
1946	7 February: 2nd Mountain Battery (A Field Battery RAA) commences deployment to Japan as a component of the British Commonwealth Occupation Force (BCOF), returning to Australia on 22 December 1948.[72]

Date	Event
1947	7 November: The Permanent Military Forces were renamed the Australian Regular Army.[73] At this time the regular Army artillery units consisted of A Field Battery, 53rd Field Battery, coast artillery maintenance units in NSW, WA, NT, SA, and TAS, and the School of Artillery.
1948	1 July: General recruiting of other ranks commences to reform the Citizen Military Forces. Artillery units were provided for two divisional artilleries, an independent infantry brigade, an armoured brigade, and corps troops.[74]
1949	25 May: The first regular Army field branch regiment, 1st Field Regiment RAA, is raised.[75]
1949	15 September: The Royal Australian Artillery Regiment and The Royal Australian Artillery (Militia) are amalgamated as The Royal Australian Artillery. The privilege of Right of the Line over the Australian Light Horse lapses by the same authority.[76]
1949	28 November: His Majesty King George VI granted the RAA permission to adopt the Motto of the RA, *Quo Fas et Gloria Ducunt* (Where right and glory lead).[77]
1950	10 March: A scarlet lanyard was authorised for wear by officers, warrant officers, and NCO of the RAA who were required to carry a whistle in the exercise of their command.[78]
1952	2 June: The last anti-tank regiment of RAA was re-roled as a light regiment.[79] The Anti-tank branch was abolished and the role was transferred to the Royal Australian Armoured Corps.[80]
1952	White lanyard authorised for wear by officers, warrant officers, and NCO of the RAA who were required to carry a whistle in the exercise of their command.[81] In 1956 this lanyard was permitted to be worn by all ranks RAA, and in 1963 A Field Battery RAA were authorised to wear it on the left shoulder.[82]
1953	13 September: The last regular Army coast artillery unit, Headquarters 25th Coast Regiment RAA, is disbanded after serving continuously since it was raised as the Regimental Staff, New South Wales Artillery, on 22 August 1876.[83]
1953	26 November: Her Majesty Queen Elizabeth II accepts the appointment of Colonel-in-Chief to The Royal Australian Artillery.[84]
1954	26 May: The current pattern of headdress badge was approved incorporating a field gun with a scroll bearing the battle honour UBIQUE (Everywhere) and a St Edwards Crown above, and scrolls below the gun bearing the motto *Quo Fas et Gloria Ducunt*.[85]
1955	1 September: 105th Field Battery RAA embarked for service in Malaya, commencing the first of two-year operational rotations of an Australian field battery as a component of 28th Commonwealth Infantry Brigade Group, and later 28th Australian, New Zealand and United Kingdom (ANZUK) Brigade, finishing on 9 January 1974 with the return to Australia of the final elements of 106th Field Battery RAA.[86]
1962	25 October: The last heavy anti-aircraft regiment RAA was re-roled as a light anti-aircraft regiment.[87] The high-level air defence role utilising surface-to-air guided weapons was transferred to the Royal Australian Air Force.
1962	19 September: Her Majesty Queen Elizabeth II grants the Royal Australian Artillery the formal title The Royal Regiment of Australian Artillery, with the short title of Royal Australian Artillery. On the same date HM notifies her desire to be known in future as the Captain-General of the Regiment in lieu of her former title of Colonel-in-Chief.[88]
1962	26 October: Coast branch RAA abolished, with its remaining CMF units transferred to Anti-Aircraft branch or disbanded.[89]

Date	Event
1964	24 May: A rotating operational deployment of a light anti-aircraft battery to RAAF Butterworth in Malaysia during Confrontation with Indonesia commences with 111th Light Anti-Aircraft Battery RAA, and ends with the return to Australia on 6 May 1969 of 110th Light Anti-Aircraft Battery RAA.
1965	27 April: Advance elements of 102nd Field Battery RAA moved from Malaysia to Borneo during Confrontation with Indonesia. Battery deployed for operations in Western Sarawak, Borneo, under command of 4th Light Regiment RA from 4 May-27 July 1965.[90] It returned to Malaysia by 14 August 1965.
1965	14 September: 105th Field Battery moved to South Vietnam, commencing an ongoing rotational RAA operational deployment in support of 1st Australian Task Force that expanded to a field regiment and a detachment, divisional locating battery, on 22 April 1966,[91] and ended with the return to Australia of 104th Field Battery on 20 December 1971.
1971	1 August: The Banner of Queen Elizabeth II is presented to the RAA in a ceremony at Paddington, NSW, to replace the 1904 King's Banner.[92]
1972	25 April: The RAA Kings Banner is laid up in perpetuity in the Australian War Memorial.
1974	31 May: The title 'Air Defence' replaces 'Anti-Aircraft' in unit designations.[93]
1990	21 August: A detachment from 16th Air Defence Regiment deployed aboard HMAS *Success* for Operation Damask in the Persian Gulf, September 1990-February 1991
1992	31 December: Command, Liaison and Observation Group elements of 107th Field Battery RAA deployed to Baidoa, Somalia, for Operation Solace.
1999	In September 1999 Arty Tac, 108th Field Battery Command and Liaison Group and 108th Field Battery Gun Line (less guns) deployed with 2nd Battalion Royal Australian Regiment to East Timor on Operation WARDEN. A Field Battery JOST elements deploy to East Timor with 3rd Battalion Royal Australian Regiment on 21 September 1999. The remainder of the Battery deployed to East Timor by 14 October 1999, with the guns prepositioned in Darwin. Battery command and observation parties on rotation provided civil-military and humanitarian support until 2006.[94]
2001	October: A Troop, 16th Air Defence Regiment, deployed aboard HMAS *Kanimbla* for Operation Slipper in the North Arabian Gulf, 2 December 2001–4 March 2002.
2003	May: A detachment of 16th Air Defence Regiment deployed on HMAS *Manoora* for Operation Falconer in the Persian Gulf.
2005	April: Artillery Command Liaison and Observation group formed around 101st Battery Headquarters, augmented with weapon locating elements from 131st Surveillance and Target Acquisition Battery, deploys for Operation Catalyst to Iraq with 2nd Cavalry Regiment RAAC as part of the Al Muthanna Task Group. Batteries on rotation provided similar support. In 2006, this task transitioned to Overwatch Battle Group West, and continued until 2008.[95]
2006	May: Following deployment of an RAA-staffed Evacuee Handling Centre from 4th Field Regiment as part of the Ready Battalion Group deployment on 19 April 2006, 101st Medium Battery (Combat Team Thor) deploys to the Solomon Is. in infantry role as part of Operation ANODE II for 4 months. Batteries on rotation provided similar support until 2013.[96]
2006	25 May: 108 Field Battery (G Company), 4th Field Regiment (operating as infantry) deploy as part of the International Stabilisation Force in East Timor and the deployment of the ANZAC Timor Leste Battle Group to which RAA batteries on occasion provided an infantry company. This commitment continued until April 2013.[97]

Date	Event
2006	18 September: The first of two Joint Offensive Support Teams from 8th/12th Medium Regiment deploying as part of approximately 400 personnel forming the Australian Reconstruction Task Force – 1 Operation SLIPPER, arrive in Afghanistan. Batteries on rotation provided support to subsequent task forces. This commitment changed to mentoring in 2010 and continued until 2014.[98]
2008	13 March: A troop of 15 gunners from 8th/12th Medium Regiment, after training for six months in the United Kingdom as part of a bilateral program, deploy with 7th Regiment Royal Horse Artillery in support of United Kingdom Operation Herrick in Helmand province, Afghanistan. RAA batteries on rotation provided similar support until 2011.[99]
2008	14 May: 102 Battery is granted the Honour Title 'Coral' for dedicated service and sacrifice made by its members at the Battle of Coral in Vietnam on 13 and 16 May 1968.[100]
2010	April: Gunners from 8th/12th Medium Regiment provided the first contingent of the Artillery Training Team – Kabul (ATT-K), and helped establish the Afghan School of Artillery.[101]
2021	01 August: The Royal Regiment of Australian Artillery commemorates the 150th Anniversary of unbroken permanent artillery service to Australia's former Colonies and to the Commonwealth of Australia.
2022	5 November: The Governor-General of the Commonwealth of Australia, His Excellency General the Honourable David Hurley, AC, DSC (Retd) presides at the presentation and consecration of the Queen's Banner (1871-2021) to the Royal Regiment of Australian Artillery at Victoria Barracks, Sydney. The Banner Parade marked the renewal of Her Late Majesty Queen Elizabeth II's *Queen's Banner (1871-1971)* to the *Queen's Banner (1871-2021)*.
Ubique	From 1871 to 2021, Australian gunners deployed on multiple operations beyond the above select deployments: in particular, on many peace operations in recent decades. Their service is recognised here.

Endnotes

Chapter 1

1 General Staff, War Office, *Field Artillery Training 1914*, Ch. VII, 'Employment of Artillery in War', Principles of Employment, Section 145, *Objects of Fire,* His Majesty's Stationery Office, London, 1914.

2 Australian Military Forces, *The Division in Battle, Pamphlet No 5, Artillery, 1969,* paragraph 101, Canberra 1969.

3 Australian Army, *Royal Regiment of Australian Artillery* webpage, https://www.army.gov.au/our-people/organisation-structure/army-corps/royal-regiment-australian-artillery, accessed 15 October 2021.

4 Australian Army, *Land Warfare Doctrine 3-4–1, Employment of Artillery,* 2009.

Chapter 2

1 Oppenheim, Peter, *The Fragile Forts; The Fixed Defences of Sydney Harbour 1788–1963*, Australian Military History Publications, Sydney, 2005, pp 6-8.

2 Section references: Horner, David, *The Gunners, A History Of Australian Artillery,* Allen and Unwin, St Leonards NSW, 1995, pp 17-23; Grey, Jeffrey, *A Military History of Australia*, Third edition, Cambridge University Press, Melbourne, 2008, pp 20-27, 44-5; Dennis, Peter; Grey, Jeffrey; Morris, Ewan; Prior, Robin; Connor, John, *The Oxford Companion to Australian Military History*, First Edition, Oxford University Press, Melbourne, 1995, p 325.

3 *Historical Records of the New South Wales Regiment of the Royal Australian Artillery,* Royal Australian Artillery Historical Society Library, pp 2-5.

4 General Order No 1 of 1 January 1885. Note: This battery's direct descendant was disbanded as 1st Military District Fixed Defences in June 1947.

5 *Officers' List of the Australian Military Forces* 1912. Entry relating to appointment of the first Officer Commanding. Note: Its direct descendant was disbanded in June 1953 as Tasmania Command Coast Artillery.

6 *Report of the Military Defences Enquiry Commission*, Votes and Proceeding of the New South Wales Legislative Assembly, 1881, Session, Part 4, p 602.

7 Bunbury, Lieutenant Colonel W St P, 'The Beginnings of the School of Gunnery at Middle Head, Sydney', *Stand To*, November-December 1962, p 17.

8 *Historical Records of the New South Wales Regiment of the Royal Australian Artillery,* p 9.

9 Dennis, Peter et al, *The Oxford Companion to Australian Military History,* p 222.

10 Horner, *The Gunners*, p 32; National Archives of Australia MP153/16, *Defences of King George's Sound And Thursday Island.*

11 *New South Wales Government Gazette No 719/1889,* 5 September 1899; *Queensland Government Gazette No 60 dated 26 August 1899*; *Victorian Government Gazette No 75 dated 15 September 1899.*

12 Bridges, Captain W T, 'Modern Coast Defence', *The Journal And Proceedings Of The United Service Institution Of New South Wales, 1893,* Vol V, pp 16-42.

13 Bridges, Captain W T, 'Modern Coast Defence', *The Journal And Proceedings Of The United Service Institution Of New South Wales, 1893,* Vol V, pp 16-42.

14 Buckhill, Major John, *Submarine Mines and Torpedoes as applied to Harbour Defence, Southampton*, self-published, 1888, p v; Kitson, Michael, *An attack on Melbourne: A case study of the defence of Australia's major ports in the early 1890s*, Australian War Memorial, https://www.awm.gov.au/articles/journal/j35/kitson, updated 28 August 2020; Marmion, Robert J, *Gibraltar of the South Defending Victoria: An analysis of colonial defence in Victoria, Australia, 1851–1901*, University of Melbourne, Parkville 31 March 2009; Victorian Parliament, *Reports and Suggestions Relative to the Defences of Victoria*, March 1882, p 5.

15 Fort Nepean – Understanding the trace – Part 3: Point Nepean Battery Development – 1885-1887, https://www.mhhv.org.au/fort-nepean-understanding-the-trace-part-3-point-nepean-battery-development-1885-1887/ accessed 03 February 2024.

16 Coxen, Major WA, 'Development of Field Artillery Equipment', *Journal and Proceedings of the United Service Institution of New South Wales,* Volume XVI, 1904, p34-35; Horner, David, *The Gunners*, p 33-38.

17 *Treatise On Ammunition, 10th Edition*, War Office, London, 1915, reprinted by the Naval And Military Press in association with the Imperial War Museum, Chapter V.

18 New South Wales General Order No 128 of 1893 http://trove.nla.gov.au/newspaper/article/236024679

19 Section references: Wilcox, Craig, *Australia's Boer War: The War in South Africa 1899–1902*, Oxford University Press, Victoria, 2002, p 398; Walsh, Leo, 'Machine Gun Section 1st QMI', *The Custodian*, Fort Lytton Historical Association, Volume 1, Issue 2, Autumn 2009, p 8; Cubis, Richmond, *A History of 'A' Battery, New South Wales Artillery (1871–1899), Royal Australian Artillery (1899–1971),* Elizabethan Press, Sydney, 1978.

20 Cubis, *A History of 'A' Battery*, p 106.

21 Glyde, Keith, 'Honorary Distinction or Colour: The Royal Australian Artillery King's Banner', *Cannonball,* Journal of the Royal Australian Artillery Historical Company, No 95, Winter 2019, p 54-60.

Chapter 3

1 Commonwealth Parliamentary Papers, *Defence Forces of the Commonwealth*, 18 July 1901, General 1901-02, Vol 2, No A13.

2 Military Forces of the Commonwealth of Australian General Order No 101; Commonwealth Military Order 160/1911, 25 April 1911.

3 Commonwealth of Australia, *Defence Act 1903*.

4 Palazzo, Albert, *The Australian Army: A History of its Organisation 1901-2001*, Oxford University Press, South Melbourne, Victoria, 2001, pp 27-34.

5 Horner, *The Gunners*, pp 56-58; Glyde, Keith, 'The Director of Artillery', *Cannonball* No 88, Spring 2014, p 18.

6 Brook, Lieutenant Colonel (Retd) David, 'The District Officer - A Forgotten Appointment in The Royal Australian Artillery', *Cannonball* No 95, Winter 2019, pp 44-50.

7 *Schedule of Armaments of the Fixed Defences of the Commonwealth, 1903,* Appendix to Horner, *The Gunners;* Oppenheim, Peter, *The Fragile Forts*, pp 139-40, 191–193, 197.

8 Commonwealth Parliamentary Papers, *Military Forces of the Commonwealth,* 7 April 1902, General 1901-02 Session, Vol 2, No. A36.

9 Horner, *The Gunners*, pp 56-58.

10 Horner, *The Gunners*, p 62.

11 Bidwell, S and Dominick, G, *Fire-Power: The British Army Weapons and Theories of War 1904–1945*, Pen and Sword Military Classics, South Yorkshire, 2004, Chapter 1.

12 Oppenheim, Peter, *The Fragile Forts,* p 195.

13 *Treatise On Ammunition, 10th Edition*, Chapter V.

14 Palazzo, *The Australian Army*, p 46.

15 National Archives of Australia, *Adjutant-General to Secretary Department of Defence, 3 February 1914*, Series No A2023, Item A5/2/40.

16 Palazzo, *The Australian Army*, p 50.

17 National Archives of Australia, *Report On an Inspection of the Military Forces of the Commonwealth of Australia, 24 April 1914*, Series No A5954, Item 830/1, pp 38-9.

Chapter 4

1 9am on 5 August 1914, eastern Australian time.

2 Bean, C E W, *Anzac to Amiens, A Shorter History of the Australian Fighting Services in The First World War,* Australian War Memorial, Canberra, Fifth Edition, 1968, Chapter II.

3 Scott, Ernest, *Official History of Australia in The War of 1914–18, Volume XI, Australia During the War*, Angus and Robertson, Sydney, 1938, pp 35-37.

4 Bean, *Anzac to Amiens*, p 27; Commonwealth Of Australia, *Defence Act 1914* (No 36 of 1914).

5 Roberts, Chris and Stevens, Paul, *The Artillery at Anzac, Adaptation, Innovation, Education*, Big Sky Publishing Pty Ltd, Newport, Australia, 2021, pp 35-41.

6 Section reference: Bean, *Anzac to Amiens,* Chapters VII and VIII.

7 Section references: Bean, *Anzac to Amiens*, Chapter IX; Roberts, Chris and Stevens, Paul, *The Artillery at Anzac,* Chapters 3, 4 and 5.

8 Aspinall-Oglander, Brigadier General C F, *Military Operations, Gallipoli, Volume II,* Naval and Military Press/Imperial War Museum, reprint of 1932 edition, p 116.

9 Section references: Bean, *Anzac to Amiens*, Chapter X; Roberts, Chris and Stevens, Paul, *The Artillery at Anzac,* Chapter 6.

10 Bean, C E W, *Official History of Australia in The War of 1914–1918, Volume II, The Story of Anzac,* Thirteenth Edition, Angus and Robertson, Sydney 1944, pp 612-3.

Chapter 5

1   In this chapter, material relating to the organisation of the AIF the battles it fought and their outcomes are sourced from: Bean, *Anzac to Amiens,* Chapters XII - XV; Westerman, William and Floyd, Nicholas, *Clash of the Gods of War; Australian Artillery and the Firepower Lessons of the Great War,* Big Sky publishing, Newport Australia, 2020.

2   Morris, Major General B M, 'The Australian Siege Brigade 1916–1918', *Stand To,* September 1957-October 1958.

3   AWM4 13/10/20, *War Diary Headquarters 1st Australian Divisional Artillery,* May 1916, Part 1.

4   Lee, Roger, *The Battle of Fromelles 1916,* Australian Army Campaign Series 8, Army History Unit, Canberra, 2010.

5   AWM4 1/29/6 and 1/29/7 Part 1, *War Diary General Staff Headquarters I Anzac Corps, July and August 1916.*

6   Brooke, Lieutenant Colonel A F, 'The Evolution of Artillery in the Great War Part IV', *Journal of the Royal Artillery,* Volume LII, Number 3, 1925/26, p 378; Farndale, General Sir Martin KCB, *History of The Royal Regiment of Artillery, Western Front1914–1918,* The Royal Artillery Institution, Woolwich, London, 1986, p 344.

7   Farndale, *History of The Royal Regiment of Artillery, Western Front 1914–1918,* p 334.

8   Section references: AWM 0987123. Stationery Service (SS) 139/4, *Artillery in Offensive Operations, March 1917,* British Expeditionary Force, France; Farndale, *History of The Royal Regiment of Artillery, Western Front,* p 344, 335, 367, 368.

9   Evans, Nigel, 'Artillery Intelligence and Counter Battery 1939–1945' in *British Artillery in World War 2* at nigelf@ tripod.com; Smith, Alan H., *Do Unto Others; Counter Bombardment In Australia's Military Campaigns,* Big Sky Publishing, Newport New South Wales, 2011.

10   AWM4 13/13/11, *War Diary Headquarters 4th Australian Divisional Artillery, April 1917;* AWM4 13/11/14, *War Diary Headquarters 2nd Australian Divisional Artillery, May 1917.*

11   AWM4 13/12/14, *War Diary Headquarters 3rd Australian Divisional Artillery June 1917.*

12   AWM4 13/4/5, 6 and 7, *War Diary General Officer Commanding Royal Artillery I Anzac Corps September to November 1917.*

13   AWM 28, *Recommendation Files for Honours and Awards, AIF, 1914–1918 War, 1842 SGT L.E. Barrett;* AWM 8, *Unit Embarkation Rolls, 3rd Light Horse Regiment, 1914–1918 War;* Interview with the Barrett Family; National Achieves of Australia: B884, WW2 Service Records, S1729 PTE L.E. Barrett; War Service Record of the First Australian Field Artillery Brigade 1914–1919.

14   Brooke, *The Evolution of Artillery in the Great War,* Volume LIII, Number 2, pp 248-249.

15   Lax, Mark, 'The First Air Observation Posts', in Westerman, William and Floyd, Nicholas, *Clash of the Gods of War,* Chapter 16.

16   Farndale, *History of The Royal Regiment of Artillery, Western Front 1914–1918,* p 335.

17   AWM4 13/13/23, *War Diary Headquarters 4th Australian Divisional Artillery, April 1918;* AWM4 23/15/26, *War Diary 15th Infantry Brigade, April 1918,* Part 1; Horner, *The Gunners,* pp 168, 169.

18   AWM4 13/13/26, *War Diary Headquarters 4th Australian Divisional Artillery, July 1918.*

19   Section references: AWM4 13/4/16, *War Diary Headquarters Royal Artillery Australian Corps, August 1918;* and AWM 13/7/29, *War Diary Brigadier-General Heavy Artillery Australian Corps, August 1918,* Part 1.

20   See for example 'Fifth Australian Divisional Artillery Instruction No2' of 5th August 1918 in AWM4 13/14/31, *War Diary Headquarters 5th Australian Divisional Artillery, August 1918,* Part 1.

21   Evans, Nigel, 'Artillery Intelligence and Counter Battery 1939–1945; Smith, Alan H., *Do Unto Others..*

22   Section reference: AWM4 13/4/17, *War Diary Headquarters Royal Artillery Australian Corps, September-October 1918.*

23   AWM 28, *Recommendations Files for Honours and Awards, AIF, 1914-18 War, 3584 C.V. Paynter;* AWM 8, *Unit Embarkation Rolls, 4th Light Horse Regiment, 1914-1918 War;* National Archives of Australia: B2455, WW1 Service Records, 3584 Gunner C.V. Paynter.

24   AWM4 13/14/33, 'The Breaking of the Hindenburg Line, Operations 29th September to 2nd October 1918', *War Diary Headquarters 5th Australian Divisional Artillery, October 1918,* Part 2.

25   AWM4 13/4/17, *War Diary Headquarters Royal Artillery Australian Corps, September-October 1918;* AWM4 13/25/34, *War Diary Headquarters 36th Artillery Group, November 1918,* Part 1.

26   Monash, John, *The Australian Victories in France in 1918,* Hutchinson and Company, London, 1920, p 13.

27   Horner, *The Gunners,* p 187.

Chapter 6

1   Grey, *A Military History of Australia,* Chapter 6.

2   Glyde, *The Director of Artillery,* pp 18–19.

3   Horner, *The Gunners,* pp 190–191; Palazzo, Albert, *The Australian Army,* pp 90–101.

4   Palazzo, *The Australian Army*, pp 104–105; Horner, *The Gunners,* p 192.

5   Horner, *The Gunners,* pp 191-192.

6   Horner, *The Gunners*, pp 196–198; Australian Army Order 580/1925 dated 5 December 1925, *Amendment No 1 to Tables of Composition, Organisation and Distribution of the Australian Military Forces 1925-26.*

7   Australian Army Order 357/1927.

8   Australian Army Order 12/1936.

9   Palazzo, *The Australian Army*, p 110; Jess, Lieutenant General Sir Carl, *Report On the Activities of the Australian Military Forces 1929–1939*, AWM1 20/9 Part 1.

10 Critics included Colonel (later Lieutenant General) Henry Wynter. e.g. see Wynter, Henry Douglas (1886–1945), Australian Dictionary of Biography. National Centre of Biography, Australian National University.

11 Section references: Fullford, R K, *We Stood and Waited; Sydney's Anti-Ship Defences 1939–1945,* Royal Australian Artillery Historical Company Inc., Manly, NSW, 1994, pp 6, 75, 102; Palazzo, *The Australian Army*, pp 115, 127.

12 Palazzo, *The Australian Army*, p117 -118; Horner, *The Gunners*, p 210.

13 Horner, *The Gunners*, pp 208-209; Jess, *Report On the Activities of the Australian Military Forces 1929–1939.*

Chapter 7

1   Horner, *The Gunners*, Chapter 10; Fullford, *We Stood and Waited*, pp 8-9, 209-216; Palazzo, *The Australian Army*, pp 155–156.

2   'Royal Australian Air Force, Integrated Air and Missile Defence', accessed 9 September 2023, https://www.airforce.gov.au/our-work/projects-and-programs/integrated-air-and-missile-defence-system; Australian Defence Doctrine Publication 3.16 – Counter-Air, edition 2; Australian War Memorial. 'Unit War Diaries, 1939–45 War – Headquarters Anti-Aircraft Group (Northern Queensland) January – May 1943', https://www.awm.gov.au/collection/C2660904 accessed 9 September 2023; Bowden, Vivian, 'The story of IFF (Identification Friend or Foe)', IEE Proceedings A (Physical Science, Measurement and Instrumentation, Management and Education, Reviews), Volume 132, Issue 6 (1985), pp 435–437; Department of the US Army, Field Manual 3-01, U.S. Army Air and Missile Defense Operations (Washington, D.C., 22 December 2020).

3   Palazzo, *The Australian Army*, pp 136–148; Jess, *Report On the Activities of the Australian Military Forces 1929–1939.*

4   Burch, *History of the School of Artillery*, Chapter 3. The Sydney Fire Command was a chain of defensive coastal fortifications established to protect the port of Sydney.

5   Bridges, Captain W T, 'Modern Coast Defence'; Fullford, R K, *We Stood and Waited*; Maurice-Jones, Colonel K W DSO, *The History of Coast Artillery in the British Army*, Royal Artillery Institution, London, 1959.

6   Pemberton, Brigadier A L, *The Development of Artillery Tactics and Equipment,* The War Office, London, 1950.

7   Section references: Horner, *The Gunners*, Chapter 10; Grey, *A Military History of Australia*, pp 141, 146, 152; Smith, Neil C, *Robin Force: The Australian Defence of New Caledonia, World War Two*, Gardenvale, 2001.

8   Cecil, Michael K, *Fire! The 25-Pounder in Australian Service,* Trackpad Publishing, Surrey UK, 2021, Chapter 5.

9   Operational chronologies and descriptions of the Mediterranean actions are sourced from: Long, Gavin, *The Six Years War; Australia in the 1939-45 War,* Australian War Memorial and the Australian Government Printing Service, Canberra 1973, Chapters 4 and 9.

10 AWM52 4/1/13/6, *War Diary Royal Australian Artillery Headquarters 6th Australian Division, January to June 1941.*

11 Section references: Grey, *A Military History of Australia*, pp 159–161; AWM52 4/1/5/3, *War Diary Royal Australian Artillery Headquarters I Australian Corps, January to May 1941.*

12 Section references: AWM52 1/5/20/5, *War Diary 9th Australian Division General Staff Branch April 1941, Part 1*; AWM52 4/11/2/7, *War Diary 3rd Australian Light Anti-Aircraft Regiment, April 1941.*

13 Australian War Memorial, Collection, accessed 16 August 2021; National Archives of Australia, Collection, accessed 18 August 2021.

14 Bidwell, Shelford and Graham, Dominick, *Firepower, The British Army Weapons and Theories of War 1904–1945*, Pen and Sword Military Classics, Barnsley, South Yorkshire, p 256.

15 AWM52 4/2/12/4 and 5, *War Diary 2/12th Field Regiment, April, June and July, and October 1941.*

16 Section references: *AWM52 4/11/2/7, War Diary 3rd Australian Light Anti-Aircraft Regiment, April 1941; AWM52 4/2/3/10, War Diary 2/3 Australian Field Regiment March - May 1941.*

17 Murphy, W E, *2nd New Zealand Artillery,* Historical Publications Branch, Wellington, New Zealand, 1966, quoted in Horner, *The Gunners*, p 263.

18 Section reference: 'Report on Operations', AWM52 4/1/14/9, *War Diary RAA Headquarters 7th Australian Division, July-August 1941.*

19 RAAHC, *Gunners of Renown*, https://artilleryhistory.org/gunners_past_and_present/gunners_of_renown_and_gunners_tales/gunners_of_renown/gunners_of_renown_home_page.html , accessed 18 August 2021; Australian War Memorial, Collection, accessed 15 August 2021.

20 Section references: 'Reports on Operations', AWM52 4/1/16/10 and 17, *War Diary RAA Headquarters 9th Australian Division, August-September and November-December 1942.*

Chapter 8

1 Operational chronologies and descriptions in this chapter are sourced from: Long, *The Six Years War,* Chapter 6.

2 Australian War Memorial, AWM 192, *Recommendations Files for Honours and Awards, AIF, 1939-1945 War, NX149078 Gunner W.T. Hudson MM;* Daily Telegraph, *Family of naked gunner ensures brave act in Darwin is not forgotten,* 2 March 2017; National Archives of Australia: *B883, WW2 Service Records, NX149078 (N108358) Gunner W.T. Hudson.*

3 Descriptions of the 8th Division's artillery action in have been sourced from AWM52 4/1/15/4 and 5, *War Diary RAA HQ 8th Australian Division, January and February 1942.*

4 Section references: Horner, *The Gunners,* pp 309-320, 423; Fullford, *We Stood and Waited,* pp 213, 216-221.

5 Fullford, *We Stood and Waited,* pp 191-2.

6 Horner, *The Gunners,* p 381-384; Fullford, *We Stood and Waited,* pp 48-49.

7 Section references: Long, *The Six Years War,* Chapter 7; Horner, *The Gunners,* pp 336-342.

8 Section references: AWM52 4/1/20/2, *War Diary Headquarters RAA New Guinea Force, January to April 1943;* AWM52 4/2/1/19 and 20, *War Diary 2/1st Field Regiment September 1942 to February 1943;* and AWM52 4/2/5/16 and 17, *War Diary 2/5th Field Regiment July 1942 to February 1943;* Threlfall, Adrian, *The Development of Australian Army Jungle Warfare Doctrine and Training, 1941 -1945.* Doctor of Philosophy Thesis, Victoria University, 2008.

Chapter 9

1 Operational chronologies and descriptions under this heading are sourced from: Long, *The Six Years War,* Chapters 10 and 11.

2 Section references: Long, *The Six Year's War,* p 290; Horner, *The Gunners,* pp 353-358; Palazzo, Albert, *Organising for Jungle Warfare,* in Dennis, P and Grey, J (Ed.), *The Foundations of Victory: The Pacific War 1943-44,* The 2003 Chief of Army's Military History Conference, Army History Unit; Palazzo, The Australian Army, pp 174–177.

3 Cecil, *Fire! The 25-Pounder in Australian Service,* Chapter 10.

4 Bidwell and Graham, *Fire Power,* Chapter 14.

5 Section references: AWM52 4/2/6/17, *War Diary 2/6th Field Regiment, August to October 1943;* AWM52 4/9/1/4, *War Diary 1st Australian Mountain Battery, August to October 1943.*

6 Section references: AWM52 4/1/16/21, *War Diary RAA Headquarters 9th Australian Division, August-September 1943,* AWM52 4/2/4/19, *War Diary 2/4th Field Regiment, August- October 1943.*

7 Horner, *The Gunners,* p 371.

8 Australian Army, *The Airborne landing at Nadzab* Australian War Memorial Collection; Horner, *The Gunners*; National Archives of Australia: *B833, WW2 Service Records VX39725 J.N. Pearson MC.*

9 Section references: AWM52 4/1/16/21-24, *War Diary RAA Headquarters 9th Australian Division, August 1943 to May 1944;* AWM52 4/2/6/17, *War Diary 2/6th Field Regiment, August to October 1943;* AWM52 4/2/4/20-21, *War Diary 2/4th Field Regiment, November 1943 to January 1944;* AWM 52 4/12/3/3, *War Diary 2/3 LAA Battery, January to December 1943.*

10 Section references: Horner, *The Gunners,* Chapter 16; Fullford, *We Stood and Waited,* pp 233-234; Oppenheim, *The Fragile Forts,* p 277.

Chapter 10

1 Horner, *The Gunners,* pp 399-400.

2 Long, *The Six Year's War,* p 405-408.

3 Operational chronologies and descriptions under this heading are sourced from: Long, *The Six Year's War,* Chapter 14.

4 AWM52 4/1/10/14, *War Diary HQ RAA 3rd Australian Division, July 1945 to February 1946.*

5 Section references: AWM52 4/1/10/14, *War Diary HQ RAA 3rd Australian Division, July 1945 to February 1946;* AWM52 4/1/12/10, *War Diary HQ RAA 5th Australian Division, April to August 1945;* AWM52 4/1/13/16, *War Diary HQ RAA 6th Australian Division, May 1945;* AWM52 4/2/1/35, *War Diary 2/1st Field Regiment, September 1945 to January 1946;* AWM52 4/2/17/8, *War Diary 2nd Field Regiment, August 1945;* AWM52 4/2/14/33, *War Diary 2/14th Field Regiment, April 1945;* AWM52 4/8/4/18, *War Diary 2/6th Australian Survey Battery, May-June 1945;* AWM52 4/8/8/9, *War Diary 3rd Australian Survey Battery, April-August 1945.*

6   Operational chronologies and descriptions under this heading are sourced from: Long, *The Six Year's War*, Chapter 15.

7   Section reference: AWM52 4/2/7/42 and 45, *War Diary, 2/7th Field Regiment, May and July 1945.*

8   Section reference: AWM52 4/2/12/23, *War Diary 2/12th Field Regiment, July to August 1945.*

9   Section references: AWM52 4/2/4/31, *War Diary 2/4th Field Regiment, October to November 1945*; AWM52 4/2/5/22, *War Diary 2/5th Field Regiment, April to December 1945*; AWM52 4/2/6/29, *War Diary 2/6th Field Regiment, July to August 1945*; AWM52 4/4/2/40, *War Diary 2/2nd Tank Attack Regiment, August to September 1945*; AWM532 4/13/1/8, *War Diary 2/1st Composite Anti-Aircraft Regiment, August to December 1945.*

10 Horner, *The Gunners*, pp 423-4.

11 Fullford, *We Stood and Waited*, pp 218-219.

Chapter 11

1   Palazzo, *The Australian Army*, pp 193–196.

2   Long, *The Six Years' War*, p 473; Horner, *The Gunners*, pp 426-427.

3   Section references: Grey, *A Military History of Australia*, Chapter 9; Palazzo, *The Australian Army*, pp 203-211; Burch, *History of The School of Artillery*, pp 75-76; Glyde, *The Director of Artillery*, p 20.

4   Horner, *The Gunners*, pp 433-437.

5   Breen, A E (Gus), 'Operation Fauna December 1952' in Pears, Maurie and Kirkland, Fred, *Korea Remembered*, Regimental Books, 1998: *Gunners past and present, Brigadier John Robert Salmon, CBE*, RAAHC website, accessed 18 Aug 2021.

6   Dennis, Peter et al, *The Oxford Companion to Australian Military History*, p 178; Grey, *A Military History of Australia*, p 206.

7   Broadcast by Prime Minister R G Menzies, 22 September 1950 in *National Broadcasts by the Prime Minister, The Defence Call to The Nation*, Government Printer, Melbourne, 1950.

8   Section references: Horner, *The Gunners*, pp 438 - 441; Palazzo, *The Australian Army*, pp 237-238.

9   Horner, *The Gunners*, pp 445-446.

10 Dennis, Peter et al, *The Oxford Companion to Australian Military History*, p 231 and 560; Grey, *A Military History of Australia*, p 217-219; Palazzo, *The Australian Army*, pp 230-237.

11 Horner, *The Gunners*, pp 449-452; Burke, A R, *105th Battery, Royal Regiment of Australian Artillery, A Concise History*, Arthur Burke, Brisbane, 2005.

12 Section references: Horner, *The Gunners*, p 452-454; Palazzo, *The Australian Army*, pp 245, 257; Killender, Jim, *Gunners of Victoria*, Unpublished Manuscript; *The Air Observation Post in World War II*, RAAF Museum, Point Cook; Cecil, *Fire! The 25-Pounder in Australian Service*, Chapters 11 and 12; NAA MP742/1; 240/5/405, *Organisation and Establishment-1 Field Regiment RAA.*

13 Movement light searchlight units were designed to provide light so that ground troops could fight, move and work during the hours of darkness. Reflecting light off the clouds was known as 'artificial moonlight'.

Chapter 12

1   Section references: Dennis, Peter et al, *The Oxford Companion to Australian Military History*, p 463; Horner, *The Gunners*, pp 454-458; Grey, *A Military History of Australia*, p 228; Australian Army, *The Pentropic Division in Battle (Provisional) Part 1,Part 5, Organisation and Tactics, 1960.*

2   Army Routine Order 14/62 dated 2 November 1962, Letter from Buckingham Palace to the Governor-General of Australia, cited in Jobson, *Royal Regiment of Australian Artillery Customs and Traditions*, Directorate of Artillery, Artillery Centre, p 19; NAA: A2880; 27/8/16.

3   Oppenheim, *The Fragile Forts*, p 292-293; Fullford, *We Stood and Waited*, p 237.

4   Section reference: Horner, *The Gunners*, pp 458-461.

5   Data in the succeeding two paragraphs has been sourced from: *British Artillery Technical Fire Control After World War 2* at www.nigelef.tripod.com/directory, accessed 22 February 2022.

6   Section reference: Smith, AH, *Gunners in Borneo, Artillery During Confrontation 1962–1966*, Royal Australian Artillery Historical Company, Sydney, 2008, pp 79-90, AWM95 3/3, *War Diary 102 Field Battery, May to July 1965.*

7   Dennis, Peter et al, *The Oxford Companion to Australian Military History*, pp 62-63.

8   Section references: AWM95 3/5/29-41, *War Diary 105th Field Battery, August 1965 to July 1966*; Burke, *105th Battery, A Concise History*, pp 20-24.

9   Material in the subsequent paragraphs is sourced from: Horner, *The Gunners*, Chapter 20.

10 'Résumé of Battle of Long Tan' and 'FSCC Artillery Sig Log Book' in AWM 95/3/5/4, *War Diary 105th Field Battery, 1-31 August 1966, Enclosures 4 to 11.*

11 Horner, *The Gunners*, pp 488-496.

12 English, Michael, *The Battle of Long Khanh*, Army Doctrine Centre, Georges Heights, 1995; Personal Interviews, WO2 Steven Wilson.

13 Burke, *105th Battery, A Concise History*, pp 20, 30.

14 Section reference: Ahearn, Colonel (Retd) I F, 'South Vietnam, The First Battle of Coral 12th-13th May 1968, The Real Story', *Cannonball* Number 84, September 2012.

Chapter 13

1 Section references: Palazzo, *The Australian Army*, pp 286-292, 314-318; Grey, *A Military History of Australia*, pp 255-257; Horner, *The Gunners*, pp 497-501.

2 Palazzo, *The Australian Army*, pp 294-300; Grey, *A Military History of Australia*, pp 260-261.

3 Horner, *The Gunners*, pp 506-512, Department of Defence, *Australian Defence (1976 Defence White Paper)*, Commonwealth of Australia, November 1976, pp 10, 13.

4 Palazzo, *The Australian Army*, pp 325-326.

5 Burke, *Concise History of 105th Field Battery*, p 31.

6 The Redeye was later replaced by the RBS-70 Very-Low-Level Air Defence system in 1987.

7 The L118/L119 was equipped with two different gun barrels. The L118 configuration, the L19 barrel fired the longer-range UK 'Abbott' family of piezo-electric-fired ammunition, while in the L119 configuration, the L20 barrel fired the US-standard M1 family of percussion-fired ammunition.

8 'Equipment Updates', *RAA Liaison Letter*, Edition 1, 1991, Directorate of Artillery, Canberra.

9 Section references: Horner, *The Gunners*, pp 512 -514; Palazzo, *The Australian Army*, pp 328-329.

10 From 1989, the Group also comprised a Parachute Surgical Team, detached administratively to 8th/12th Medium Regiment.

11 'Headquarters Land Command Artillery Report', *RAA Liaison Letter*, August 1993.

12 Dibb, Paul, *Review of Australia's Defence Capabilities: Report to the Minister for Defence*, Australian Government Publishing Service, Canberra, March 1986, pp 134-142; Department of Defence, *The Defence of Australia (1987 Defence White Paper)*, Commonwealth of Australia, March 1987; Horner, *The Gunners*, pp 515-7.

13 Burch, *History of The School of Artillery*, p 120.

14 Horner, *The Gunners*, p 517.

15 Palazzo, *The Australian Army*, p 348; Brangwin, Nicole; Church, Nathan; Dyer, Steve and Watt, David, *Defending Australia: A history of Australia's Defence White Papers*, Department of Parliamentary Services, Canberra, 20 August 2015, p 22.

16 Grey, *A Military History of Australia*, p 265.

17 Palazzo, *The Australian Army*, pp 348-353; APH, 'The evolution of the Australian Defence Force Gap Year program', http://www.aph.gov.au/About_Parliament/Parliamentary_Departments/Parliamentary_Library/pubs/rp/rp1314/ADFGapYear, 08 May 2014, accessed 28 Nov 21; 'Message from the Director', *RAA Liaison Letter*, 1991, Edition 1, p 1.'

18 Brangwin et al, *Defending Australia: A history of Australia's Defence White Papers*, pp 24, 32-33; Department of Defence, *Defending Australia: Defence White Paper 1994 (DWP 94)*, Commonwealth of Australia, 1994.

19 'A View from the Pond', *RAA Liaison Letter*, 1996, p 5.

20 Palazzo, *The Australian Army*, p 360.

21 'Director's Message', *RAA Liaison Letter*, 1997.

22 Palazzo, *The Australian Army*, p 359.

23 Palazzo, *The Australian Army*, pp 364-365.

24 'Colonel Artillery's Message', *RAA Liaison Letter*, 1998/9, Offensive Support Division, Combined Arms Training Centre, Puckapunyal, Victoria; '1st Field Regiment Report', *RAA Liaison Letter*, 2000.

25 Fire Support Company, 6th Motorised Battalion, *Standard Operating Procedures*, 1998.

26 'Land Command Artillery Report', *RAA Liaison Letter*, 2001.

27 Deputy Head of Regiment, 'Land Warfare Development Centre and Defence Materiel Organisation Reports', *RAA Liaison Letter*, 2002, School of Artillery, Combined Arms Training Centre, Puckapunyal Victoria.

28 Department of Defence, *Chief of the General Staff Directive 10/96*.

29 The Auditor-General, *Audit Report No.33 2000–2001 Performance Audit: Australian Defence Force Reserves*, Commonwealth of Australia 2001, pp 45-47.

30 Dennis, P (et al), *Oxford Companion to Australian Military History*, pp 457-461.

31 Horner, *The Gunners*, p 519; '16th Air Defence Regiment Report', *RAA Liaison Letter* 2/1990.

32 Grey, *A Military History of Australia*, pp 266-269. These included missions to Northern Iraq (1991); Western Sahara (1991-4); Cambodia (1991-3); Somalia (1992-5); the former Yugoslavia (1992-3, 1997); Rwanda (1994); Bougainville (1994, 1997-2003); Mozambique (1994-5); Haiti (1994-5); Guatemala (1997); and Kosovo (1997).

33 *Grey, A Military History of Australia*, pp 273-274.

34 Department of Defence, *Australia's Strategic Policy, 1997 Strategic Review, (ASP 97),* Commonwealth of Australia, p 8.

35 Department of Defence, *ASP 97,* pp 8, 51; Horner, David. *Australia's Military History for Dummies*, Wiley Publishing Australia Pty Ltd, Queensland, p 381.

36 Palazzo, *The Australian Army*, p 365.

37 'Colonel Artillery's Message', *RAA Liaison Letter,* 1998/9.

38 Commonwealth of Australia, *ASP 97,* pp 8, 51.

39 Horner, David, *Australia and the New World Order: From Peacekeeping to Peace Enforcement: 1988–1991, The Official History of Australian Peacekeeping, Humanitarian and Post-Cold War Operations, Volume II*, Cambridge University Press, Melbourne, 2011, pp 410-490.

40 Abraham Gubler, 'Return to the Hollow Force?', *Asia-Pacific Defence Reporter,* Venture Media, Miranda, Australia, July 2008.

41 8th/12th Medium Regiment moved to Darwin in December 1999, and detached 'A' Field Battery to 4th Field Regiment during the INTERFET operation in Timor-Leste. 8th/12th Medium Regiment began re-raising 102nd Field Battery in January 2000.

Chapter 14

1 'Deployment of A Field Battery to East Timor', *RAA Liaison Letter*, 2000; '4th Field Regiment Report', *RAA Liaison Letter*, 2000; Griggs, Major T, 'Another Successful Civilian-Military Operation', *RAA Liaison Letter*, 2001; Thomson, Mark, *ASPI Special Report Issue 5 – The Final Straw: Are our defence forces overstretched?* Australian Strategic Policy Institute, Barton, May 2007.

2 Horner, David, *Making the Australian Defence Force: The Australian Centenary History of Defence,* Oxford University Press, Melbourne, 2001, pp 32-3.

3 'Unit Reports', *RAA Liaison Letter*, 2000-2004 inclusive; Brennan, Terry, '20 Surveillance and Target Acquisition Regiment', *RAA Liaison Letter*, Autumn 2007; Palazzo, *The Australian Army*, pp 371-372. Note: as social norms evolved, the 'U' in 'UAV' changed from 'Unmanned' to 'Unattended' and finally 'Uncrewed'.

4 Department of Defence, *Defence 2000: Our Future Defence Force*, Commonwealth of Australia, 2000, pp xi, 79-80; Brangwin et al, *Defending Australia: A history of Australia's Defence White Papers*, 20 August 2015, p 37.

5 Palazzo, *The Australian Army*, pp 375-377.

6 Department of Defence, *Defence 2000: Our Future Defence Force*, p 83; 'Capability Development and DMO Project and Fleet Synopsis', *RAA Liaison Letter*, Spring, 2003.

7 'Head of Regiment Report', *RAA Liaison Letter,* 2001; 'Land Command Artillery Report', *RAA Liaison Letter,* 2001.

8 '16th Air Defence Regiment Report', *RAA Liaison Letter,* 2002.

9 1st Ground Liaison Group, *History of 1st Ground Liaison Group - 23 Oct 1963 to 15 Jan 2012*, Unit PowerPoint Presentation (unpublished), 2012.

10 Department of Defence, The War in Iraq: ADF Operations in the Middle East in 2003, https://www.defence.gov.au/publications/lessons.pdf, Department of Defence, 23 February 2004, accessed 04 December 2019; Department of Defence, *Defence Annual Report 2002-2003*, pp 3-4.

11 Bryant, Wes J, 'U.S. Strike Cells: Dispelling the Myths', *Articles of War*, https://lieber.westpoint.edu/us-strike-cells-dispelling-myths/, 15 June 2022, accessed 20 November 2023.

12 *History of 103 Medium Battery as at January 2015*, Australian Artillery Association Website, accessed 10 September 2021.

13 '8/12th Medium Regiment Report', *RAA Liaison Letter,* Spring 2005; '131st Surveillance and Target Acquisition Battery', *RAA Liaison Letter,* Spring 2005; Major, Sergeant B C, 'Iraq Experiences of a Weapon Locating Radar Number One', *RAA Liaison Letter*, Autumn 2006.

14 *History of 103 Medium Battery.*

15 Thomson, Mark, *ASPI Special Report Issue 5 – The Final Straw: Are our defence forces overstretched?* Australian Strategic Policy Institute, Barton, May 2007, p 4.

16 '7 Brigade Army website newspaper clipping', *RAA Liaison Letter,* 2001.

17 Department of Defence, *Defence Annual Reports*, 2000-01, 2001-02, 2002-03, 2003-04, 2004-05.

18 'Unit Reports', *RAA Liaison Letter*, 2000-2004 inclusive; Burke, *105th Battery, A Concise History*, p 40.

19 'Unit Reports', *RAA Liaison Letter*, 2000-2005 inclusive.

20 Section references: Department of Defence, *Defence Annual Report 2005-6,* Chapter 2, Outcome 3; Chief of Army, *Order of The Day: The Hardened and Networked Army*, dated 15 December 2005; Chief of Army, *Order of The Day, The Hardened and Networked Army*, dated 10 March 2006; Ryan, Lieutenant Colonel S, 'Hardened and Networked Army and Plan STAN: An Artillery View', *RAA Liaison Letter*, Spring 2006.

21 Thomson, Mark, *ASPI Special Report Issue 5.*

22 Swinsburg, Lieutenant Colonel P R, 'Development of 20th Surveillance and Target Acquisition Regiment', *RAA Liaison Letter*, Spring 2006.

23 Fourays, *History*, Australian Army Aviation Association inc., https://www.fourays.org/history/, accessed 01 December 2023; Lax, Mark, 'The First Air Observation Posts', https://www.artilleryhistory.org/history_seminar_series/seminar_no_4_august_2016/presentation_3.html , accessed 01 December 2023.

Chapter 15

1 Thomson, Mark, *ASPI Special Report Issue 5*, p 4.

2 Chief of Army, *Order of The Day: A Larger Army,* dated 24 August 2006, *RAA Liaison letter*, Spring, 2006.

3 Thomson, Mark, *ASPI Special Report Issue 5*, p 2.

4 'Land Command Artillery Report', *RAA Liaison Letter*, Spring 2006.

5 'Head of Regiment Report', *RAA Liaison Letter*, Spring, 2007; Office of Chief of Army, *Chief of Army Directive 07-2007,* dated 31 May 07.

6 *Nicole Brangwin,* 'Women in the ADF', Parliament of Australia (aph.gov.au),https://www.aph.gov.au/About_Parliament/Parliamentary_Departments/Parliamentary_Library/FlagPost/2015/December/Women_in_the_ADF, posted 01 December 2015, accessed 09 October 2023.

7 'Head of Regiment Report', *RAA Liaison Letter*, Spring 2007; 'Head of Regiment Report', *RAA Liaison Letter*, Autumn 2008.

8 Australian National Audit Office, *Report 31, 2008-2009*, p 29.

9 Department of Defence, *Defence Annual Report*, 2008-2009, p 212.

10 Army Headquarters, Chief of Army Address to Centre for Defence & Strategic Studies, *Army and the Management of Concurrency*, July 2006; Defence Annual Report 2007-8 Volume 1 p 67; 'Unit Reports', *RAA Liaison Letters,* 2002-2005.

11 *History of 103 Medium Battery;* 'Unit Reports', *RAA Liaison Letters*, 2006-2013 inclusive.

12 See Close, W C, 'Operations in East Timor's Rural Districts', *RAA Liaison Letter* Autumn 2006, pp 110–111; Klomp, D M, 'Anzac Battle Group', *RAA Liaison Letter* Autumn 2007, pp 39-41; Close, W C, 'Timor Leste & Golf Company', *RAA Liaison Letter,* Spring 2008, pp 38-41; Grant, Peter, 'Timor Leste', *RAA Liaison Letter* Autumn 2009, p 30; Correspondence between author (Floyd) and Official History Project East Timor Volume 2 authors (W Westerman, A Richardson), Sep 2021; United Nations, 'UN peacekeeping mission ends operations as Timor-Leste continues on path to 'brighter future', https://news.un.org/en/story/2012/12/429232, 31 Dec 2012, accessed 12 Sep 2021.

13 Edwards, D M, 'RAA Commitment to Overwatch Battle Group (West) and AATI-VI,' *RAA Liaison Letter*, Spring 2006, pp 97–100.

14 Lee, Lieutenant B J, 'Overwatch Battle Group (West)', *RAA Liaison Letter*, Autumn 2008.

15 Edwards, Major D M, 'RAA Commitment to Overwatch Battle Group (West) and AATTI-IV', *RAA Liaison Letter*, Spring 2006. Note: as social norms evolved, the 'U' in 'UAV' changed from 'Unmanned' to 'Unattended' and finally 'Uncrewed.'

16 *History of 103 Medium Battery*, op cit.

17 Dennis, Peter et al., *The Oxford Companion to Australian Military History* (Second Ed.). Melbourne: Oxford University Press Australia & New Zealand, 2008. The first ADF CH-47 Chinooks, then operating as the Aviation Support Element, had deployed into Afghanistan in 2006.

18 The term *Forward Observer* was altered to *Joint Fires Observer* to reflect the growth in accessing joint fires. Similarly, the term *Forward Air Controller* was altered to *Joint Terminal Attack Controller* to reflect the ability to terminally control all forms of joint fires.

19 Worsley, Major A, 'Lingo Changes with the Times', *RAA Liaison Letter*, Spring 2009; Kenny, Lieutenant Colonel S and Furini, Lieutenant Colonel C, 'OP Trade & Structure', *RAA Liaison Letter*, Spring 2008.

20 'Unit Reports', *RAA Liaison Letters* 2006-2010 inclusive.

21 Concurrently, Australian Commando force elements with the Australian Special Operations Task Group were operating with integral mortar teams.

22 Brennan, Terry, '20th Surveillance and Target Acquisition Regiment', *RAA Liaison Letter*, Autumn 2007, pp 94-95; Dutton, Matthew, 'Operations in Afghanistan', *RAA Liaison Letter*, Autumn 2008, pp 32-33; Worsley, Adam, 'Bringing on the Rain': RTF 3 Offensive Support', *RAA Liaison Letter*, Spring 2008, pp 112–113. Note: 'Skylark' UAVs had deployed briefly to Uruzgan in early 2006, in support of the Special Forces Task Group.

23 The Term 'Unmanned Aerial System' (UAS) describes the entire capability system (airframes, ground control station, command & control nodes, observation and advice elements), whereas the term 'UAV' describes the airframes specifically.

24 Brennan, Terry, '20th Surveillance and Target Acquisition Regiment', *RAA Liaison Letter*, Autumn 2007; Dutton, Matthew, 'Operations in Afghanistan'; Worsley, Adam, 'Bringing on the Rain', pp 112–113.

25 'Chief of Army Address to Regimental Conference 2004', *RAA Liaison Letter*, Autumn 2005.

26 'Commander Land Command Artillery's Report', *RAA Liaison Letter*, Autumn 2006; 'Firing Up: Army's New Generation RBS70 Arrives', *RAA Liaison Letter*, Autumn 2006; 'Defence Materiel Organisation Report', *RAA Liaison Letter*, Spring 2006; 'Defence Materiel Organisation Report', *RAA Liaison Letter*, Autumn 2008.

27 Crawford, Lieutenant Colonel R, 'Mortars for Reserve Gunners?', *RAA Liaison Letter* Spring 2008; Toohill, I, 'Gunners Converted', *RAA Liaison Letter*, Spring 2009.

28 Schwarz, B, 'New task force faces biggest killer', *Defender—Spring 2006*, Australian Defence Association, 2006.

29 Worsley, Major A, 'Lingo Changes with The Times', *RAA Liaison Letter*, Spring 2009.

30 Kenny, Lieutenant Colonel S and Furini, Lieutenant Colonel C, 'OP Trade & Structure', in *RAA Liaison Letter*, Spring 2008.

31 Minister for Defence, 'Media Release 17/2008: Australian Artillerymen Deploy to Afghanistan in Support of UK Operations, dated 13 March 2008', *RAA Liaison Letter*, Autumn 2008.

32 Furini, C D, '8/12 Medium Regiment Order of the Day', *RAA Liaison Letter* Autumn 2008; El Khaligi, Lieutenant K, 'Helmand Stories', *RAA Liaison Letter*, Spring 2009; Department of Defence, https://news.defence.gov.au/media/media-releases/australian-gunners-final-mission-afghanistan, 25 March 2011, accessed 07 Oct 2021.

33 Furini, C D, '8/12 Mdm Regt Order of the Day', *RAA Liaison Letter* Autumn 2008, p 15.

34 For the activities of this Troop see: *History of 103 Medium Battery*.

35 Final Protective Fire (FPF) missions involve gunfire directed to fall immediately in front of defending troops to break up and or destroy an enemy assault.

36 DefenceWeb, *Enter the Dragon*, https://www.defenceweb.co.za/land/land-land/enter-the-dragon/ 1 Apr 2009, accessed 19 Feb 2021; Hastings, S, photo supplied; Personal Interviews, WO2 Steven Wilson.

37 *History of 103 Medium Battery*

38 Hartley, Lieutenant R, *Post Activity Report (PAR) of Troops in Contact (TIC) at FOB Budwan 05 October 2010*, October 2010 (unpublished).

39 El Khaligi, Lieutenant K, 'Helmand Stories'.

40 *Defence White Paper 2009*, p 77.

41 'Chief of Army Address to Regimental Conference 2004', *RAA Liaison Letter*, Autumn 2005; *History of 103 Battery*.

42 *Defence White Paper 2009*, p 77; 'Defence Materiel Organisation Report', *RAA Liaison Letter*, Spring 2008.

43 Department of Defence, *Defence White Paper 2009: Defending Australia in The Asia Pacific Century*, Commonwealth of Australia, Canberra, pp 13–14, 74; Chief of Army, 'Email to Army: Adaptive Army', *RAA Liaison Letter*, Spring 2008; *RAA Liaison Letter*, Autumn and Spring, 2009.

44 Kennedy, Lieutenant Colonel M and Doran, Lance Corporal M, 'Changes in Artillery', *Army Newspaper*, 3 March 2011, republished in *RAA Liaison Letter*, Autumn 2011.

45 Hill, Lieutenant Colonel D, 'Evolution of 4th Regiment 2008-2015 and Beyond', in *RAA Liaison Letter*, Autumn 2015.

46 *RAA Liaison Letter*, Autumn 2013.

47 Defence Media Release, 'C-RAM in Afghanistan', in *RAA Liaison Letter*, Autumn 2011; Satchell, Jeremy, 'CRAM – Enhanced Force Protection', *RAA Liaison Letter* Autumn 2011, p 28; *Defence White Paper 2009*, p 77.

48 *History of 103 Medium Battery*.

49 *History of 103 Medium Battery*.

50 Personal Interviews, WO2 Steven Wilson; *RAA Liaison Letter*, Autumn 2013.

51 'Unit Reports', *RAA Liaison Letter* 2010-13 inclusive.

52 Crawford, R, 'Recollections of Chief of Staff HQ Task Force Uruzgan (TF-U)', Letter to author (Floyd), 15 Oct 2021.

53   *History of 103 Medium Battery*; Reilly, S T, 'Fort Alamo: Artillery Training Advisory Team-Two', *RAA Liaison Letter*, Autumn 2013, pp 29-30.

54   Section References: Media Release, *New structure and capability for Army*, Minister for Defence, Minister for Defence Materiel and Parliamentary Secretary for Defence; *Plan Beersheba*, www.parlinfo.aph.gov.au; Department of Defence, *Defence White Paper 2013*, Commonwealth of Australia, 2013, p 85.

55   Butterly, Nick, 'Defence cuts 'put troops at risk'', *The West Australian*, 30 May 2012, https://thewest.com.au/news/australia/defence-cuts-put-troops-at-risk-ng-ya-314386, accessed 05 Dec 2022; Commonwealth Government, 'Transcript of joint press conference, Canberra', *PM Transcripts*, https://pmtranscripts.pmc.gov.au/release/transcript-18545, accessed 05 Dec 2022; Ireland, Judith, 'Government foreshadows more cuts to Defence spending', *The Canberra Times*, 3 May 2012, https://www.canberratimes.com.au/story/6170781/government-foreshadows-more-cuts-to-defence-spending/, accessed 05 Dec 2022;

56   Head of Regiment, 'St Barbara's Day Greeting 2012', *RAA Liaison Letter* Autumn 2013. The batteries were: 2/10th Light Battery (5/6th Bn RVR); 23rd Light Battery (4/3rd Bn RNSWR); 7th Light Battery (2/17th Bn RNSWR); 6/13th Light Battery (10/27th RSAR; 5/11th Light Battery (9RQR); 3rd Light Battery (11/28th RWAR).

57   The decision also precipitated the cessation of awarding the Mt Schanck Trophy, which had been presented to the champion Reserve battery for one hundred years since 1912.

Chapter 16

1   Head of Regiment, 'Head of Regiment Report', *RAA Liaison Letter*, Spring 2014.

2   Shanasy, Major E., 'Back in the Fight', *RAA Liaison Letter* Autumn 2013; Hill, Lieutenant Colonel D, 'Evolution of 4th Regiment 2008-2015 and Beyond', *RAA Liaison Letter* Autumn 2015.

3   '110th Air-Land Battery Report', *RAA Liaison Letter* 2016.

4   '2nd Division Joint Fires Cell Report', *RAA Liaison Letter* Spring 2017.

5   '9th Regiment Report', *RAA Liaison Letter,* Winter 2018 and Summer 2019.

6   Australian Parliamentary Library, *Background to the Afghan Withdrawal: A Quick Guide*, https://www.aph.gov.au/About_Parliament/Parliamentary_Departments/Parliamentary_Library/pubs/rp/rp2122/Quick_Guides/BackgroundToAfghanistanWithdrawal, 26 August 2021, accessed 13 May 2022.

7   Alternately styled *Islamic State of Iraq & the Levant* (ISIL).

8   1st Ground Liaison Group, *History of 1st Ground Liaison Group – 23 Oct 1963 to 15 Jan 2012*, Unit PowerPoint Presentation (unpublished), 2012.

9   See, for example, '4th Regiment and 8/12th Regiment Reports', *RAA Liaison Letter*, Winter 2018; and '1st Regiment Report', *RAA Liaison Letter*, Summer 2019.

10   Bailey, J B A, *Field Artillery and Firepower*, Annapolis, MD: Naval Institute Press, 2004, p 372; Combat Studies Institute, *Global War on Terrorism Occasional Paper 4: Field Artillery in Military Operations Other Than War: An Overview of the US Experience*, Combat Studies Institute Press, Fort Leavenworth, Kansas [undated], p 26.

11   Department of Defence, Operation *OKRA – Iraq*, https://www.defence.gov.au/operations/okra, accessed 12 Sep 2021.

12   Department of Defence, *Defence White Paper 2016*, Commonwealth of Australia, pp 68, 96, 98.

13   Commonwealth of Australia, *Defence Strategic Update 2020*, pp 38-40.

14   Minister for Defence, *Media Release: Contract Signed for New Air Defence System*, dated 20 June 2019; Minister for Defence *Media Release: Request for Tender Release for Protected Mobile Fires*, dated 3 September 2020; Kuper, Stephen, 'What a Coalition win means for the Defence Portfolio', *Defence Connect*, https://www.defenceconnect.com.au/key-enablers/4054-and-the-winner-is-coalition-returned-and-what-it-means-for-defence, 19 May 2019, accessed 29 Nov 21.

15   Commonwealth of Australia, *Defence Strategic Update 2020*, pp 38-40.

16   'Trusted networks' support important security services including user authentication, exhaustive network device admission control, and end-device condition verify, policy-based access control, traffic filtering, and automated remediation of non-compliant devices and auditing.

17   'Head of Regiment Report', *RAA Liaison Letter*, Winter 2009.

18   Department of Defence, 'Artillery Modernisation Plan (Draft),' *Australian Army*, undated, accessed 04 December 2021.

19   Department of Defence '2020 Force Structure Plan,' *Commonwealth of Australia*, available at: https://www.defence.gov.au/about/publications/2020-force-structure-plan.

20   Department of Defence, Commonwealth of Australia, *2020 Defence Strategic Update,* Canberra, 01 July 2020.

21   Nicholson, B, 'StrikeMaster: a Bushmaster variant with a big bite', *The Strategist*, ASPI, 7 Mar 2022.

22 Photograph supplied courtesy of Hanwha Defense Australia on 30 Jun 2022.

23 Commonwealth of Australia, *National Defence: Defence Strategic Review*, 2023, p 105.

24 Commonwealth of Australia, *National Defence: Defence Strategic Review*, 2023, p 19.

25 Dougherty, Major R, 'Specialist combat brigades' restructure unveiled for Australian Army', *Defence Connect*, https://www.defenceconnect.com.au/land/12876-major-specialist-combat-brigades-restructure-unveiled-for-australian-army, 28 September 2023, accessed 14 October 2023.

26 Department of Defence, 'Artillery Modernisation Plan (Draft),' undated.

Chapter 17

1 Monash, John, *The Australian Victories in France in 1918* p 96.

Appendices

1 Horner, *The Gunners*, pp 56, 58-59.

2 Westerman, William and Floyd, Nicholas, *Clash Of The Gods Of War*, Appendix, Table V.

3 Westerman, William and Floyd, Nicholas, *Clash Of The Gods Of War*, Appendix, Table VI.

4 Horner, *The Gunners*, pp 194-196.

5 Horner, *The Gunners* pp 218-219; Palazzo, *The Australian Army*, pp 117-118.

6 Horner, *The Gunners*, pp 220-222.

7 Horner, *The Gunners*, pp 229-230.

8 Horner, *The Gunners*, pp 309-314.

9 Horner, *The Gunners*, pp 312-314.

10 Horner, *The Gunners*, p 354.

11 Horner, *The Gunners*, pp 375-376.

12 Horner, *The Gunners*, p 396.

13 Horner, *The Gunners*, pp 430-431: Palazzo, *The Australian Army*, pp 208-210.

14 Horner, *The Gunners*, pp 429; Palazzo, *The Australian Army*, pp 211.

15 Horner, *The Gunners*, pp 438-440; Palazzo, *The Australian Army*, p 238.

16 Palazzo, *The Australian Army*, pp 261-263.

17 Horner, *The Gunners*, pp 501-502.

18 Palazzo, *The Australian Army*, pp 351-353.

19 Palazzo, *The Australian Army*, p 379.

20 Floyd, N and McFarlane, J, 'The Future Ready Royal Australian Artillery – A Perspective | Part 1: Framing the Issue', *The Cove*, https://cove.army.gov.au/article/future-ready-royal-australian-artillery-perspective-part-1-framing-issue, 26 January 2023, accessed 11 Nov 2023.

21 *NSW Government Gazette No 100 of 21 August 1854*.

22 *South Australian Government Gazette No 39 of 14 September 1854*. Note: It is currently perpetuated in the South Australian element of the 6th/13th Light Battery RAA.

23 *Victorian Government Gazette No 113 of 13 November 1855*. Note: Its direct descendant is the current 2nd/10th Light Battery RAA.

24 War Office Minute dated 2 October 1858; War Office Letter to Secretary of State for the Colonies dated 10 October 1858 [WO 32/8250, *Request to use the title 'Royal' by Volunteer Corps in Victoria*; PRO 416-6580, Records of the War Office (as filmed by the AJCP) Fonds WO/Series AJCP Reel No: 7235]. Earliest official use of the title in Victoria after receipt of approval is *Victorian Government Gazette No 30 of 4 March 1859*.

25 *Journals of the House of Assembly, Volume XV, 1867, Paper No 9*. Note: It is now perpetuated as the Hobart element of the 6th/13th Light Battery RAA.

26 *Queensland Government Gazette No 80 of 30 August 1862* appointing the Captain-Commandant, Queensland Volunteer Artillery. Note: Its direct descendant is the current 5th/11th Light Battery RAA.

27 *General Volunteer Order No 76 of 7 March 1862*. Note: The Instructor in Gunnery resigned on 31 December 1863 and use of the facility appears to have lapsed by October 1864 with the establishment of a drill yard at Lower Macquarie Street for the volunteers.

28 Laws, Lieutenant Colonel M E S, *Battery Records of the Royal Artillery 1859-1877,* RA Institution, Woolwich, 1970. Grey, Jeffrey. *A Military History of Australia.*

29 *Victorian Government Gazette No 70 of 21 October 1870*. An earlier Victorian Government memorandum (xx Jul 1870) directed the Victorian Military Forces Commandant, Colonel William Anderson to commence preparations to raise the unit.

30   *NSW Government Gazette No 190 dated 1 August 1871*. Note: The direct descendants of this initial unit were disbanded as elements of 25th Coast Regiment RAA between 1952 and 1953, and it is now perpetuated by 'A' Battery RAA.

31   *Victorian Government Gazette No 25 of 21 April 1871* appointing the Commanding Officer effective 1 January 1871. The Permanent Victorian Artillery was raised under the new *Victorian Discipline Act 1870*, establishment 150 all ranks. Note: Its direct descendant was disbanded as 3rd Military District Coast Artillery in September 1947.

32   *Government Gazette of Western Australia No 3 of 21 January 1873*. Note: The name was altered at the Western Australian Governor's direction, following the partial transition to gun drill from early 1871 and a general parade of the Troop on 01 July 1872. Its direct descendant is the current 3rd Light Battery RAA.

33   *The Official Directory and Almanac of Australia*, Australian Mutual Provident Society, 1883, p 354. See Trove, https://nla.gov.au/nla.obj-2887633250, accessed 20 Nov 2023; General Order (GO) 151/80: "In compliance with instructions from the Government, and in accordance with the vote of Parliament, the Victorian Artillery Corps is disbanded from this date."

34   *Victorian Government Gazette No 83, 11 August 1882*. The new unit was raised as the Victorian Artillery Corps, and operated under the *Victorian Discipline Act 1870*.

35   NAA: AP161/1; Item 15, *Historical Records of the South Australian Permanent Artillery*, appointment of Commanding Officer. Note: Its direct descendant, Central Command Coast Artillery, was disbanded in June 1953.

36   *Supplement to NSW Government Gazette No 84 of 27 February 1885*, and NSW *Blue Book* for the Year 1885, compiled from official returns in the Registrar General's Office, Part IV, Colonial Secretary, p 48, New South Wales Contingent. Note: the contingent embarked at Sydney on 3 March 1885, and disembarked at Sydney on 23 June 1885. It was disbanded on 3 July 1885.

37   NSW *Blue Book* for the Year 1885, compiled from official returns in the Registrar General's Office, Part IV, Colonial Secretary, p 41, appointment of Military Instructors. Note: Its direct descendant is the current School of Artillery.

38   General Order No 1 of 1 January 1885. Note: Its direct descendant was disbanded as 1st Military District Fixed Defences in June 1947.

39   *Officers' List of the Australian Military Forces* 1912, entry relating to appointment of the first Officer Commanding. Note: Its direct descendant was disbanded in June 1953 as Tasmania Command Coast Artillery.

40   *Victorian Government Gazette No 125 dated 9 October 1891*.

41   NAA B5718, *Report of the Council of Defence' dated 28 July 1892*; *Victorian Defence Forces List, 1st January 1893*. The Victorian Permanent Artillery was later retitled the *Victoria Regiment, Royal Australian Artillery* on 13 September 1899.

42   *Government Gazette of Western Australia Extraordinary No 10 of 1 March 1893*; *Government Gazette of Western Australia No 16 of 6 April 1893*. Note: Its direct descendants were disbanded as components of 27th Coast Regiment RAA in August 1953.

43   Promulgated in *Queensland Government Gazette No 60 of 26 August 1899*.

44   Notified in *NSW Government Gazette No 719 of 5 September 1899*.

45   Notified in *Victorian Government Gazette No 75 of 15 September 1899*.

46   General Order 101/1902 of 4 July 1902.

47   General Order 169/1903 of 25 July 1903.

48   *The Australian Regulations and Orders for the Military Forces of the Commonwealth, Provisional Edition, 1904*, Part I, paragraph 1, Precedence of Corps.

49   General Order No 243 of 20 October 1904; General Order No 258 of 8 November 1904.

50   Despatch No 22, The Under Secretary of State to the Governor-General of Australia.

51   Military Order 405/1910 of 26 November 1910.

52   Military Order 160/1911 of 25 April 1911.

53   Proclamation by the Governor-General of Australia notified by Military Order 438/1914 of 4 August 1914.

54   Scott, Ernest, *Official History Of Australia In The War Of 1914-18, Volume XI*, pp 35-37.

55   Proclamation by the Governor-General of Australia notified by Military Order 465/1914 of 18 August 1914.

56   Military Order No 316 of 1 June 1915; *Commonwealth of Australia Gazette No 47 of 29 May 1915*, effective 21 May 1915, notified in Military Order No 323 of 1 June 1915.

57   Military Order 261/1919 of 31 May 1919, reconfirmed by Appendix A to AHQ 26437 of 25 November 1949.

58   Amendment, Serial No 1, to *Tables of Composition, Organization and Distribution of the Australian Military Forces, 1925-26*.

59   *Tables of Composition, Organization and Distribution of the Australian Military Forces, 1927-28*.

60 Australian Army Order 357/1927 of 16 July 1927.

61 Military Board Circular Memorandum No 337 dated 19 June 1930.

62 Australian Army Order 71/1935 of 31 March 1935, terminated by Appendix A to AHQ 2373 of 9 February 1951.

63 Australian Army Order 12/1936 of 31 January 1936.

64 *Commonwealth of Australia Gazette No 62 of 2 September 1939.*

65 *Commonwealth of Australia Gazette No 104 of 12 October 1939.*

66 Military Board Memo No 5407 of 27 January 1940 authorising the conversion of 2/5th Field Regiment to 2/5th Anti-Tank Regiment.

67 Army Headquarters Operation Instruction No 12 of 24 February 1941.

68 Military Board Instruction G.112/1941 of 31 August 1941. Cadres were to be complete and in training by 1 October 1941.

69 *The London Gazette No 35360, (Second Supplement) 25 November 1941*, p. 6825.

70 General Routine Order G.241/1943 of 26 March 1943.

71 General Routine Order G.784/1943 of 3 December 1943. In practice Military Board Instruction G.111/1941 of 31 August 1941 had replaced the term 'Coast Defence Artillery' (apparently referring to equipment) with 'Coast Artillery', and unit designations had been changing as early as May 1943.

72 AWM52 4/9/2/12, War Diary 2nd Mountain Battery BCOF, January-June 1946

73 Military Board Instruction No 191 of 7 Nov 47, NAA: A2653; Military Board Agenda 1947, Volume 4, Agenda 141/1947

74 The appointment of Commanding Officers, Adjutants, and Quartermasters had occurred on 1 April 1948, and the remaining officers were appointed on 1 May 1948.

75 Australian Army Order No 54/1949 of 31 Jul 1949.

76 *The Defence Act and Regulations and Orders for the Australian Military Forces and Senior Cadets*, AMR&O 83. (R.68) (1), as amended by Serial No 54 promulgated by Statutory Rules 1949, No 68, notified in the *Commonwealth of Australia Gazette of 15 September 1949*.

77 Letter dated 28 November 1949, Private Secretary to the King, to His Excellency The Governor-General of Australia, NAA: A2880, 27/8/16; Australian Army Order No 6 of January 1950.

78 Para 3 to Military Board (MGO) letter B2531 of 10 Mar 1950, NAA: SP1008/1, 544/2/7152; Para 2 to Military Board (MGO) letter B7411 of 02 Aug 1951, NAA: MP742/1; 61/10/26.

79 *The Army List of Officers of the Australian Military Forces*, Volume I, The Active List, 1st April 1953, p. 485, entry for HARRIS, Thomas Albert ED, CO 3 A Tk Regt until 2 June 1952, CO 3 Lt Regt from 3 June 1952.

80 *Australian Military Forces Study Précis Book 5, Artillery*, Directorate of Military Training, Artillery 1, January 1954, Organization of Artillery Units, paragraph 14(a).

81 MBI 86/1952, *Standing Orders for Dress (Provisional)*, paragraph 30, Whistles, sub-paragraphs (a), and (b).

82 Military Board (MGO) letter B06167 of 01 Jun 1956, NAA: MT1131/1, A87/1/96, pp. 8-9; *Dress Manual 1963*, paragraph 312.

83 AHQ Memo 5/431/114(A3) dated 1 June 1953, NAA: MP729/8, 5/431/114.

84 *Commonwealth of Australia Gazette No 76 dated 26 November 1953.*

85 AWM113: MH25/1/1 Part 2; *Regimental badges and Buttons – Corps, Armoured and Light Horse Units, Miscellaneous, 1952-1956*. Specification MGO/Aust 991, Appendix No 47, Issue No 2 dated 26 May 1954.

86 DRA Liaison Letter, September 1955, p 1 ; Eaton, H B, *Something Extra: 28 Commonwealth Brigade 1951-1974*, The Pentland Press Limited, Durham, 1993.

87 Establishment III/221/2 (TE), held by DPLANS-A, Army Headquarters, redesignating 9 HAA Regt as 9 LAA Regt.

88 Army Routine Order 14/62 of 2 November 1962.

89 Army Headquarters letter 60/441/228 of 26 October 1962

90 Annex B to Military Board Instruction 261-1 of 22 April 1966, Amendment No 2 of 10 January 1967.

91 Annex B to Military Board Instruction 216-1 of 22 April 1966, Amendment No 2 of 10 January 1967.

92 *Presentation of The Queen's Banner to The Royal Regiment of Australian Artillery 1971*, Programme of Ceremony.

93 Organization Instruction 22/74, reorganize and redesignate 16 LAA Regt as 16 AD Regt (Lt).

94 'A Field Battery', *RAA Liaison Letter, 2000*, p 11; '4th Field Regiment', *RAA Liaison Letter, 2000*, p 15.

95 Mott, S, 'Gunners: Supporting the Al Muthanna Task Group', *RAA Liaison Letter, Spring 2005*, pp 61-62; *101st Battery History as at 2015*, 2015.

96 Mott, S G T and Sinclair, D J, 'Combat Team Thor', *RAA Liaison Letter,* Spring 2006, p 108.

97 Minister for Defence and Minister for Foreign Affairs - Joint Media Release - International stabilisation force in Timor-Leste concludes mission, 21 November 2012. Australian War Memorial, *East Timor, 1999-2013*, https://www.awm.gov.au/collection/CN37, accessed 08 July 2022.

98 Defence Media Release, *Aussie Reconstruction Task Force On The Ground*, https://parlinfo.aph.gov.au/parlInfo/search/display/display.w3p;query=Id%3A%22media%2Fpressrel%2F1AEW6%22, accessed 04 Jun 2022; Barrow, Captain R R, 'Offensive Support in a Counter Insurgency Environment', *RAA Liaison Letter,* Spring 2007, pp 69-73.

99 J Fitzgibbon (Minister for Defence), Defence Media Release, *Australian artillerymen deploy to Afghanistan in support of UK operations*, https://parlinfo.aph.gov.au/parlInfo/search/display/display.w3p;query=Id:%22media/pressrel/4IWP6%22, 13 March 2008, accessed 04 Jun 2022.

100 Hetherington, Corporal Andrew, 'Coral Title a First', *Army Newspaper*, 29 May 2008.

101 Reilly, ST, 'Fort Alamo: Artillery Training Advisory Team-Two', *RAA Liaison Letter,* Autumn 2013, pp 29-30.